tax aspects
of

Deferred
Compensation

tax aspects
of
Deferred
Compensation

Ernest O. Wood, CPA
Arthur Young & Company, Pittsburgh

John F. Cerny, CPA
Arthur Young & Company, Milwaukee

Englewood Cliffs, N. J.   Prentice-Hall, Inc.

PRENTICE-HALL INTERNATIONAL, INC., *London*
PRENTICE-HALL OF AUSTRALIA, PTY, LTD., *Sydney*
PRENTICE-HALL OF CANADA, LTD., *Toronto*
PRENTICE-HALL OF INDIA PRIVATE LTD., *New Delhi*
PRENTICE-HALL OF JAPAN, INC., *Tokyo*

LIBRARY OF CONGRESS
CATALOG CARD NUMBER-
69-15594

PRINTED IN THE UNITED STATES OF AMERICA

B & P

Since the first edition of this book was published, there have been many changes in the principles relating to deferred compensation. This second edition has been expanded to include consideration of these new principles and to reflect changes of emphasis in the field. The self-employed retirement plan, for example, has received considerable attention recently because of increased tax benefits, and accordingly a new chapter has been added to this edition on the subject of tax planning for the professional man. Investment of trust funds has been expanded into a full chapter. New executive compensation plans have been covered. The importance of pension planning in the area of mergers and acquisitions is highlighted in a full chapter. The future of the private pension system is re-examined.

The deferment of taxes through the deferment of compensation is by no means a new development in the history of U. S. taxation. The initial candle was lighted by the Revenue Act of 1921, which provided an exemption for employees' trusts relating to profit-sharing and stock bonus plans. Through the years the way grew brighter as additional beacons were fired, although the darkness continually threatened.

In 1926 pension plans joined profit-sharing and stock bonus plans as deferred-compensation devices. In 1928 and 1942 limitations were placed upon the amount of employer deductions. The year 1942 saw the capital gains treatment of lump-sum distributions and stricter qualification requirements. The restricted stock option had its genesis in the Revenue Act of 1950, and deferred compensation for self-employed persons flickered to life in 1962. The 1964 Act blew out the restricted stock option light and provided a dimmer replacement, the qualified stock option.

Taxpayers have been guided by these and other lights while Congress, the lamplighter of taxation, stands at the edge of the shadow, with match in one hand and snuffer in the other. This area of taxation is subject to constant change. There is no reason to believe that the principles and procedures of today will be the standards of tomorrow. In January 1965 the President's Committee on Corporate Pension Funds released its report of recommendations to improve the "basic soundness and equitable character" of private retirement plans. Included in this report are recommendations to increase vesting provisions, accelerate funding, place a limitation on investments, and eliminate the capital gains treatment of lump-sum distributions. What the future holds remains in the shadows.

Important as future developments may be, it is the principles and procedures of the present that are of primary concern to those who must deal with deferred-compensation plans today. The authors have written this book, which is based largely upon their own experience, in the hope that it will be of assistance to the tax practitioners, tax executives, and personnel managers who also work in this area of taxation.

—E. O. W. & J. F. C.

ACKNOWLEDGMENTS

Assistance and counsel come from many sources. The authors gratefully acknowledge the help which they have received from their partners and associates. They particularly appreciate the contributions made by Richard J. Bannon of Chicago and by Irwin Ettinger, Donald Hayes, Edwin Mruk, and Victor Noschese, all of New York. There is always one person of whom special mention must be made. In this case, it is Albert Newgarden, Editor of *The Arthur Young Journal,* for his advice, encouragement, and assistance throughout the writing and production of this volume. The authors also owe a debt to H. Avery Rafuse, Vice President, John Wood Company, who collaborated with them in the writing of the first edition. And, lastly, they tip their hats to Don Summa, Director of Taxes, Arthur Young & Company, who urged them on.

CONTENTS

tax aspects
of

Deferred
Compensation

Ends and Means of Employee Compensation

OBJECTIVES OF A COMPENSATION PROGRAM
CURRENT COMPENSATION
FRINGE BENEFITS
INCENTIVE BONUS ARRANGEMENTS
RETIREMENT PROGRAMS
PENSION VS. PROFIT-SHARING PLANS
OTHER METHODS
MANAGEMENT DECISIONS
CONCLUSION

OBJECTIVES OF A COMPENSATION PROGRAM

Some of the basic objectives of a compensation program, as viewed by the owners of a business, are:

—To bring competent people into the organization at all levels.

—To keep competent people in the organization.

—To motivate people to perform at a consistently high level of effectiveness.

—To attract qualified personnel into the supervisory and management ranks.

—To keep abreast of competitive and prevailing conditions in the industry or locality.

As viewed by those who will participate in it, on the other hand, a compensation program is measured by a different and more personal set of objectives. Typically, employees are interested in a compensation program that will provide them with:

— Sufficient income to permit them to enjoy the same standard of living as their peers or associates in their own company or in other companies in the general community.
— An opportunity to provide some security for their family, through insurance or other means, in the event of their death.
— Protection against the economic hazards of major illness or disabling accidents.
— The prospect of eventually being able to retire with a reasonable income.
— Some protection against the effects of inflation.

In any company, the most effective compensation program can be developed only after full consideration has been given to all aspects of both the owners' goals and the employees' goals. In most companies today, however, the program will consist of some combination of most or all of the following elements:

1. Current compensation (base salary).
2. Supplementary compensation:
   a. Fringe benefits.
   b. Incentive bonus arrangements.
   c. Retirement programs (pension plans, profit-sharing plans, etc.).

It is not our purpose here to consider in any detail the elements of a sound basic pay structure. As its title indicates, this volume is concerned exclusively with *deferred*-compensation plans, and specifically with the tax aspects of such plans. It should be emphasized, however, that a sound and equitable salary structure is the foundation of any good compensation program.

CURRENT COMPENSATION

If it is to attract and retain competent people, a company must pay salaries which are competitive in the marketplace, regardless of the quality or extent of its supplementary compensation program. Furthermore, almost all other forms of compensation — insurance programs, pension plans, profit-sharing arrangements, stock bonus plans, etc. — are directly related to the amount of each participant's base salary.

A sound salary administration program is an important management tool in defining the duties and responsibilities of each position in the company. It places each position in proper relationship to all other positions. In this regard, it cannot be too strongly emphasized that not only rank-and-file employees but executive personnel have a keen interest in properly established base salaries. Any existing inequities or unreasonable disparities are strongly felt, and until they are removed neither rank-and-file employees nor executives will react wholeheartedly to incentive arrangements.

Too often a company neglects to consider its corporate objectives, both long- and short-term, in developing or reviewing its overall compensation program. There have been instances where companies have provided too generous and too costly fringe benefits at the expense of basic salaries, with the result that, sooner or later, they have found themselves unable to compete in the local labor market. Studies have indicated, for example, that in industries which employ substantial numbers of female workers, far greater importance is attached by rank-and-file employees to base salaries than to fringe benefits — yet there are many companies in this category whose fringe-benefit costs are extremely high.

FRINGE BENEFITS

So-called fringe benefits play an important part in conjunction with current compensation, and include a large number and variety of items which tend to satisfy employees' needs and reduce their fears. Because the resulting freedom from anxiety allows the employee to concentrate greater effort upon his job requirements, the use of fringe benefits often has the effect of increasing employee productivity.

Group life, accident and health, hospitalization, surgical, and medical catastrophe insurance, both for employees and for their dependents, are useful and increasingly common types of fringe benefits. So too are vacations, sick leave, holidays, and the allowance of time off for key events in the life of the individual employee.

INCENTIVE BONUS ARRANGEMENTS

Close behind current compensation and fringe benefits in frequency of use are incentive bonus arrangements based on profit levels, production standards, or other measures of performance. Such arrangements are, of course, predicated on two assumptions: (1) that better-than-average performance should be rewarded and (2) that human beings are so constituted, psychologically, that some stimulus is usually needed to generate better-than-average performance. One type of stimulus which many companies have found to be particularly effective in overcoming the natural forces of inertia and generating better-than-average performance is the incentive bonus arrangement. Needless to say, any such arrangement must be developed with specific reference to the particular needs and resources of the company concerned and the particular economic and business conditions under which it is operating.

It is at this point, after management has met and dealt with the problems of current compensation, fringe benefits, and incentive bonus arrangements, that retirement programs deserve consideration.

RETIREMENT PROGRAMS

From the company's viewpoint, a planned retirement program permits the orderly release of older employees and their succession by younger and presumably more energetic employees. Generally, a planned retirement program that is qualified under the Internal Revenue laws will cost a company less than one that is not qualified—the difference being that investment income and capital gains of the qualified plan are tax-deferred, whereas the earnings of the nonqualified plan are not. In this regard, it has often been painfully revealing to compare a company with an established qualified retirement program, the costs of which have been assumed proportionately over the productive years of the employees covered, with a company that does not have such a program, when both are inevitably faced with the problem of releasing older employees.

The company which has overlooked this cost currently, frequently finds that it must assume a greater burden at the time its employees retire.

From the employee's viewpoint, a planned retirement program should provide maximum security (consistent with his circumstances) for himself and his family; a hedge against inflation; and a deferral of Federal income tax, with an opportunity for capital gains treatment (or perhaps no tax at all) on the payments to be made.

A well-designed retirement program should provide adequate income, as measured by the employee's standard of living prior to retirement. It is widely agreed today that an adequate retirement income should approximate 60% of pre-retirement pay for lower-paid employees, 50% for the middle-income group, and 40% for higher-paid employees. In practice, however, these percentages are generally obtainable only by those employees who have long service with a company. Underlying any determination of retirement benefits, of course, are such considerations as what the company can afford, what local practices are in this regard, and to what extent the employees are eligible for retirement benefits under the social security system.

PENSION VS. PROFIT-SHARING PLANS

It might be useful, at this point, to consider briefly the relative advantages and disadvantages of two basic types of retirement programs qualified under the Internal Revenue laws: the pension plan and the profit-sharing plan.

The pension plan establishes a definite retirement program for employees, with stated benefits payable upon retirement. The employer (and, if the plan is contributory, the employee) must meet the actual cost of the benefits to be provided. Under the profit-sharing plan, on the other hand, the employer agrees to place some percentage of company profits in trust for its employees, with those profits being distributed at some later date to those retiring under the plan. A profit-sharing plan can be used to perform some of the functions of a pension plan by deferring all distributions until the retirement time specified, at which time the amount allocated to the employee may be paid out in the form of a life income. A profit-sharing plan does not guarantee any specific amount to the employee, but from the employer's point of view it does have a theoretical advantage in that the contributions to be made to the trust each year are based on the amount of profits earned during the year. Such limitation of contribution based on profits has an attraction to small, closely held companies, in that they do not feel they are burdened by a fixed commitment — no profits, no contribution. So, too, many companies feel that there is a less harmful effect on employee morale when no contribution is made to a profit-sharing plan because of no profits than there is when no contribution is made to a pension plan.

Because of differences in vesting requirements between pension and profit-sharing plans, it may be more desirable from the employer's viewpoint to adopt a pension plan. Under a pension plan, vesting is not required until the employee retires, whereas under the usual type of profit-sharing plan a participating employee acquires a 10% vested right in his interest annually from the date he becomes a member of the plan, thus requiring ten years before 100% vesting is achieved. (Note that some District Directors are now requiring that benefits vest within five years. However, there appears to be considerable disparity in this regard, not only from one District to another but in the treatment accorded different plans by the same District Director.) Employees terminating employment under a profit-sharing plan are entitled to receive their vested amounts, the nonvested balance being reallocated to participating employees who continue in the service of the company. Although payment of vested amounts may be deferred until the terminated employee reaches retirement age, this creates administrative problems in keeping track of the employee until retirement age. Under a pension plan, employees terminating service prior to retirement usually forfeit all amounts credited on their behalf other than their own contributions plus interest. The forfeited amounts are used to pay for the cost of the benefits of the employees who remain, and in effect reduce future company contributions for this purpose.

As a general rule, the greater the vesting, the lesser the "holding power" of the plan upon employees. Thus, pension plans generally tend to have greater holding power than profit-sharing plans, since their vesting provisions are usually less liberal.

One feature of a profit-sharing plan that may be particularly objectionable is that, for practical purposes, it can provide little or no past service benefits, particularly for key employees, whereas a pension plan can do so immediately upon adoption. Hence, a newly adopted profit-sharing plan cannot adequately provide for the immediate or impending retirement of older employees, whereas a pension plan can meet this need.

Finally, contributions by the company to a profit-sharing plan are limited to 15% of the compensation of the employees covered under the plan, whereas no similar percentage limitation applies to pension plan contributions. For both types of plans, an overall "reasonable compensation" test must be met. This requires that the total amount of the pension or profit-sharing contributions and the employee's other compensation be regarded as reasonable under the Internal Revenue laws. If a company covers the same group of employees with both a qualified profit-sharing plan and a pension plan, however, the overall contribution that the company may make is limited to 25% of the compensation of the employees covered.

Either plan may provide for employee contributions which may be as much as 6% on an involuntary basis and 10% on a voluntary basis, making a permissible total of 16%. Employees who are participants in both plans may contribute to both and thus increase the permissible total to 26%. [Rev. Rul. 65-178, Part 4(h); Rev. Rul. 59-185.] This furnishes an investment vehicle for employees in which the accumulation of earnings is not subject to tax until a later date, and then possibly at the more favorable capital gains rate.

OTHER METHODS

Though we have dwelt at some length upon pension and profit-sharing plans, it is certainly not our intention to minimize the part that stock options, employee savings plans, self-employed retirement plans, nonqualified executive compensation plans, and their many variations can play in the overall compensation program. Under the appropriate circumstances, such plans fulfill an important need, and alert management will be quick to use them when the occasion arises, fully aware of the unique incentive power of such plans in the context of today's tax structure.

MANAGEMENT DECISIONS

Any company setting out to establish a pension, profit-sharing, or other retirement program faces a number of important management decisions. The range of these decisions is broad and their consequences are far-reaching. They relate, for example, to such matters as eligibility for membership through the formula for benefits; the instrumentality for administration; the diversity of terms in the plan as to vesting, forfeitures, retirement dates, and funding; and basic investment policy.

It is essential that management have at least a broad general knowledge of the various approaches available and their consequences, if its decisions are to be informed. The natural tendency will be for management to seek expert advice and guidance in this area, and this is unquestionably a sound policy. However, the decisions themselves are so far-reaching in their implications that they should not be simply delegated to the expert. The role of the expert is, or should be, to acquaint management with the various approaches which are available and their implications with respect to personnel policy, accounting, employee motivation and morale, succession planning, hiring and recruiting practices, and other important management considerations.

CONCLUSION

At best, the above is but a brief outline of some of the basic objectives and methods of employee compensation. It is intended primarily to provide a general frame of reference for the chapters that follow, in which we will consider the technical details and effects of various types of retirement programs and other deferred-compensation plans in the light of today's Federal income tax laws. Anyone would be well advised, before making a final decision concerning any form of deferred compensation, to consult with his certified public accountant, his attorney, his insurance agent, an actuary, and (if appropriate) a trust officer.

The Role of the Professional Adviser

THE TEAM APPROACH

SERVICE TO THE COMPANY

SERVICE TO THE TRUST

SERVICE TO PARTICIPANTS

THE TEAM APPROACH

Successful planning for employee retirement carries the employer into such highly technical fields as tax law, state and local statutes, actuarial computations, and investment planning. With the exception of large corporations which maintain compensation planning departments, the employer is seldom able to travel in this area without the assistance of outside professional advisers. The outside assistance which he requires is available, in whole or in part, from a number of sources. He may look to his attorney, his banker, his insurance agent, his certified public accountant, actuaries, pension planners, and others. The professional adviser to whom he looks may be fully competent to advise him through all the steps which he must take. It is more likely, however, that he will have to consult several sources — i.e., he will have to rely upon a team in order to construct a retirement plan program which satisfies both the employer and the employee. If the job is particularly complex, the employer may use the talents of a full team. The composition of the team will depend, in part, upon the type of plan that the employer seeks. Usually, the team includes an attorney and a certified public accountant. Depending upon the type of plan under consideration, the team may also include an actuary, a trust officer, and an insurance specialist.

Each member of the team brings to the joint effort a specialized view and talent. The attorney brings the ability to draft a plan or trust instrument in accordance with sound legal principles. The actuary brings his expertise in assembling and analyzing the data necessary to establish the costs of carrying out the plan. The trust officer brings his experience in the conservation and management of trust assets. The insurance specialist brings a detailed knowledge of the various types of insurance contracts by which the objectives of the program may be achieved. The certified public accountant brings the full range of knowledge of his client's business affairs and his accounting and tax skills.

This is not to say that the role of any one of these advisers should be limited to the aforementioned peculiar skills. Each of these specialists may range far beyond these enumerated activities if he has prepared himself in the arts and skills of employee retirement planning. There are many lawyers who are competent to advise their clients on most aspects of this technical field. The same can be said of insurance specialists, bankers, actuaries, and other pension counselors. On the other hand, there are certain functions which should be restricted, or which by their nature are restricted, to specific members of the team. For example, the drafting of legal documents is commonly considered to be the practice of law, and this is a matter for the attorney. Likewise, the attorney is the person to resolve the legal questions which might relate to the employment status of individuals, the legal liabilities of employers, the status of noncompetitive clauses, and the legal aspects of collective bargaining under the plan. As a further example, the certified public accountant is the party to conduct audits and certify financial statements. As a consequence, some measure of teamwork is required.

The purpose of the team is to serve the best interests of the employer. While the functions of the various members of the team may overlap in certain areas, the end product of the team should reflect the best abilities of the individual members working in harmony. For example, the banker may know more than any other member of the team about possible investment programs. The attorney may be well versed in the legal limits placed upon trust investments. The certified public accountant may have knowledge of the present and future financial capabilities of the employer to assume the cost of a pension or profit-sharing program, of the business and tax advantages to be gained, and of the benefits to be realized in the area of employee relations and morale.

Within the framework of the team, the scope of any individual member's work will depend upon his ability and the requirements made of him. A particular member may be working with another member in a narrow area; he may also be working in a separate area by himself. It is difficult to enumerate all the functions which any given member may perform. The authors, being certified public accountants, set forth below those functions which they see as being within the capabilities of the CPA who has developed the appropriate technical skills. They do not intend to suggest that only the CPA may do these things; other members of the team may also be capable of performing these tasks. The CPA is used as an example.

An attorney might use the same list, making certain substitutions. For example, the attorney would exclude from his list the audit and certification functions and would include the preparation of legal documents. By way of further example, the attorney might not wish to exclude the section which discusses independent evaluation of various types of plans because the attorney often serves as an impartial adviser in this area.

SERVICE TO THE COMPANY

1. Suggestion of guidelines for the development of a plan suited to the specific needs of the company. Because of his intimate knowledge of the financial and tax position of the company, his familiarity with the desires of management and shareholders, and his knowledge of the company's employee relationships, the CPA is particularly qualified to suggest such guidelines to his client. During the initial phases of developing a plan, the CPA may wish to advise his client concerning such points as the following:

> Eligibility requirements.
> Contributory vs. noncontributory plan (if contributory, whether voluntary, involuntary, or both, and percentage limits).

Contribution formula.
Allocation of contributions.
Vesting provisions and allocation of forfeitures.
Selection of administrative committee.
Responsibilities of administrative committee.
Selection of trustee.
Methods of distributing benefits (lump sum, etc.)
Funding methods.

2. Independent evaluation of the various types of plans and methods of funding.

3. Preparation of the request for a determination letter from the Internal Revenue Service.

4. Preparation of Form 2950, setting forth the information required by Regulations 1.404(a)-2.

5. Advice concerning the payment of employer contributions in order to obtain maximum tax and financial advantage.

6. Advice on accounting for employee retirement costs and the presentation of the costs and related data in the financial statements in accordance with generally accepted accounting principles, with particular reference to Accounting Principles Board Opinion No. 8.

7. Computation of contributions under a profit-sharing plan containing a predetermined formula.

SERVICE TO THE TRUST

1. Installation of the accounting system of the trust.

2. Examination of the financial statements of the trust for the purpose of expressing an opinion on the adequacy of the statements, thus providing protection for the participants and the employer.

3. Preparation of Form 990-P, the annual tax return of the trust.

4. Preparation of the annual report required by the Federal Welfare and Pension Plans Disclosure Act.

5. Preparation of other reports required by Federal and state agencies.

6. Advice regarding permissive trust investments in accord-

ance with the income tax regulations, with particular reference to employer use of trust. (See page 239.)

7. Assistance in the valuation of the assets of the fund.

SERVICE TO PARTICIPANTS

1. Advice and assistance in relation to the submission of information to plan participants as required by Federal and state agencies.

2. Assistance in advising participants as to the income, gift, and estate tax consequences of employee contributions to the retirement fund, withdrawals and distributions from the fund, exercise and disqualification of options, etc .

Qualified Pension, Profit-Sharing, and Stock Bonus Plans

GENERAL STATEMENT

The Code provides under Section 501(a) that a trust created or organized in the United States and forming all or part of a pension, profit-sharing, or stock bonus plan is exempt from income taxes if certain conditions are met concerning the following:

1. Benefits.
2. Diversion of funds.
3. Coverage.
4. Discrimination.

A trust must qualify throughout the taxable year to be exempt for any portion of the year. [Regs. 1.401-1(c).] However, as far as number or class of employees covered by a pension or profit-sharing plan is concerned, the plan is considered as qualifying for the whole of any taxable year of the plan if on anyone day in each quarter it satisfies the requirements. [Sec. 401(a)(6).]

PENSION PLANS

DEFINITIONS. A pension plan within the meaning of Section 401(a) is a plan established and maintained by an employer primarily to provide systematically for the payment of definitely determinable benefits to employees over a period of years, usually for life, after retirement. Neither the benefits nor the contributions are determined by reference to profits. Benefits are generally measured by years of service and compensation. Contributions are based on the cost of the benefits, except for money-purchase plans, in which case contributions are fixed — i.e., they do not vary with profits.

In computing the costs of a trusteed plan or a plan of the deposit administration type of group annuity, the interest and other assumptions used should not be so conservative as to anticipate for a long period of years the most unfavorable experience likely to occur at any time in the future. The assumptions should be consistent with reasonable expectations as to average experience. [Rev. Rul. 63-11 and Rev. Rul. 64-84.] Revenue Ruling 63-11 also sets forth the conditions under which a minimum interest rate assumed should be at least 3½%. The Treasury Department takes the position that the assumption of an unrealistically low interest factor in effect builds up a contingency reserve in the trust for which the Treasury will not allow a current deduction.

A plan can become overfunded where, after past service costs are fully funded, credits arise because of dividends and forfeitures but the employer continues to make contributions based on normal cost without regard to such dividends and forfeitures. It is overfunded if assets, not counting employer contributions which have not been deducted, exceed accrued liabilities to beneficiaries. A contribution deduction is not allowed to an overfunded plan. [Rev. Rul. 64-159.] For this purpose, any consistently followed asset valuation basis resulting in reasonable costs is acceptable. [Rev. Rul. 63-11; Rev. Rul. 64-84.]

Contribution deductions to a qualified employee pension plan are governed by Section 404 and are not affected by the employer's accounting treatment for book and financial statement purposes [Rev. Rul. 68-34.]

On the ground that benefits are not otherwise "definitely determinable," the regulations require that any pension trust funds arising from forfeitures on termination of services be used to reduce future contributions by the employer, and not to provide increased benefits for the remaining participants. [Regs. 1.401-1(b)(1)(i); Regs. 1.401-7(a).] The 1962 Act put this provision in the law. [Sec. 401(a)(8).] This rule is equally applicable to pension plans of the money-purchase type. [Rev. Rul. 65-178, Part 2(m) and Part 7(a).]

Although the existence of fixed benefits normally precludes a fixed contribution, the Revenue Service has approved a pension trust negotiated between the employer and a union, requiring both fixed contributions and fixed benefits, where the contributions were based upon an actuarial computation. [P.S. No. 64.] Approval has also been given to a provision for an increase or decrease in benefits related to the market value of the assets from which the benefits are payable, and to a provision for adjustment according to a specified and generally recognized cost-of-living index. [Rev. Rul. 65-178, Part 2(m).]

A pension trust may qualify under Section 401(a) even though the employer does not contribute to the trust fund (created from employee contributions) but does obligate himself to pay the full amount of stipulated retirement benefits after the trust funds have been exhausted. [Rev. Rul. 65-178, Part 2(b); Rev. Rul. 54-152; Rev. Rul. 68-25.] A trust may be funded by someone other than employer or employees. [Rev. Rul. 65-178, Part 2(g); Rev. Rul. 63-46.]

A self-insured, trusteed plan providing normal pension benefits for a time certain with no life contingencies may qualify. [Rev. Rul. 57-312.]

INCIDENTAL BENEFITS. A pension plan may provide for the payment of a pension due to disability and may also provide for the payment of incidental death benefits through insurance or otherwise. However, a plan is not a pension plan if it provides for the payment of benefits not customarily included in a pension plan, such as layoff benefits or benefits for sickness, accident, hospitalization, or medical expenses. [Regs. 1.401-1(b)(1)(i).] See, however, Section 401(h) for permissive medical plans for retired employees. [Reg. 1.401-14(a).] A death benefit payable under a qualified pension plan will be considered incidental where the value of the death benefit does not exceed the benefit that would have been paid had the benefit been funded under a typical retirement income contract. [Rev. Rul.

61-121; Rev. Rul. 65-178, Part 2(n)(1).] In the case of a pension or annuity plan, the life insurance protection is not greater than 100 times the monthly annuity—e.g., $1,000 of life insurance for each $10 of monthly annuity. [Rev. Rul. 65-178, Part 2(n)(1).] A plan will qualify where it provides that a death benefit after retirement will be paid which is equal to 50% of the salary of the participant in the last year before retirement and where the death benefit will cost less than 10% of the cost of the pension plan as determined by excluding the cost of such a death benefit. [Rev. Rul. 60-59.]

WITHDRAWALS. A pension plan may permit the withdrawal of voluntary contributions (as contrasted with employer contributions, compulsory employee contributions, and increments), provided (1) that the withdrawals do not affect a member's participation in the plan, the employer's past or future contributions on his behalf, or the basic benefits provided by both the participant's and the employer's nonwithdrawable contributions, and (2) that no interest is allowed on the withdrawals either at the time of withdrawal or in computing benefits on retirement. [Rev. Rul. 65-178, Part 2(o).] A contributory plan which is amended so as to make it a noncontributory plan, accompanied by a refund of employee contributions and reduced benefits, will not lose its exempt status. [Rev. Rul. 61-79.] Upon discontinuance of his participation under a pension plan, an employee may withdraw his own contribution plus the interest actually earned on his contribution without affecting the qualification of the plan. [Rev. Rul. 65-178, Part 2(o).]

SUSPENSION OF CONTRIBUTIONS. Suspension of contributions will not affect the qualification of a pension plan if (1) the benefits to be paid or made available under the plan are not affected at any time by the suspension and (2) the unfunded past service cost at any time does not exceed the unfunded past service cost as of the date of establishment of the plan. Otherwise, the suspension will be treated as a termination or partial termination of the plan, and the exemption will be reexamined. [Rev. Rul. 56-596.] Assuming no changes in coverage, etc., if the current service cost plus the interest on the unfunded past service cost are paid annually, the unfunded past service cost will remain constant.

TRUSTS. A single pension plan or trust may qualify for an entire group of corporate employers, regardless of whether or not the employers are "affiliated" for purposes of filing a consolidated return. [Regs. 1.401-1(d).]

PROFIT-SHARING PLANS

DEFINITIONS. A profit-sharing plan under Section 401 is a plan which is established and maintained to enable employees or their beneficiaries to participate in the profits of the employer's trade or business. The plan must contain a definite predetermined formula for allocating the contributions and for distributing the funds accumulated under the plan. Distribution must be provided for after a fixed number of years, upon the attainment of a stated age, or upon the occurrence of some event such as layoff, illness, disability, retirement, death, or severance of employment. A formula for allocating the contributions among the participants is definite if, for example, it provides for an allocation in proportion to the basic compensation of each participant. [Regs. 1.401-1(a) and (b).]

PROFIT-SHARING FORMULA. The regulations under the 1939 Code, prior to retroactive amendment in 1956, required also that a profit-sharing plan be based on "a definite and predetermined formula for determining the profits to be shared." This restriction was held invalid by several courts. In the leading case, it was held that a lump-sum contribution out of profits could constitute the corpus of an exempt profit-sharing trust, even though there was no "formula" related to the corporation's profits and no provision for any future contributions. [*Lincoln Electric Co. Employees' Profit-Sharing Trust,* 190 F.2d 326 (6th Cir. 1951):]

The regulations state that merely making a single or occasional contribution out of profits for employees does not establish a plan of profit-sharing, and they require that there be recurring and substantial contributions out of profits for the employees. [Regs. 1.401-1(b)(2).] However, discontinuance of contributions will not affect the qualification of a profit-sharing plan if there is a granting of fully vested rights upon discontinuance. [Rev. Rul. 65-178, Part 6(d)(2).] See also Section 401(a)(7).

Although the regulations no longer require a definite and predetermined formula for determining the profits to be shared, they do contain two other requirements: (1) a definite predetermined formula for allocating among the participants the contributions made to the plan and (2) a definite predetermined formula for distributing funds which are accumulated either after a fixed number of years (not less than two) [Rev. Rul. 65-178, Part 2(c)] on the attainment of a stated age, or on the happening of a particular event. However, in order to take advantage of the special grace period for accrual-basis taxpayers (see page 89), an employer without a predetermined formula must, during the taxable year on account of which the contribution is made, incur a liability to make the contribution. [Regs. 1.404(a)-1(c).]

INCIDENTAL BENEFITS. A profit-sharing plan is primarily a plan of deferred compensation, but the amounts allocated to the account of a participant may be used to provide for him or his family incidental life or accident or health insurance. [Regs. 1.404-1 (b) (1) (ii).] The Revenue Service does not permit an unlimited use of profit-sharing funds for life insurance premiums, but it does permit such use to the extent of an amount which, when added to the total contributions and forfeitures previously allocated to the purchase of ordinary life insurance for the participant, is less than one-half of the total contributions and forfeitures allocated to the employee's account. [Rev. Rul. 65-178, Part 2(n) (2).] If no part of the life insurance element continues after retirement, such element prior to retirement is considered to be incidental to the primary purpose of the plan. [Rev. Rul. 60-83.]

Where profit-sharing funds have not been accumulated for at least two years, the payment of premiums for accident and health insurance therefrom are treated as incidental if, in the aggregate, such payments do not exceed 25% of the funds allocated to the account of the participant for whom the insurance is acquired. If such funds are used to purchase both ordinary life and accident and health insurance, the amount expended for accident and health insurance, plus one-half of the premiums paid for ordinary life insurance, may not in the aggregate exceed 25% of the funds allocated to an employee's account. [Rev. Rul. 61-164; Rev. Rul. 65-178, Part 2(n)(3).]

If an affiliated group of corporations maintains a profit-sharing or stock bonus plan, employees may share in the profits of the group. [Regs. 1.401-1(a)(2)(ii) and (iii).]

FORFEITURES. Forfeitures arise when a profit-sharing plan participant withdraws from the plan prior to the time that he achieves a 100% vested interest. The various methods of allocating forfeitures are as follows:

1. Allocation among the remaining participants in proportion to their account balances.
2. Allocation among the remaining participants on the same basis as that on which the current employer contribution is allocated.
3. Allocation among the participants on the basis of the number of years of participation in the plan.
4. Allocation on an equal basis among all remaining participants.
5. Application of forfeitures to reduce the next employer contribution. [Rev. Rul. 65–178, Part 7.]

The Internal Revenue Service favors treating a forfeiture as an additional current employer contribution and allocating it on the same basis as that on which the normal employer contribution is allocated — i.e., on the basis of current compensation. Allocation of forfeitures on account balances, while not preferred, may be used provided such a method does not result in discrimination.

No particular problem is presented for the single-employer plan in allocating forfeitures except for choosing between the various methods in order to avoid discrimination.

Experience discloses difficulties with a single plan for affiliated employers. In this situation, the following question may arise: May the forfeitures arising in one company be reallocated to all employees of the other affiliated company or must the forfeitures be reallocated to the employees of the company for whom the forfeited employee worked? While many companies do spread the forfeitures over all employees of the affiliated group, the position of the Revenue Service is that the forfeiture must be retained among the employees of the corporation giving rise to the forfeiture. [P.S. No. 51, Part B.]

WITHDRAWALS. A plan which provides for supplemental unemployment insurance benefits may qualify [Special Ruling, December 29, 1955], as may a profit-sharing plan (but not a pension plan) which permits participants to withdraw funds in times of financial need. [Rev. Rul. 56–693.] An employee may elect each year to participate in the trust or to take his entire share in cash. [Rev. Rul. 65–178, Part 2(h).] But see *Hicks v. U. S.*, 314 F.2nd 180

(4th Cir. 1963) for a decision which might be contra. [See also Rev. Rul. 63–180; Rev. Rul. 56–497.] A plan may qualify which provides cash payments to some employees and deferred payments to other employees if it satisfies the other conditions of Section 401. [Rev. Rul. 65–178, Part 4(d).]

A profit-sharing plan can qualify even if it allows certain active participants with at least 60 months of participation to withdraw all employer contributions, including those made within the last two years. [Rev. Rul. 68–24.]

STOCK BONUS PLANS

A stock bonus plan is a plan established and maintained by an employer to provide benefits similar to those of a profit-sharing plan, except that deductible contributions by the employer are not necessarily dependent upon the existence of profits or surplus and the benefits are distributable in stock of the employer company. For the purpose of allocating and distributing the stock of the employer a stock bonus plan is subject to the same requirements as a profit-sharing plan. [Regs. 1.401-1(b)(1)(iii).]

(a) REQUIREMENTS FOR QUALIFICATION

BENEFITS

EXCLUSIVE EMPLOYEE BENEFIT. The first condition to be met for qualification of a pension, profit-sharing, or stock bonus plan is that contributions are to be made by the employer, or employees, or both, and the corpus and income of the fund accumulated are to be distributed to the employees or their beneficiaries. The plan must be for their exclusive benefit. [Sec. 401(a)(1).]

PARTICIPANTS. The term "beneficiaries" includes not only the employee's estate or dependents and the natural objects of his bounty but also any person designated by him to share in the benefits of the plan after his death. [Regs. 1.401-1(b)(4).] A qualified plan may restrict the "beneficiaries" to the estate of the employee, dependents of the employee, or persons who are the natural objects of the employee's bounty. [Rev. Rul. 65-178, Part 2 (1).] An employee may not irrevocably elect, prior to retirement, to defer until after death his vested benefits. [Rev. Rul. 56-656.]

A plan may be for the exclusive benefit of employees or their beneficiaries where only former employees are covered. [Regs. 1.401-1(b)(4).] The plan must cover some employees, active or retired. [Rev. Rul. 65-178, Part 2(j).] A qualified plan will cease to qualify at such time as the employer has no employees, active or retired. [Rev. Rul. 55-629.]

The position of the Revenue Service is that the entire plan is disqualified if any participant is not an "employee." See the chapter on foreign operations beginning at page 133. An attorney or other professional person may be an employee if he qualifies as such for other purposes, including social security and income tax with-holding, even though he has an independent income from his professional practice. A principal in an association taxable as a corporation under Section 7701 and a full-time life insurance agent may qualify to participate. A stockholder may be a participant if he is an employee. [Rev. Rul. 65-178, Part 2(j).]

PERMANENCY. In order to qualify, the plan must be intended to be permanent when set up. The regulations do not specify a minimum period of time for which the plan must be in existence in order to qualify. Instead they indicate what might happen if the plan were to be terminated or abandoned within a few years after it has taken effect. First, the regulations sound the warning that an early termination may be evidence that the plan was never a qualified plan. [Regs. 1.401-1(b)(2).] Second, special rules are laid down limiting the amount of money that may be applied under a pension plan for the benefit of any of the 25 highest paid employees, if the plan is terminated within ten years after it is established or within ten years after an amendment increasing the possibility of discrimination as to contributions and benefits. [Mim. 5717, modified by Rev. Rul. 61-10.] Third, the interests of participants must become vested when the plan is terminated, or upon complete discontinuance of contributions. [Sec. 401(a)(7).]

The Commissioner has ruled, however, that the test of permanency is met where, under a union negotiated contract, a pension plan cannot be changed for five years and then may be modified in accordance with the terms of a contract to be re-negotiated at that time, the assumption being that the plan itself is continuous even though the contract is of limited duration. [Rev. Rul. 55-681.] A termination in the first year of operation due to employee dissatisfaction has been permitted. [*Kane Chevrolet Co.*, 32 T.C. 596 (1959).]

A discontinuance of contributions is in reality a termination of a qualified plan. On the other hand, a suspension of contributions is an event which may or may not evolve into a discontinuance. In order to determine whether a suspension actually is a discontinuance, it is necessary to take into consideration the following factors, in addition to the provisions of the plan itself [Rev. Rul. 60-2]:

1. Whether a discontinuance is called a suspension in order to avoid the vesting requirement.
2. Whether the contributions are recurring and substantial.
3. Whether the lack of contributions is likely to continue indefinitely.
4. Whether, as of the end of any year for which no substantial contribution has been made, the lack of full vesting for employees whose services have already terminated has created the prohibited discrimination in favor of continuing participants.

INVESTMENTS. Financial transactions between the employees' trust and the employer must be for the benefit of the participants under the plan. This requirement does not prevent others from also benefiting from such a transaction. See chapter on investment of trust funds, page 239.

The following are examples of transactions between an employer and an exempt trust which might be considered nonbeneficial to the participants under the plan:

1. Purchase of employer stock for the purpose of:
   a. Buying out a troublesome shareholder.
   b. Providing liquidity for the estate of a deceased shareholder.
   c. Shifting control between shareholders.
   d. Bolstering a market for the shares.
   e. Providing a new market for the shares.

2. Loan of money by the trust for the purpose of:
   a. Furnishing funds at a time when the employer is unable to borrow through normal channels.
   b. Furnishing funds without adequate security, or with too little or too much interest.

REVALUATION OF INVESTMENTS. Usually the equity securities held by pension trusts are valued at cost and the obligations at cost or amortized cost. If there is substantial unrealized appreciation on the securities, it may be proper to recognize the unrealized appreciation in determining the amount of the employer's annual contribution and the unfunded past service costs. (See page 76 for definition of the term "past service cost.") The Treasury Department has permitted unrealized appreciation to be taken into consideration provided the plan is in no present danger of being underfunded and the method of recognizing the appreciation is consistently followed. [Rev. Rul. 57-549.] Recognition of unrealized appreciation may provide evidence that the plan is overfunded. [Rev. Rul. 64-159.]

Generally, any reasonable valuation method is acceptable if the adopted method is followed consistently and does not result in the manipulation of values. [Rev. Rul. 63-11; Rev. Rul. 64-84.] Some methods which have been used are as follows:

1. Use of market value or short-term average of market.
2. Bankers Trust method, under which adjusted cost is written up each year by 3%.
3. Long-range yield method. If market exceeds adjusted cost, a write-up is made equal to 7% of adjusted cost less dividends received. Gains on actual sales reduce the adjusted cost. Losses increase the adjusted cost.
4. Revenue Ruling 57-549 method, under which a constant percentage of the difference between the market value and adjusted cost represents the annual write-up.
5. Transfer of a single trust to a pooled trust. When the transfer is made the securities must be recorded in the pooled trust at market values.

A pension or annuity plan is fully funded at any given time if the cost of benefits which have accrued to that time has been paid.

A determination in this respect is made at the end of a taxable year. If the total contributions for all years through the end of the taxable year, plus the increments thereon, are sufficient to provide the benefits accrued to that time, determined in accordance with the plan, no further deductions are allowable for additional contributions since such additional contributions would not be ordinary and necessary business expenses. [Rev. Rul. 57-89; Rev. Rul. 59-153; Rev. Rul. 64-159.]

Similarly, if there are enough funds under the plan to provide the benefits which have accrued through the taxable year, additional contributions are not expenses for such year or any prior year. Additional contributions may be prepayments or tax-free accumulations which may revert to the employer on termination of the trust as a balance due to an actuarial error. In either case they are not deductible. [Regs. 1.401-2(b)(1).]

A deduction for a contribution under a pension or annuity plan depends upon the methods, factors, and assumptions which are used to compute the costs of the plan, and on the applicable limitation. If the assets in the fund are consistently valued at cost, and if under such method the accrued benefits have not been fully paid for, the plan is not overfunded although the assets valued at market may be more than enough to fully provide for the accrued benefits. Realized gains, however, must be taken into account. [Speech by Isadore Goodman delivered at a Briefing Conference on Pension and Profit-Sharing Trusts sponsored by the Federal Bar Association, Washington, D.C., January 21, 1966; *Prentice-Hall Pension and Profit-Sharing Service*, ¶ 19,033.5.]

The year in which the employer's contribution is reduced as a result of recognizing the appreciation will depend upon the actuarial method used for determining the cost of a pension plan. If the "single premium" method is used, for example, the write-up may be absorbed in one year or in a relatively few years, while the "level premium" method may require a spreadout of 15 to 20 years.

In the case of a profit-sharing or stock bonus plan, or of a self-administered money-purchase pension plan, any securities held by the trust must be valued at fair market value at least once a year on a specified inventory date, and each participant's account must then be adjusted in accordance with the valuation. No amounts may be withheld from allocation in a profit-sharing or stock bonus plan through the setting up of reserves. [Rev. Rul. 65-178, Parts 2(s) and (t).]

Example: Jones has a one-tenth interest in the funds of the XYZ Company's profit-sharing plan trust. Prior to the annual valuation, Jones's interest was stated at $24,000. As a result of the annual valuation at fair market value the total fund increased by $35,000. After the annual valuation, Jones's account is stated at $27,500.

DIVERSION OF FUNDS

The second condition to be met for qualification is that it must be impossible under the trust for funds to be diverted to any other purpose until all liabilities under the trust to employees or their beneficiaries have been satisfied. [Sec. 401(a)-(2).]

In the case of a pension trust, after all liabilities under the plan are satisfied the employer may recover any remaining surplus provided such surplus is the result of an erroneous actuarial computation. [Regs. 1.401-2(b)(1).] Allocations under profit-sharing and stock bonus plans are not based on amounts necessary to provide stipulated retirement benefits, and consequently there can be no erroneous actuarial computation and thus no recovery. [Rev. Rul. 65-178, Part 3(e).]

A pension plan will not fail to qualify merely because it provides that, except as to claims of the employer, the rights of the employee are not subject to claims of creditors. [Rev. Rul. 65-178, Part 3(b).]

A plan may qualify even though it contains a provision for recovery of conditional contributions in the event that the Commissioner rules that the plan is not qualified. No diversion of funds exists. [Rev. Rul. 65-178, Part 3(c).]

COVERAGE

PERCENTAGE REQUIREMENTS. The third condition to be met for qualification is that the plan must cover one of the following classifications [Sec. 401(a)(3)]:

1. Seventy percent or more of all employees.
2. Eighty percent or more of all employees who are eligible

if 70% or more of all employees are eligible for coverage. Under this classification, coverage can be extended to as few as 56% of all employees.

3. A classification set up by the employer and found by the Commissioner not to be discriminatory in favor of officers, shareholders, supervisory personnel, or highly compensated employees.

For the purposes of the percentage requirements of classifications 1 and 2 above, the following employees may be excluded:

1. *Minimum service employees* — those persons who have not been employed for the minimum period of service prescribed by the plan. The prescribed minimum service period cannot exceed five years (three years if there is an owner-employee participating). See the chapter on retirement plans for the self-employed, beginning on page 115.

2. *Part-time employees* — those persons whose customary employment is for not more than 20 hours in any one week.

3. *Seasonal employees* — those persons whose customary employment is for five months or less in any calendar year.

Employees temporarily on leave — e.g., persons in the Armed Forces — must be included if otherwise eligible. Full-time life insurance salesmen are included if they qualify as employees for social security purposes. Persons ineligible because of age alone must be included in the computation of total employees. [Regs. 1.401-3(a) (2).]

Example: The ABC Company adopts a trusteed pension plan. The plan provides that any full-time employee is eligible to participate if he has at least three years' service and is at least 30 years of age. An analysis of ABC's personnel records shows the following:

1. Eligible employees 1,350
2. Employees not eligible because of age 300
3. Employees not eligible because of length of service 175
4. Employees not eligible because of part-time work 100
5. Employees not eligible because of seasonal work 75
6. Total employees 2,000

In this situation the coverage test is met if at least 1,080 employees are covered by the plan. The computation is as follows:

7. Total employees for percentage test (line 6 above minus lines 3, 4, and 5) 1,650
8. Total employees eligible to participate (line 7 minus line 2) 1,350
9. The "70% of all employees" test is met (percentage of line 8 to line 7) 82%
10. The "70% of all employees" test would have required coverage of (70% of 1,650) 1,155
11. The "80% of 70%" test requires coverage of (80% of 1,350) 1,080

CLASSIFICATION. In lieu of meeting the percentage requirements, an employer may set up a classification of employees, but the classification must not discriminate in favor of officers, shareholders, supervisors, or highly compensated employees. Plans can qualify which are limited to employees who are within a prescribed age group, have been employed for a stated number of years, have been employed in certain designated departments, or are in other classifications. The effect of limiting coverage must not result in discrimination in favor of employees within the enumerations with respect to which discrimination is prohibited. [Regs. 1.401-3(d); Rev. Rul. 65-178, Part 4(c).]

If all current employees are eligible regardless of length of service, and only those future employees who will complete five years of service can become eligible, the plan will qualify even though there are some employees who have less than five years of service. [Rev. Rul. 65-178, Part 4(e).]

The Revenue Service states that limiting coverage to salaried or clerical employees only, by excluding hourly workers, will not in and of itself qualify a plan. To qualify, the classification must not discriminate in favor of officers, shareholders, employees whose principal duties consist in supervising the work of other employees, or highly compensated employees.

A pension plan covering salaried employees only qualified under the following circumstances:

Total employees	109	100.0%
Employees eligible for coverage	26	23.9%
Highly paid employees covered	11	42.3%

However, the Revenue Service states that the percentages derived from the facts of the ruling cannot be used as a standard in all cases. [Rev. Rul. 66-12; Rev. Rul. 68-244.]

A profit-sharing plan limited coverage to salaried employees who were 30 years of age or older and had worked for at least six months. Seventeen of the employer's 20 employees were hourly employees. Two of the three salaried employees qualified under the plan. The two were officers and supervisors earning substantially more than the hourly employees. The plan did not qualify. [Rev. Rul. 66-13.]

A corporate employer established a profit-sharing plan for the benefit of its full-time salaried employees. The employer has 60 employees, six of whom are salaried and are plan participants. Of the six covered, five are officer-shareholders, each of whom earns an annual salary of $26,000. The other participant has an annual salary of $6,160. Employees excluded are hourly paid and are represented by a union. Earnings of each of the 54 excluded union employees are considerably less than the five officer-shareholder employees. The employer contended that in negotiating with the union in connection with contract demands he has a strict obligation to bargain in good faith with the duly designated representative of the employees in the bargaining unit over wages, hours, and other conditions of employment, and that he cannot unilaterally include union employees in a profit-sharing plan. The plan failed to qualify. [Rev. Rul. 66-14.]

An employer established a profit-sharing plan for the benefit of his full-time salaried employees. The plan excludes those employees for whom the employer contributes to a pension or welfare plan, under a collective bargaining agreement. The employer has 62 employees, six of whom are salaried and are plan participants. Fifty-six hourly-rated employees are ineligible for participation because they are covered under a union collective bargaining agreement. Three of the six covered employees are shareholders, officers, and supervisors, and the remaining three are considered to be highly compensated.

When the salaried employees' profit-sharing plan and the hourly-rated employees' pension plan are viewed together as a unit, the percentage requirements of Section 401(a)(3)(A) are met. However, the profit-sharing plan does not qualify because it is discriminatory. The employer contributes 15% of the base salaries of participants to the profit-sharing plan but contributes only 4% of the total payroll of participants to the hourly-rated employees' pension plan. [Rev. Rul. 66-15.]

A plan covering three out of 20 employees qualified. [*Ray Cleaners, Inc.*, TCM 1968-6.]

A pension plan covering only salaried employees who were managers, stockholder-employees, and supervisors did not qualify. [*John Duguid & Sons, Inc.*, 278 Fed. Supp. 101 (D.C. New York, 1967); *Ed and Jim Fleitz, Inc.*, 50 T.C. No. 35 (1968).]

A profit-sharing plan failed to qualify when regular salaried employees were covered and hourly-paid employees excluded. Six out of fourteen employees, or 43% of all employees, of the employer, participated. The Tax Court, however, considered the percentage of employees covered adequate for qualification. Of the six covered, only three employees were in the supervisory category. The Court reasoned that, although five of the covered employees, including the president, were paid more than the hourly employees, the actual compensation level did not make them highly paid under the circumstances of the case. Here, a relatively small difference existed between the top salaried employee, other than the president, and the highest hourly-paid employee. However, the Second Circuit reversed and held the plan to be discriminatory in favor of highly compensated employees. [*Pepsi-Cola Niagara Bottling Corp.*, 48 T.C. 75 (1967), rev'd. (2nd Cir. 1968).]

A profit-sharing plan was held not to be discriminatory where benefits were reallocated by reason of forfeitures from departing rank-and-file employees to a stockholder-employee. The Revenue Service refuses to follow this case. [*Sherwood Swan & Co., Ltd.*, 42 T.C. 299 (1964) *nonacq.*, aff'd. (9th Cir. 1965); Rev. Rul. 66-251.]

The Revenue Service has ruled that a corporation engaged in a joint venture with another corporation is required to take the employees of the joint venture into account and its distributive share of compensation paid to them in determining qualification under Section 401(a) of the corporation's profit-sharing plan as to coverage and nondiscrimination requirements. [Rev. Rul. 68-370.]

A plan will not necessarily fail to qualify merely because it covers only the employer's one employee. [Rev. Rul. 65-178, Part 4(a); Rev. Rul. 55-81.] Where, however, the sole stockholder is the only employee who is continuously employed, a plan covering him only will not qualify. [Rev. Rul. 63-108.] Unofficial sources indicate that qualifications may be obtained for plans of "one-man" corporations—i.e., those with no employees other than the sole shareholder.

The Revenue Service has ruled that a pension plan meeting the percentage coverage requirements of Section 401(a)(3)(A) in which four out of a total of 15 employees were eligible and participated in the plan qualified, even though all the participants were shareholders and highly compensated employees. It ruled that the plan was not discriminatory within the meaning of Section 401(a)(4) merely because it fails to provide benefits for ineligible employees. The fact that the plan in operation covered only shareholders and highly compensated employees doesn't make it discriminatory because the plan covered all eligible employees and met the percentage coverage requirements. The eligibility requirement that excludes seasonal employees is clearly acceptable — i.e., those employees whose customary employment is not for more than 20 hours in any one week, and employees whose customary employment is not for more than five months in any calendar year. [Sec. 401(a)(3)(A); Rev. Rul. 68-301.]

DISCRIMINATION

The fourth condition to be met for qualification is that the contributions and benefits must not discriminate in favor of employees who are officers, shareholders, supervisory personnel, or highly compensated employees. [Sec. 401(a)(4).]

This discrimination provision is of particular concern to the Revenue Service. Every qualified plan is eventually examined by the Service to determine whether discrimination existed in the plan at the time of its inception or subsequently crept into the plan through actual operation. [*Harold D. Greenwald*, 44 T.C. 137, 366 F. 2nd 538 (2nd Cir. 1966).]

The possibility of discrimination varies with each plan and circumstance. Discrimination is somewhat of a state of mind, and as such is subject to the judgment of the taxpayer and the Revenue Service. Consequently, no specific guidelines can be laid down to define discrimination. Section 401(a)(5), however, does set forth five classifications of employees which in themselves are *not dis-*

criminatory as to coverage under Section 401(a)(3)(B) or as to contributions and benefits under Section 401(a)(4):

1. One which excludes employees whose sole compensation is subject to social security taxes — i.e., whose whole compensation is $7,800 or less.
2. One which is limited to salaried or clerical employees.
3. One in which contributions or benefits bear a uniform relationship to total compensation or to basic or regular rates of compensation.
4. One in which contributions and benefits based upon the first $7,800 of wages differ from contributions and benefits based upon compensation in excess of $7,800.
5. One in which contributions and benefits differ because of retirement benefits created under state or Federal laws.

A plan which is limited to salaried employees is not discriminatory on the sole basis of that limitation alone. Such a plan might be discriminatory in favor of prohibited employees, however, when all facts are considered. This situation may arise in the case of a small corporation.

Example: The Minute Company has 105 employees, of whom 100 are hourly workers and five are salaried. Of the five salaried employees, two are share holders and three are supervisors. It would be impossible to qualify a salaried-employees-only plan in this case.

The Internal Revenue Service has issued proposed regulations explaining new integration rules to reflect the increase in the social security wage base under 1967 amendments to the law to $7,800 and proposes a new integration rate of 30%. [Prop. Regs. 1.401-3, 1.401-11, and 1.401-12.] The Revenue Service will accept plans which integrate under existing rules pending the issuance of final regulations. Thus, new plans integrated at $4,800 are allowed to provide a retirement benefit of up to 37.5% of average earnings, and plans integrated at $6,600 are allowed to provide benefits of up to 27.27% [Rev. Rul. 67-10.] (But see page 263.)

A plan which is limited to salaried employees is not discriminatory on the sole basis of that limitation alone. Such a plan might be discriminatory in favor of prohibited employees, however, when all facts are considered. (See comments above.)

The five classifications in Section 401(a)(5) are not exclusive. The regulations [Regs. 1.401-3(d)] provide that under appropriate circumstances the following classifications may be nondiscriminatory:

1. Employees over a certain age.
2. Employees with stated length of service.
3. Employees in designated company departments.
4. Any other classification of employees which does not favor officers, shareholders, supervisors, or highly compensated employees.

The exclusion from a plan of employees who earn less than $7,800 is not necessarily discriminatory provided that the plan benefits for over-$7,800 employees, when coupled with social security benefits, are not proportionately greater when compared to total compensation than social security benefits are for the $7,800-and-under employees. However, until regulations are amended, the Revenue Service will not rule on qualification of plans above the $6,600 level. [Rev. Rul. 67-10; Rev. Rul. 67-261.]

CONTRIBUTIONS

A qualified plan may require employee contributions. If a contributory plan is offered to all the employees, but the contributions required of the employee participants are so burdensome as to make the plan acceptable only to the highly paid employees, the classification will be considered discriminatory in favor of such highly paid employees. [Reg. 1.401-3(d).] Generally, the Revenue Service will consider compulsory employee contributions up to 6% of compensation as not being burdensome. [Rev. Rul. 65-178, Part 4(g).]

A plan may provide for voluntary contributions by employees of up to 10% of their compensation, provided that the employer's contribution or the benefits are not geared to employee contributions. [Rev. Rul. 65-178, Part 4(h).] The voluntary contribution is in addition to the compulsory contribution. It is also understood that each plan may have a voluntary contribution of up to 10% even though employees participate in more than one plan — e.g., if they participate in both a pension and a profit-sharing plan.

VESTING

Numerous provisions for vesting of employees' rights are in use. The provisions include complete and immediate vesting, complete vesting after completion of a stated term of service or attainment of an age, graduated vesting over a period of years, and no vesting until retirement. The facts in each case determine whether the vesting provision contains the element of discrimination. For example, a plan which allows no vesting until retirement where most of the participants are migratory will not qualify. [Rev. Rul. 65-178, Part 4(i), 5(c).]

CIVIL RIGHTS ACT

The Civil Rights Act of 1964 prohibits discrimination in employment practices and applies to any employer in an industry affecting interstate commerce who has 25 or more employees. Discrimination is prohibited on the basis of race, color, religion, sex, or national origin. The law is administered by the Equal Employment Opportunity Commission.

A difference in optional or compulsory retirement age if based on sex violates Title VII. The law provides no specific fine or other penalty for violation and has no real enforcement power. If the violator refuses to comply, an employee can then bring his own civil suit against the violator. An employer who does not comply can lose his Government contracts. The effective date of the new ruling is July 1, 1968. [EEOC—Pension and Retirement Plans Compliance with Civil Rights Act—29 CFR, Part 1604.]

(b) CERTAIN RETROACTIVE CHANGES IN PLAN

An employer may find that a plan is defective and cannot be qualified. In such a case, he may correct the defect at any time during the period which begins with the effective date of the plan and ends with the 15th day of the third month following the year which contains the effective date. The qualified status will date back to the original effective date, provided, of course, the corrected plan is made retroactive to that date. In actual practice, the limitation of the grace period to 2½ months may not be strictly enforced. This statutory relief provision does not apply to amendments to existing plans. [Sec. 401(b).]

Example: A calendar-year employer adopts a pension plan in 1965, effective as of March 1, 1967. On February 25, 1968, after discussions with the Revenue Service, the plan is amended so as to meet the qualification requirements. The amendments are made retroactive to March 1, 1967. The plan is qualified from that date.

(c) DEFINITIONS AND RULES RELATING TO SELF-EMPLOYED INDIVIDUALS AND OWNER-EMPLOYEES

(d) ADDITIONAL REQUIREMENTS FOR QUALIFICATION OF TRUSTS AND PLANS BENEFITING OWNER-EMPLOYEES

(e) EXCESS CONTRIBUTIONS ON BEHALF OF OWNER-EMPLOYEES

The above subsections relate to retirement plans for the self-employed individual as provided by the Self-Employed Individuals Tax Retirement Act of 1962. This subject is treated in summary in a separate chapter (see page 115).

(f) CERTAIN CUSTODIAL ACCOUNTS

As a medium of funding, a custodial account, in lieu of a trust, may be established with a bank, trust company, or domestic building and loan association as those terms are defined in Section 581 of the Code, or a corporation subject to the supervision and examination of a state banking authority. The custodian of the account will be treated as the trustee of the account for all purposes relating to a qualified retirement plan. The custodial account is treated as an exempt trust for all purposes of the Code. It is exempt from income tax under Section 501(a). It must file information returns and supply the other information that an exempt trust must supply. [Regs. 1.401-8(c).]

The investments which may be made through a custodial account are limited to two types:

1. *Stock in a regulated investment company.* The term "regulated investment company" means one which falls within the meaning of Section 851(a) of the Internal Revenue Code of 1954 — that is, one which is registered under the Investment Company Act of 1940 either as a management company or as a unit investment trust, or which is a common trust fund or similar fund excluded from the definition of "investment company" and not included in the definition of "common trust fund" by Section 584(a) and which issues only redeemable stock.

2. *Annuity, endowment, or life insurance contracts issued by an insurance company.*

If cash is invested in "open-end" mutual funds, the shares must be registered in the name of the custodian or its nominee, and the employee-participant must be the beneficial owner. The requirement as to beneficial ownership does not mean that the participant must have a nonforfeitable right to the shares. If a participant forfeits his interest in the plan, his interest in the stock is reallocated to other participants in the plan. [Regs. 1.401-8(b) (4).]

If the investment is in annuity, endowment, or life insurance contracts with an insurance company, the contracts must be held by the custodian until distributed under the terms of the plan. [Regs. 1.401-8(b) (1).]

The requirement that a custodial account's funds must be invested solely in mutual funds or insurance company contracts means that the employer contribution, the employee contribution, and the earnings on both contributions must be invested. It also applies to capital gains on the sale of stock, capital gain dividends, and refunds. It does not prohibit the custodian from accumulating cash in a checking or savings account prior to investment. [Regs. 1.401-8(b) (3).]

While the statute provides for two types of investments for the custodial account, only one type may be chosen. The investment must be solely in stock of a regulated investment company or solely in contracts with an insurance company. A single plan, however, may have more than one custodial account. If there are two custodial accounts, one may be invested in stock and the other may be invested in contracts.

A plan may also use custodial accounts and an exempt trust. [Regs. 1.401-8(a).]

(g) "ANNUITY" DEFINED

The term "annuity" includes a face-amount certificate as defined in Section 2(a) (15) of the Investment Company Act of 1940; however, any certificate issued after December 31, 1962 must be nontransferable unless owned by the trustee of a qualified trust or a custodial account. A face-amount certificate is an investment contract which may be purchased by a single-sum payment or a series of payments over a period of time. The payout at maturity is in the form of a lump-sum amount or in installments. [Regs. 1.401-9.]

(h) MEDICAL, ETC., BENEFITS FOR RETIRED EMPLOYEES AND THEIR SPOUSES AND DEPENDENTS

For taxable years beginning after October 23, 1962, a pension or annuity plan may provide for the payment of sickness, accident, hospitalization, and medical expenses of retired employees, their spouses, and their dependents under certain circumstances. For an employee to be considered retired there must be a separation from employment. In order for such a plan to be effective, the following requirements must be met:

1. The plan must not discriminate in favor of officers, shareholders, supervisory employees, or highly compensated employees as to coverage, contributions, or benefits. This requirement applies to both the medical and the retirement portions of the plan. [Regs. 1.401-14(b)(2).]
2. Contributions to fund the medical benefits may be on either a contributory or noncontributory basis without regard to whether the funding of retirement benefits are on a similar basis. [Regs. 1.401-14(b)(3).]
3. The plan must specify the type and amount of benefits which are available. [Regs. 1.401-14(c)(1).]
4. The medical benefits and the life insurance protection under the plan must be subordinate to the plan's retirement benefits. [Regs. 1.401-14(c)(1).] For purposes of

this requirement the life insurance protection means the excess of the amount which would be paid upon death of the employee over the amount of reserve available to provide retirement benefits. Medical benefits are considered subordinate if at all times the accumulated total of contributions for medical benefits and life insurance protection does not exceed 25% of the accumulated total contributions under the plan, excluding contributions to fund past service costs. The accumulations begin with the first year in which a contribution is made for medical benefits.

Example:	1966	1967	1968
Annual contributions:			
Medical	$ 18,000	$ 20,000	$ 28,000
Insurance	21,000	24,000	30,000
Retirement	129,000	138,000	120,000
Total	$168,000	$182,000	$178,000
Accumulated totals:			
Medical	$ 18,000	$ 38,000	$ 66,000
Insurance	21,000	45,000	75,000
Retirement	129,000	267,000	387,000
Total	$168,000	$350,000	$528,000
Percentage of medical and insurance contributions to total contributions	23%	24%	27%

The 1968 amounts are in excess of the allowable limits.

5. A separate account must be established and maintained for the contributions made to fund the benefits. [Regs. 1.401-14(c)(2).] The funds need not be invested separately but can be commingled with other funds of the retirement plan. If the funds are not invested separately, the income from the investments must be allocated to the medical account in some reasonable manner.

6. The employer's contribution to the separate account must be reasonable and acertainable. [Regs. 1.401-14(c)(3).] The amount of the employer's contribution is taken into account in determining whether compensation is reasonable (see page 315), but it is not considered in determining the amount which is deductible under Section 404 as a

contribution to a qualified retirement plan (see page 73). [Regs. 1.404(a)-3(f).]

7. Prior to the time that all liabilities under the medical plan are satisfied, no part of the separate account can be used for any other purpose. For example, the funds cannot be used to reduce the employer's contribution or to provide retirement benefits. The funds may be used to pay necessary and appropriate administration expenses relating to the medical-benefits accounts. [Regs. 1.401-14(c)(4).]

8. The plan must provide that after all liabilities under the medical plan are satisfied, any surplus in the separate account must be returned to the employer. [Regs. 1.401-14(c)(5).]

9. Forfeitures prior to the termination of the plan must be applied to reduce employer contributions to fund medical benefits. [Regs. 1.401-14(c)(6).]

(i) CROSS REFERENCE

This subsection is a cross reference to Section 501(a), which covers exemption from tax of a trust qualified under this section (see page 203).

Taxability of Beneficiary of Employees' Trust

(a) TAXABILITY OF BENEFICIARY OF EXEMPT TRUST

Contributions by an employer to an exempt employees' trust are not taxable to the participants at the time the contribution is made, with the exception of certain premiums paid on life insurance. The employees, or their beneficiaries, are taxable only in the year in which amounts are actually distributed or made available to them. When amounts are distributed or made available to an employee or other beneficiary of an exempt trust, they are taxed as an annuity except as stated below. [Sec. 402(a)(1).] It is immaterial in the case of contributions to an exempt trust whether the employee's rights in the contributions to the trust are forfeitable or nonforfeitable, either at the time the contribution is made to the trust or thereafter. [Regs. 1.402(a)-1(a)(1)(i).]

PRINCIPLES OF TAX DEFERMENT

The principle of a qualified plan is to permit the employer to deduct contributions currently, and to defer taxation of amounts allocated to the employee to the time they are distributed to him. At that time the employee will normally be in a lower tax bracket.

The rule of tax deferment, however, is subject to certain restrictions and limitations:

1. Employer contributions or earnings of a qualified trust applied to the purchase of retirement income, endowment, or other contracts providing life insurance protection payable upon an employee's death are taxable to the extent of the cost of the life insurance protection portion to the employee for the year in which it is so applied. [Sec. 72 (m)(3); Regs. 1.402(a)-1(a)(3).] (See page 56.) This rule also applies to a nontrusteed group annuity contract providing group permanent life insurance protection.

2. Special rules apply when a distribution to an employee or his beneficiary is made in stock or other securities of the employer corporation or a parent or subsidiary. [Regs. 1.402(a)-1(b).] Any net unrealized appreciation in the

value of such securities received as part of a distribution complying with the rules of long-term capital gain is not taken into account. If a distribution is made during employment, net unrealized appreciation is taken into account only with respect to such securities purchased with contributions made by the employer. (See page 52.)

3. If the distribution is in the form of a nontransferable annuity contract, the cash surrender value is not taxable to the employee except at the time, and to the extent, that he converts it to cash. Similarly, the same treatment is accorded the cash value of an insurance contract distributed by a qualified trust, if within 60 days after the distribution it is irrevocably converted into a contract under which no part of any death benefit is excludible from income as proceeds from life insurance.

4. If employees contribute and the employer withholds such contribution from the salary or wages due an employee, the amount so withheld is taxable to the employee at the time it is withheld. The amount is considered to have been constructively received before it was applied.

5. If a plan or trust agreement provides for an employee's irrevocable election, before his interest becomes distributable, to defer its distribution to a fixed or determinable future time, his interest is not made available to him before that time. It is immaterial in this instance whether he makes the election by positive action or merely by inaction. But see *Hicks v. U.S.*, 314 F.2d 180 (4th Cir. 1963) for a decision which on peculiar facts, as described on page 47, held to the contrary. Such a provision in a qualified plan is extremely helpful in preventing immediate taxation to employees who are affected by corporate mergers, consolidations, and other organizational changes in which qualified plans are discontinued and their assets transferred to the plans of the surviving companies. [Rev. Rul. 55-423.]

6. Withholding is not required with regard to payments made to or from the qualifying trust, or under a qualifying annuity plan. [Regs. 1.3401(a)(12)-1.] However, the trustee or other payor is required to file an information return, on Form 1099, as to each beneficiary to whom there is

distributed or made available an amount which is taxable to the extent of $600 or more. [Regs. 1.6041-2(b); Rev. Rul. 56-176.]

CONSTRUCTIVE RECEIPT

An election given employees to take currently part or all of an employer's contribution to a qualified plan does not necessarily make the amount "available" to those employees who have not elected to receive cash. For example, all eligible employees in a qualified profit-sharing plan are given an election to take their share in cash, or to have the employer contribute to the plan. The Revenue Service has ruled that such an election of itself does not disqualify the plan, as long as those who elect not to take cash are sufficient in number to make the plan nondiscriminatory. [Rev. Rul. 56-497.] There is a clear implication in this ruling that those who have elected to defer their share under the plan are not deemed to have received it. The key point seems to be that any election exercised before the close of each year, at a time when the amount of the contribution is not known, avoids the problem of constructive receipt.

On the other hand, a plan which gave employees an election which could be made at any time after 15 years of participation to withdraw their entire share was held to result in "available" taxable income after expiration of the first 15 years, whether or not the option was exercised. [Rev. Rul. 57-260.]

An amount is not "available" to an employee if he either suffers a serious detriment or gives up the "available" amount by making a prior irrevocable election to defer receipt of his share until some future time. The detriment or deferment must be substantial. Giving up further participation in the plan or losing all prior service credits in the event of re-employment are detriments which are substantial. [Rev. Rul. 55-423; Rev. Rul. 55-425.] Also, if a withdrawal is subject to a committee's approval on furnishing proof of financial necessity, the amount is not "available." [Rev. Rul. 55-424.]

No income is realized by an employee who is given a right to elect between cash and restricted stock in payment of compensation for services, provided the right to elect is exercised before the beginning of the year for which the services are rendered, until the restrictions on the stock lapse or the stock is sold, or cash is elected. [Rev. Rul. 68-86.]

In *Hicks v. U.S.*, 314 F.2d 180 (4th Cir. 1963), it was held that an employee constructively received 60% of his share of the profit-sharing contribution, even though it was paid into the trust at his direction. The Hicks profit-sharing plan described the elective portion "as if paid by such employee," thereby labeling it an employee's contribution. Furthermore, the elective portion could be withdrawn at any time subject only to a modest 5% penalty.

The Revenue Service has issued a ruling since the *Hicks* decision describing the manner in which taxation may be deferred on the portion of an employer's profit-sharing contribution which the employee elects to have paid into a plan. It suggests that the elective portion be subject to the same rules of distribution as the rest of the employee's share, and that the elective portion be described as an employer's contribution, not an employee's contribution. The amount should not be accessible to the employee at will, nor should it be subject to a nominal penalty only. [Rev. Rul. 63-180.]

Also to be considered is the fact that problems of discrimination are likely to be encountered in elective cash-pay profit-sharing plans. This may happen if all of the lower-paid employees elect current cash payments whereas the higher-paid employees elect deferment. In such a case, the plan may not qualify for tax exemption.

CAPITAL GAINS

DEATH OR OTHER SEPARATION. If, because of an employee's death or other separation from employment, the total distributions then payable to him by a qualified trust are paid in one taxable year of the recipient, the amount of such distribution is treated as the proceeds from the sale of a capital asset held over six months. [Sec. 402(a)(2).]

Capital gain treatment is available if the employee upon separation receives in one taxable year the entire balance of his credit at that time, even though he has received prior distributions during the continuance of the trust. [Sec. 402(a)(3)(C).] The capital gain provision applies even though in a later year an additional amount, attributable to the last year of service, is credited to the account of the employee and distributed. [Regs. 1.402(a)-1(a)(6)(ii).] The later distribution, however, will be taxed as ordinary income. [Rev. Rul. 56-558.] A lump sum paid to a death beneficiary is entitled to capital gain treatment even though the employee had previously received some annuity payments after retirement. [Regs. 1.402(a)-1(a)(6)(ii).] The provision does not apply, however, if the employee commences to receive an annuity after retirement and then accepts a lump sum in satisfaction of the remaining annuity payments, unless all payments are received in one taxable year. [Regs. 1.402(a)-1(a)(6)(iii).]

If a separated employee receives a total distribution consisting of cash and an annuity contract, the cash is long-term capital gain in the year of receipt even though the annuity is not taxable until payments under it are received. [Rev. Rul. 65-267.]

Where an employee receives an annuity contract as a total distribution and surrenders it in a subsequent taxable year, the amount received is ordinary income. [Rev. Rul. 65-268.]

TERMINATION OF A TRUST. The capital gain treatment does not apply to a lump-sum payment received upon a termination of the trust while the taxpayer remains an employee. [*Edward Joseph Glinske,* 17 T.C. 562 (1951); *Beecher v. U.S.,* 226 F. Supp. 547 (D.C. Ill., 1963).] Even a complete distribution at retirement age does not qualify where the employee continues to render some services and receives his regular salary beyond the year in which he receives the distribution. [Rev. Rul. 56-214.] Capital gain treatment does not apply to a total distribution received upon termination of a trust where a taxpayer continues to render service without compensation. [Rev. Rul. 57-115.]

BUSINESS TRANSFERS. As a result of certain business transfers, a "separation from service" may occur even though the employees of the old business are transferred to the new business. The Revenue Service has ruled that the following qualify as separations: (1) a reorganization under Section 368(a) (1) (C) in which the assets are retransferred to a subsidiary of the transferee [Rev. Rul. 58-94]; (2) a liquidation of a subsidiary where Section 334 (b) (2) is applicable [Rev. Rul. 58-95]; (3) a sale of all assets for cash [Rev. Rul. 58-96]; (4) a sale of the assets of a division [Rev. Rul.

58-97]; and (5) a liquidation of a corporation into a partnership where eligible stockholder-employees become ineligible partners. [Rev. Rul. 58-98.] A separation does not occur where a subsidiary's employees participate in a parent's trust and the subsidiary is separated from the parent. [Rev. Rul. 58-99.]

The liberal Revenue Service rulings must, however, be read in the light of several court decisions which cast some doubt as to the rulings' validity in defining the term "separation from the service." These decisions have held that "separation" does not occur where the employee continues in the same job with the same employer following a change of stock ownership and control. But, more important, the language used in the opinions may raise questions in connection with the Revenue Service rulings which have stated that there is a "separation from service" in reorganization-type situations. The decisions note Congressional limitations on the concept of "separation from service" because of Congress's fear that corporate taxpayers might abuse the law. This fear is based on the possibility that there can be a technical disappearance of a corporate entity in a tax-free reorganization not involving "a substantial change in the make-up of employees." This subject is further discussed in the chapter entitled "Business Combinations," beginning at page 265.

CONSULTATION AGREEMENTS AFTER RETIREMENT. Since the capital gain advantage is available upon "separation from service," a lump-sum payment from a qualified plan might not qualify for capital gains if the recipient is required to render services or to be available for consultation after retirement under a deferred-compensation contract. (A controlling stockholder after the sale of his stock to an acquiring corporation continued in an advisory capacity, and amounts received were taxable as ordinary income. [*William S. Bolden*, 39 T.C. 829 (1963).] But see Letter Ruling, December 22, 1960, at ¶ 11,981 of the *Prentice-Hall Pension and Profit-Sharing Service* contra.) If the work performed or required after retirement is as an independent consultant, in contrast to an employer-employee relationship, the latter being tested under the definition for Federal employment tax purposes, capital gains may be obtainable, but at present it is not entirely free from doubt. Many deferred-compensation contracts contain the requirement that the employee continue rendering services. Since the definition of "separation from service" is not fully resolved, it may be desirable, in certain instances, to eliminate the service and consultation clauses in deferred-compensation contracts where an executive is also covered by a qualified plan. Other conditions, such as refraining from competition, which are used in such contracts to avoid taxation under the doctrine of constructive receipt, may be retained without affecting the capital gains treatment on the lump-sum payment. For a terminated corporate officer acting as a liquidator, see Rev. Rul. 63-22.

TEN-YEAR RULE. A lump-sum distribution of the total amount standing to the credit of one of the 25 highest-paid employees participating in a qualified employees' pension plan and trust, paid to such employee on account of his separation from service at a time when the plan has been in existence for less than ten years, will be entitled to capital gain treatment where an agreement, adequately securing the obligations thereunder, between the distributee and the trustee guarantees repayment of any part of the distribution which is restricted under certain plan provisions should the plan be terminated within the first ten years of its existence or the full current cost of the plan has not been met at any time during this period.

An agreement between the severing employee and the plan trustee which provided as follows was found to be acceptable: In the event the employer failed to meet the full current cost within the first ten years or the plan was terminated, the employee or his estate would repay to the trust an amount equal to the actuarial value by which his monthly benefits under the plan would have been decreased under Mimeograph 5717. He agreed to deposit, as a guarantee of repayment, property worth 125% of the amount repayable if the plan was terminated on the date of the lump-sum distribution, and to deposit additional property if the market value fell below 110%. He could retain any income from the property. [Rev. Rul. 61-10.]

TOTAL DISTRIBUTIONS. The term "total distributions payable," as used in connection with this special long-term capital gain rule, is defined as the balance to the credit of an employee which becomes payable to a distributee by reason of the occurrence of the special event. The term is defined in this manner so that partial distributions made prior to the occurrence of the specified event will not defeat application of the capital gain treatment. [Regs. 1.402(a)-1(a)(6)(ii).]

Capital gain treatment for a lump-sum benefit paid to an employee from a qualified plan several years after separation may be available under certain conditions despite the fact the amount distributed is paid more than one year after the employee's separation from service. For example, if the employee leaves the employ of the company in one year, but doesn't receive the lump-sum benefit from the qualified plan until several years later, capital gain treatment may still be available. Taxability of the amount to the employee in any year depends upon the amount actually distributed or made available to the employee. If a substantial restriction on the employee's right of withdrawal exists in the year of his separation from service, a later lump-sum distribution to him will qualify for capital gain treatment. In this regard, any increment credited to an employee's account after his separation from service is taxable to him as ordinary income in the year of distribution because this amount does not represent a part of the balance to his credit in the trust payable on account on his separation from service. If the delay in distribution was caused by administrative problems of the plan, however, the increment may also be reported as capital gains. [Rev. Rul. 60-292.] Any increment other than the employee's share of the employer's contributions for the year of retirement credited to his account subsequent to the date of the termination of his service is taxable as ordinary income. [Rev. Rul. 62-190.]

If the entire amount credited to the employee's account is paid to the deceased employee's beneficiary within one taxable year of the beneficiary, it is a "severance distribution" taxable as capital gain. If, however, within 60 days after the distribution first becomes payable, the beneficiary exercises an election to receive an annuity in lieu of a lump sum, the annuity is ordinary income as the installments are received. [Regs. 1.402(a)-1(a)(6)(i).]

Where the qualified plans of two employers are funded through a single trust, an employee of both employers is entitled to capital gain treatment for a lump-sum distribution on termination of employment with one employer. [Rev. Rul. 66-16.]

PLANNING. In some cases a lump-sum distribution to an employee, even though taxed at capital gain rates, may be less desirable. The after-tax amount retained by the employee after having received a lump sum in the year of retirement may be considerably less than the amount he would have received had he taken an annuity over his lifetime or lesser period. This might be caused by the employee's high tax bracket in the year of retirement which may impose a greater tax burden on the amount received than the amount of tax that would have been imposed in later years on annuity payments when his tax brackets are lower because of reduced income and increased exemptions for age over 65 for himself and his wife. Thus, a tax computation made both ways is advisable in every case to determine whether the lump sum or annuity payments result in less tax cost.

INCOME AVERAGING. The elective income-averaging tax computation in appropriate circumstances should also be explored for possibilities of reduced tax cost upon distributions from qualified or nonqualified plans. The provisions of Sections 1301 to 1305 describe the computations required.

EMPLOYER'S STOCK

Where the distribution (either current or upon separation from employment) includes securities of the employer or of a "parent" or "subsidiary" corporation (as specially defined for this purpose), certain unrealized appreciation will not be taxable until the employee disposes of the securities.

In the case of current (nonseverance) distributions, the amount to be excluded is that portion of the net unrealized appreciation in the securities of the employer corporation which is attributable to the amount considered to be contributed by the employee to the purchase of such securities. [Regs. 1.402(a)-1(b)(1)(i)(b).] See column (1) in the example on page 53.

In the case of severance distributions, the exception extends to all securities of the employer. The employee's gain is computed by excluding any net unrealized appreciation in such securities. Any gain excluded under this provision is taken into account when the taxpayer ultimately disposes of the securities. Any gain upon disposition of the securities is treated as long-term capital gain to the extent of the unrealized appreciation at the time of distribution. Any gain in excess of such appreciation may be short-term or long-term, depending upon the employee's actual holding period. [Regs. 1.402(a)-1(b)(1)(i)(a).] See column (2) in the example below.

Example: Under a qualified savings plan which invests solely in employer stock, an employee contributes 5% of his salary to a trust and the employer contributes 2½%. The amount to be included in taxable income under the two conditions described above is computed as follows:

	Non-severance (1)	Severance (2)
A. Employee contribution	$1,000	$1,000
B. Employer contribution	500	500
C. F.M.V.* of stock acquired with A	1,200	1,200
D. F.M.V. of stock acquired with B	600	600
E. Dividends on A stock (invested)	100	100
F. Dividends on B stock (invested)	50	50
G. F.M.V. of stock acquired with E	120	120
H. F.M.V. of stock acquired with F	60	60
F.M.V. of distribution (C+D+G+H)	$1,980	$1,980
Less employee's contribution (A)	1,000	1,000
Net	980	980
Less appreciation attributable to employee's contribution (C−A)	200	200
Net	780	780
Less appreciation on remaining securities (D+G+H−B−E−F)	—	130
Taxable amount:		
Ordinary income	$ 780	
Long-term capital gain		$ 650

* Fair market value.

In a nonseverance distribution, the net unrealized appreciation on stock acquired with reinvested dividends is not excluded. [Rev. Rul. 67-165.]

The foregoing example illustrates a situation where there is a specific identification or tracing. If no such tracing is possible, the amount of unrealized appreciation attributable to the employee's contributions is ascertained by multiplying the unrealized appreciation of the stock distributed by a fraction the numerator of which is the employee's contributions and the denominator of which is the total of employee contributions, employer contributions, and earnings of the fund. In other words, the denominator is equivalent to the tax basis of the total fund assets if the fund were a taxpaying entity. The equation to be derived from the foregoing example (column 1 is as follows [Rev. Rul. 68-32]:

$$\frac{1,000}{1,650} \times 330 = 200$$

The purpose of this provision is to put the employee in a position similar to the one in which he would have been if he had purchased the employer securities directly rather than through the exempt trust.

Net unrealized appreciation in securities of the employer corporation which are distributed by the trust is the excess of the market value of such securities at the time of distribution over the cost or other basis of such securities to the trust. If a distribution consists in part of securities which have appreciated in value and in part of securities which have depreciated in value, the net unrealized appreciation shall be considered to consist of the net increase in value of all of the securities included in the distribution. Two or more distributions made by a trust to a distributee in a single taxable year of the distributee shall be treated as a single distribution. [Regs. 1.402(a)-1(b)(2)(i).]

The distributee's basis of the securities is the value of the securities taken into account for tax purposes in the distribution year, the portion which is taxable plus the employee's own contribution. Net unrealized appreciation which is excludable shall not be included in the basis of the securities in the hands of the distributee at the time of distribution for purposes of determining gain or loss on their subsequent disposition. [Regs. 1.402(a)-1(b)(1).]

TAX ADVANTAGES

The rules deferring taxation of net unrealized appreciation to a later time are useful as a tax planning device not only for employees of large corporations but also for stockholder-employees of closely held corporations. Stockholder-employees may accumulate capital for a retirement income program in the form of dividends by having their corporation contribute corporate securities instead of cash. If the stock is not sold, the unrealized appreciation may escape income tax entirely where the stock acquires on death a new and perhaps higher basis. It may be worthwhile in some cases for such corporations to consider changing from a trusteed plan with cash contributions to a trusteed plan with contributions payable in the stock of such corporations.

BENEFICIARIES

Although the employee is the primary beneficiary of an employees' trust he may name an individual as his beneficiary—that is, as the person to receive the distributions of the trust in the event of his death. The amounts are taxed to the beneficiary in the same manner as if they had been received by the employee. If there is no beneficiary and the distributions are made to the employee's estate, the same rule applies.

DEATH BENEFIT EXCLUSION

Long-term capital gain treatment of a lump-sum distribution is not the only tax benefit available to a beneficiary of a deceased employee. The beneficiary-recipient of the lump-sum distribution is also entitled to an exclusion of up to $5,000 under the employee death benefit provisions if not otherwise used. [Sec. 101(b).]

Example: Under the terms of an exempt pension trust an employee was entitled to retire at age 65, at which time he would receive $100 a month for a minimum of ten years. If the employee died before reaching retirement age his beneficiary was to receive the stipulated payments for the same period or could receive instead a lump-sum distribution. The employee did not contribute to the plan. He died at age 55 and his wife-beneficiary was paid a lump-sum distribution of $10,000. The wife was entitled to exclude from her gross income up to $5,000. The difference between her death benefit exclusion and $10,000 was taxable at capital gain rates.

If an employee retires and begins to receive payments under a joint and survivor annuity, the payments to his survivor after his death do not qualify for the $5,000 death benefit exclusion under Section 101(b). However, if an employee retires on a disability pension and elects a joint and survivor annuity under a plan and dies before reaching "retirement age," the death benefit exclusion will apply to the benefits payable to the survivor. Reason: Benefits attributable to employer contributions paid before the employee reaches "retirement age" are excludable as sick pay under Section 105(d), and are not considered to be an annuity. The survivor consequently is considered to be the primary annuitant and thereby entitled to the exclusion. [Rev. Rul. 61-161.]

An employee's retirement plan of a municipality provides for pensions to its employees and benefits for a widow, a minor child or a dependent mother after the death of an employee, whether before or after retirement. The Revenue Service has ruled that the amounts payable to the survivors do not constitute amounts received under a joint and survivor annuity. Such amounts are not amounts which the employee had a nonforfeitable right to receive while living, and as such an aggregate amount of $5,000 may be excludable from gross income as provided by Section 101(b). [Rev. Rul. 64-229.]

For tax purposes, under the above plan the employee's benefits and those of his survivor are to be treated as separate contracts. Tax is imposed on a joint and survivor annuity if the employee's rights are not forfeitable at the time the benefits become payable. In the circumstances of the above ruling no rights to benefits existed until the employee died, and then only if he left one of the specified dependents surviving him. Under the plan, neither the contributions which the employee made nor his retirement pension benefits were affected by the presence or absence of survivor benefits. Finally, there was no interrelation of contributions and benefits. Consequently, the benefits of the employee and those of his survivor were treated as separate contracts for tax purposes.

INSURANCE

Although annuity premiums are not taxable when they are paid by a pension trust, a different rule applies to premiums paid on a retirement income, endowment, or other contract providing life insurance protection, if the proceeds of such contract are payable to a beneficiary of the employee either directly or through the trust. The employee is currently taxable upon the premiums so paid, either from employer contributions or from earnings of the trust, to the extent that the premium is attributable to life insurance protection. [Sec. 72(m)(3); Regs. 1.402(a)-1(a)(3).]

Example: A policy purchased under a qualified plan for an employee provides an annuity of $100 per month upon retirement at age 65, with a minimum death benefit of $10,000. The insurance payable if death occurred in the first year would be $10,000. The cash value at the end of the first year is 0. The net insurance is therefore $10,000 minus 0, or $10,000. Assuming that the Commissioner has determined that a reasonable net premium for the employee's age is $5.85 per $1,000, the premium for $10,000 of life insurance is therefore $58.50, and this is the amount to be reported as income by the employee for the year. The balance of the premium is the amount contributed for the annuity, which is not taxable to the employee under a plan meeting the requirements of Section 401(a). Assuming that the cash value at the end of the second year is $500, the net insurance would then be $9,500 for the second year. With a net one-year term rate of $6.30 for the employee's age in the second year, the amount to be reported as income to the employee would be $59.85. [Regs. 1.72-16(b)(5).]

The aggregate premiums for the pure insurance cost which are taxable to the employee in prior years can be treated by the retired employee as his contribution to the plan. One result, where a person retires under a noncontributory plan using retirement income contracts paying a pension of $100 a month, is as follows: If it is assumed that the one-year term premiums on which he is taxable for life insurance protection over the years are $1,000, the employee is treated as having contributed $1,000 to his retirement pension. He is permitted to exclude from income his first ten months' pension receipts under the three-year rule. [Regs. 1.72-8(a)(1); Sec. 72(d).]

The Revenue Service has ruled that an employee's consideration for an annuity, purchased for him by the trustee of an exempt employees' trust with proceeds of a surrendered life insurance policy, does not include the portion of the premiums allocable to life insurance protection during the period the surrendered policy was outstanding. The employee's consideration under Section 72 does not include that portion of the premiums included in his gross income while the policy was outstanding because it was paid for life insurance protection. Retirement benefits payable under the annuity are treated as received under a single contract, the annuity contract. [Rev. Rul. 67-336.]

See *Prentice-Hall Pension and Profit-Sharing Service* ¶ 5301-C for comments on separate insurance and retirement programs.

The cost of incidental life insurance protection in an individual retirement income contract purchased after December 31, 1962 by an employer covered under Section 403(d) is includable in gross income of the employee for whom the contract is purchased. But the cost of insurance is deemed to be part of the employee's basis in the annuity contract. The annuity contract was purchased by an organization exempt from Federal income tax under Section 501(c)(3). [Rev. Rul. 68-304.]

If a retirement income, endowment, or other life insurance contract is distributed, its entire cash value is treated as a cash distribution. The employee may, however, defer the realization of income to the extent that, within 60 days after the distribution, he converts the cash value into an annuity contract under which no death proceeds would be treated as proceeds of life insurance. [Regs. 1.402(a)-1(a)(2).]

If death benefits are payable by an exempt trust, other than under a life insurance contract carried by it, the entire amount is treated as deferred compensation received by the beneficiary. No part of the payment is exempt as insurance proceeds, but the payment is subject to the limited $5,000 exemption for employees' death benefits. [Regs. 1.402(a)-1(a)(4); Regs. 1.72-16(c).]

Premiums paid by an employer for group (term) life insurance on his employees are not taxable income to the employees. For periods after December 31, 1963 this exemption is limited to premiums on insurance coverage not exceeding $50,000. On the other hand, an employee-participant of a qualifying trust is currently taxable on premiums paid for his benefit by the trustee on a group life insurance contract even though it affords term insurance protection only. [Rev. Rul. 54-52.] The same payment, if made by the employer, would be tax-free. Where the insurance is purchased directly by the employer under a qualified annuity plan, the regulations state that the premiums are currently taxable if the contract provides current insurance protection in the form of group permanent life insurance in addition to retirement benefits. [Regs. 1.403 (a)-1(d); Regs. 1.72-16.]

Premiums paid by the trust for group life insurance on plan participants to indemnify the trust against excessive death benefit payments are not taxable income to the participants. [Rev. Rul. 66-138.]

BASIS

If a deceased employee made contributions to the trust, or if he was taxable on employer contributions (other than by reason of life insurance premiums), the amount of such contributions not theretofore recovered tax-free by the employee is deductible from the beneficiary's taxable income. If the amount is receivable as an annuity, such contributions are a cost of the annuity. [Regs. 1.402(a)-1(a)(5),(6).]

OTHER

The death proceeds of a life insurance policy are normally exempt in the hands of a beneficiary. The Revenue Service has taken the position, however, that the proceeds of a policy purchased by an exempt trust are in the nature of deferred compensation to the extent of the cash value of the policy immediately before death, minus any premiums previously taxed to the employee. Only the amount in excess of cash value, as so reduced, is exempt as insurance proceeds. [Regs. 1.402(a)-1(a)(4); Regs. 1.72-16(c).]

Example: Under a noncontributory plan a trust carries a retirement income policy with a lump-sum death benefit of $25,000 payable to the employee's widow. If the cash value of the policy immediately before death was $11,000, the widow has $14,000 exempt insurance proceeds. The remaining $11,000 is taxable deferred compensation subject to the $5,000 exclusion for employees' death benefits. The regulations indicate that this taxable $11,000 is reduced also by the amount of any premiums previously taxed to the employee. The taxable amount is taxable as a long-term capital gain if received within one taxable year. [Regs. 1.72-16(c)(3).]

If the employee neither contributed the premiums nor was taxable upon the employer's contribution for them, then any death proceeds distributed by the trust are entirely deferred compensation. [Regs. 1.72-16(c)(4).]

Section 402(a) was amended in 1960 and made applicable to taxable years beginning after December 31, 1959 to provide that amounts paid to a nonresident alien individual by the United States, as civil service annuities and other retirement benefits for service performed by an employee of the United States, are not to be taxable to him to the extent they are attributable to a basic salary derived from services abroad. This means that for the typical nonresident alien who has worked for the United States abroad, no U.S. income tax will be payable on his pension. [Sec. 402(a)(4).]

SICK PAY EXCLUSION

An employee who receives a disability pension from a qualified plan and who has not reached "retirement age" can exclude his pension payments from gross income as sick pay, within the limits of Section 105(d). Under an employer-financed pension plan, the exclusion from income up to a rate of $75 or $100 a week is permitted. However, the exclusion does not apply to any pension payments that he receives after he reaches retirement age, under the premise that then he is not absent from work because he is no longer expected to work. Under a qualified pension or profit-sharing plan the term "retirement age" means the lowest age specified in the plan at which the employee, had he not been disabled and continued in the service of the employer, would have had the right to retire without the employer's consent to receive retirement benefits based on service to date of retirement, calculated at the rate set forth in the plan without actuarial or similar reduction because of retirement before some later specified age. [Rev. Rul. 57-76; Rev. Rul. 61-6.] Depending upon individual circumstances, different "retirement ages" may be present within the same plan for the purpose of the sick pay exclusion. [Rev. Rul. 58-544.]

MEDICAL EXPENSES

Where a profit-sharing plan provides for distribution to reimburse participants for medical expenses, amounts so distributed were at first ruled by the Service to be excludable from gross income under Section 105(b). (See Letter Ruling, February 20, 1962, at ¶ 11,984 of the *Prentice-Hall Pension and Profit-Sharing Service*.) However, the Service reversed its position later in the same year in another private ruling. (See Letter Ruling, October 1, 1962, at ¶ 11,989 of the *Prentice-Hall Pension and Profit-Sharing Service*.)

The above refers to a direct distribution from the trust to reimburse participants for medical expenses. If the trust pays premiums for health and accident insurance, the employee has always been currently taxed on the premiums paid. Since a profit-sharing plan is primarily a plan of deferred compensation, regulations require that the amounts allocated to the account of the participant which may be used to provide, for him or his family, life or accident or health insurance must be only incidental. Revenue Ruling 61-164 explains the rules when the profit-sharing trust buys health or accident insurance only, or health or accident insurance in addition to ordinary life insurance.

(b) TAXABILITY OF BENEFICIARY OF NONEXEMPT TRUST

In the case of an employees' trust which does not qualify for exemption in a given taxable year, the contributions to the trust by the employer (during its taxable year which ends with or within such taxable year of the trust) must be included in the gross income of the employee to the extent to which his interest in each contribution is nonforfeitable at the time the contribution is made.

Example: The G Company, a corporation which makes its returns on a calendar-year basis, has a pension trust which fails to qualify for exemption for its taxable year ended February 28, 1964. During 1963 the company contributed $60,000 to the trust, $2,400 of which was for the benefit of employee Z. His vesting percentage at the time of the contribution was 60%. Therefore, 60% of $2,400, or $1,440, will be includable in Z's gross income for 1963 because of the G Company's contribution to the trust. The remainder ($960) will not be taxable to Z until distribution.

When the distributions under a nonqualified plan in any year are actually made, such distributions are taxed as an annuity and in all cases as ordinary income. The amounts previously taxed to the employee on account of the employer's contributions, plus the amounts of the employee's contributions, if any, will be included in the employee's consideration paid, in determining his investment in the contract under the annuity rules.

Forfeitable contributions are not taxable until actual distribution, even though they have become nonforfeitable during an intervening year. [Regs. 1.402(b)-1(a)(1).]

(c) FOREIGN-SITUS TRUSTS

If a pension, profit-sharing, or stock bonus trust would qualify for exemption except for the fact that it is created or organized outside the United States, the trust is nevertheless considered exempt for the purpose of taxing distributions to the employees or their beneficiaries.

(d) CERTAIN EMPLOYEES' ANNUITIES

Beneficiaries of certain nonqualified trusts created by employers prior to October 21, 1942 receive the same beneficial tax treatment which applies to beneficiaries of qualified employees' trusts. This rule applies to years beginning after 1938, but does not apply to contributions to a qualifying trust made after June 1, 1949.

(e) CERTAIN PLAN TERMINATIONS

This provision was added merely to prevent hardship where certain plans were terminated on mistaken assumptions of what the law was under the 1939 Code. Thus, if there was a corporate liquidation before August 16, 1954, followed by a termination of the dissolved employer's plan and lump-sum distribution from it in 1954, the distribution would be entitled to capital gain treatment.

Taxation of Employee Annuities

(a) TAXABILITY OF BENEFICIARY UNDER QUALIFIED
    ANNUITY PLAN
    CAPITAL GAINS
    TIME OF TAXATION
    METHOD OF TAXATION

(b) TAXABILITY OF BENEFICIARY UNDER ANNUITY PURCHASED
    BY SECTION 501 (c)(3) ORGANIZATION OR PUBLIC
    SCHOOL
    SUPPLEMENTARY COMPENSATION—SALARY REDUCTION
    TRUSTEED PLANS AND EMPLOYEE CONTRIBUTIONS
    INSURANCE COMPANIES' RESERVES

(c) TAXABILITY OF BENEFICIARY UNDER NON-
    QUALIFIED ANNUITY

(d) TAXABILITY OF BENEFICIARY UNDER CERTAIN
    FORFEITABLE CONTRACTS PURCHASED BY EXEMPT
    ORGANIZATIONS

(a) **TAXABILITY OF BENEFICIARY UNDER QUALIFIED ANNUITY PLAN**

A qualified pension plan under which retirement benefits are provided through direct purchase by the employer, rather than through a trust, is an annuity plan. A qualified annuity plan must meet the same qualification requirements as a qualified trusteed pension plan as to coverage and nondiscrimination. An annuity contract or face-amount certificate, as defined in the Investment Company Act of 1940, issued after December 31, 1962, must not be transferable if any person other than the trustee of a qualified trust is the owner of the contract or certificate. [Sec. 401(g).] Refunds of premiums on account of credits such as dividends, experience rating credits, and surrender or cancellation credits must be reapplied within the current or next succeeding year of the employer toward the purchase of retirement annuities. [Sec. 404(a)(2).] The agreement between the employer and the insurer must be written.

Where, under a qualified plan, an annuity contract (as distinct from a contract containing an element of life insurance) is purchased for a participating employee, the employee is not immediately taxable, even though he has a vested interest in the contract. Nor does he (or his beneficiary) receive taxable income when the contract is distributed. Income is not realized until payments are received under the contract.

If the employer is a tax-exempt organization or otherwise not subject to Federal income tax, so that deductibility of the purchase price of the annuity is not important, the restriction is equally applicable. See, however, the exception relating to Section 501(c)(3) organizations or public schools explained on page 68.

An annuity contract for this purpose is a contract which provides primarily for periodic installment payments to the annuitant named therein, and under which the death benefits at any time cannot exceed the larger of the reserve or the total premiums paid for the annuity benefits. Thus, in any annuity contract there is no pure insurance protection at any time. The fact that the contract may provide for return of total premiums paid for the annuity benefits in case of death, and that such total premiums may exceed the reserve in the early years, will not be considered as providing insurance protection. [Rev. Rul. 55-639.]

Any other type of contract which involves life contingencies is a life insurance contract. This includes any type of contract which provides pure insurance protection (i.e., a death benefit which at any time may exceed the larger of the reserve or the aggregate premiums paid to such time), such as a retirement income contract or an endowment contract, as well as an ordinary life insurance contract. The mere fact that such a contract may contain provisions permitting the application or the conversion of this reserve, or its cash value or maturity value, to provide annuity benefits does not make such a contract an annuity contract unless and until such conversion takes place. Thus, while a life insurance contract may be converted into an annuity contract, a contract is never both at the same time. Although such terms as "life insurance/annuity," "life insurance with annuity," and "annuity with life insurance," may be used to describe contracts issued by life insurance companies, such contracts will be considered life insurance contracts for the purposes of Sections 402 and 403 of the Internal Revenue Code if they provide pure insurance protection. [Rev. Rul. 57-191.]

A qualified plan may not provide only such benefits as are furnished through the purchase of ordinary life insurance contracts which may be converted to life annuities at the normal retirement date. [Rev. Rul. 54-67.] Life insurance protection may, however, be provided under a qualified plan provided that such protection is merely an incidental feature of the plan. In the case of a pension or annuity plan, the life insurance benefit is deemed to be incidental where the insurance protection is not greater than 100 times the monthly annuity — e.g., $1,000 of life insurance for each $10 of monthly annuity. [Rev. Rul. 60-83.] As to profit-sharing plans, see Revenue Rulings 54-51, 57-213, and 60-84. [Rev. Rul. 65-178, Part 2(n)(2).]

For a discussion of the taxability to the employees of the cost of life insurance protection see page 56.

CAPITAL GAINS

As indicated previously, total distributions from a qualified trust paid to an employee or his beneficiary within one taxable year, by reason of the employee's death or other separation from service, may be entitled to long-term capital gain treatment. A similar rule applies to lump-sum payments made in connection with a qualified annuity plan, even though it is not a trusteed plan, if paid by reason of an employee's death or other separation from service, or by reason of the employee's death after retirement.

Long-term capital gain treatment is available if the following conditions are present:

1. The annuity is purchased by an employer for an employee under a plan which meets the requirements for qualified trusteed plans; *and*

2. The plan requires that refunds of contributions with respect to annuity contracts purchased under such plan be used to reduce subsequent premiums on the contracts under the plan; *and*
3. The total amounts payable by reason of an employee's death or other separation from service, or by reason of the death of an employee after the employee's separation from service, are paid to the payee within one taxable year of the payee.

If an annuity contract is distributed to the employee's beneficiary because of the employee's death and is a "total distribution," and if the beneficiary surrenders the contract in the same year for its cash value, the proceeds are treated as long-term capital gain.

Capital gain treatment is not available in respect of distributions made to any payee to the extent such distributions are attributable to contributions made on behalf of an employee while he was a self-employed individual. If an individual was covered under a qualified annuity plan both as an employee and as a self-employed individual, capital gain treatment may apply only to the portion of the distribution that is attributable to contributions credited to his account while he was an employee. [Sec. 403(a)(2).]

TIME OF TAXATION

Proceeds of a qualified plan become taxable when they are actually distributed or made available to the employee. [Regs. 1.403(a)-1(b).] If an accumulation over many years is distributed in one lump sum other than by reason of death or other separation from employment, the resulting surtax may be exorbitant. The Revenue Service has stated that an employee is taxable upon the entire fund accumulated for his benefit at the time when he becomes entitled to demand a lump-sum payment after a prescribed length of service. [Rev. Rul. 54-265.] However, the Revenue Service has stated that an amount does not become "available" to an employee if his right to withdraw is subject to a substantial condition, penalty, or prior election. Thus, an employee is not taxable if withdrawal would involve discontinuance of his participation in the trust or a forfeiture of part of his interest. [Rev. Rul. 55-423.] Nor is he taxable under the doctrine of constructive receipt where withdrawal is subject to approval by a committee upon proved financial necessity. [Rev. Rul. 55-424.] Nor is he taxable if, before the time his right of withdrawal matures, he elects to subject the amount to deferred payments. [Rev. Rul. 55-425.] Nor is he taxable where, continuing employment after the normal retirement date, he makes, before that date, an irrevocable election to receive the total benefit only upon termination of his services. [Rev. Rul. 57-260.] These rules apply to both Section 402 and Section 403. See also *Hicks v. U.S.*, 314 F.2d 180 (4th Cir. 1963); Revenue Ruling 63-180; and the discussion on pages 45 and 46.

METHOD OF TAXATION

Special tax treatment is provided for proceeds of an annuity, endowment, or life insurance contract received by an employee as an annuity where a part of the consideration for the contract was contributed by the employer and a part by the employee. In the case of such a contract, if during the first three years in which payments under the contract are made the total amount receivable by the employee will equal or exceed contributions made by the employee, then the employee's entire receipts are to be excluded from gross income until his consideration has been recovered. All payments thereafter will be fully taxable. [Sec. 72(d); Regs. 1.72-13.]

Example: Employee J was entitled to receive from his employer, on his retirement in 1967, a life annuity payable in annual installments of $700 beginning January 1, 1968. The consideration paid for the annuity was $8,000 of which the employer had contributed $6,000 and J had contributed $2,000. J is not to use the life expectancy annuity method in determining the taxable and nontaxable portions of the annuity payments. Since he will recover his consideration paid for the annuity, $2,000, during the first three years (1968-1970) in which payments under the annuity are made (he will have received $2,100), he is to use the special three year exclusion rule. Therefore, the $700 received in 1968 and the $700 received in 1969 are to be excluded from gross income; $600 of the $700 payment received in 1970 is to be excluded; and the remaining $100 is to be included in gross income. The $700 payments to be received in 1971 and later years are to be included in full in gross income.

This special exclusion rule, first provided for in the 1954 Code, applies even though the employee's annuity began before

1954. Thus, amounts actually excluded from income under the 1939 Code are to be added to amounts excluded under the 1954 Code to determine when payments are fully taxable. The rule also applies to a beneficiary of an employee provided the employee dies before receiving any amount as an annuity under the contract. It does not apply to a joint and survivor annuity where the first annuitant died in 1951, 1952, or 1953.

(b) TAXABILITY OF BENEFICIARY UNDER ANNUITY PURCHASED BY SECTION 501(c)(3) ORGANIZATION OR PUBLIC SCHOOL

Before its amendment in 1958, the law literally provided that the premiums paid by a Section 501(c)(3) organization for a non-forfeitable annuity for an employee are not to be taxed to him currently, but that he should be taxed only upon receipt of the annuity benefits. Regulations permit deferment of taxation only if the premium is merely a supplement to past or current compensation. An example of an acceptable annuity premium described in the Regulations is 10% of the employee's salary from the exempt organization. The Technical Changes Act of 1958, effective for years beginning after 1957, enlarged the regulatory but reduced the statutory provision, so that the employer's payment for an annuity, if the annuity is nonforfeitable and not purchased under a qualified plan, will be presently taxable income to the employee to the extent it exceeds the employee's "exclusion allowance." The provision was extended in 1961 by P.L. 87-370, retroactive to years beginning after 1957, for similar employer payments made by public educational institutions.

Thus, if an annuity contract is purchased for an employee by an employer which is exempt from tax as a charitable, religious, educational, or other organization under Section 501(c)(3), or which is a public school, and if the annuity is nonforfeitable and not purchased under a qualified plan, the employee will be taxable on the premium payments to the extent they exceed his "exclusion allowance." The maximum amount of premiums that the employee can exclude from his income in any year is 20% of the employee's current annual compensation times the number of years of service, reduced by the aggregate premiums paid by the employer in previous years which were excludable from the employee's gross income in such prior years, including prior employer contributions to a qualified insured annuity plan which were excludable from the employee's gross income in such prior years. The excess over this limit is included in the employee's current taxable income. Thus, the provision permits purchase of past service annuities which will be currently tax-free to the extent stated. [Regs. 1.403(b)-1(d)(3); 1.403(b)-1(g).]

Example: E became an employee of X on January 1, 1957 and continued as a full-time employee of X through the years 1957, 1958, 1959, and 1960. He received includable compensation in the amount of $10,000 for 1957, $11,000 for 1958, $12,000 for 1959, and $12,000 for 1960. X is an organization described in Section 501(c)(3), and for the years 1957, 1958, 1959, and 1960 was exempt under Section 501(a). In 1957, E became eligible, and X is contributing $400 annually toward a retirement benefit for E under a qualified insured annuity plan. Also in 1957, X commenced to purchase for E annuity contracts under which E's rights are nonforfeitable. X paid as premiums for such contracts $2,000 in 1957 and $2,000 annually thereafter.

> *1957*—The $2,000 premium paid in 1957 is fully excludable under Section 403(a)(1) of the Code prior to amendment in 1958.

> *1958*—E's exclusion allowance for 1958 is determined in the following manner: First, 20% of his includable compensation for 1958 is $2,200. Second, $2,200 times his years of service, two, is $4,400. Finally, $4,400 less any contributions excludable in a prior year—$2,000 plus the $400 payment under the qualified insured annuity plan—leaves $2,000. Accordingly, the $2,000 premium paid in 1958 is entirely excludable.

> *1959*—E's exclusion allowance for 1959 is determined in the following manner: First, 20% of his includable compensation is $2,400. Second, $2,400 times his years of service, three, is $7,200. Finally, $7,200 less any contributions excludable in prior years—including payments under the qualified insured annuity plan, $4,800—leaves $2,400. Accordingly, the $2,000 premium paid in 1959 is entirely excludable.

> *1960*—E's exclusion allowance for 1960 is determined in a similar manner: First, 20% of his includable compensation is $2,400. Second, $2,400 times his years of service, four, is $9,600. Finally, $9,600 less any contributions excludable in prior years—including payments under the qualified insured annuity plan, totaling $7,200—leaves $2,400. Accordingly, the $2,000 premium paid in 1960 is entirely excludable.

The $5,000 death benefit exclusion is applicable with special limitations to annuities purchased by Section 503(b)(1), (2), or (3) organizations which have obtained exemption under Section 501(a). [Sec. 101(b)(2)(B)(iii).] The organizations described in Section 503(b)(1), (2), and (3) are as follows:

(1) A religious organization other than a trust.
(2) An educational organization which normally maintains a regular faculty and curriculum and normally has a regularly enrolled body of pupils or students in attendance at the place where its educational activities are regularly carried on.
(3) An organization which normally receives a substantial part of its support from the United States or any state or political subdivision thereof or from direct or indirect contributions from the general public.

Prior to the amendment of the law in 1961, employees of a wholly-owned state instrumentality could not participate in the benefits granted by Section 403(b) unless the instrumentality obtained an exemption under Section 501(a) as an employer described in Section 501(c)(3). [Rev. Rul. 55-319; Rev. Rul. 60-384.] The 1961 amendment to the law changed this in part. An educational institution as defined in Section 151(e)(4) operated by the state, a political subdivision of a state, or an agency or instrumentality of any one or more of the foregoing may purchase annuity contracts for its employees and obtain for them the benefits of Section 403(b) without going through the formality of obtaining an exemption under Section 501(a).

If a Section 501(c)(3) organization or public school purchases a forfeitable annuity contract for the employee, he is not taxable at the time the contract is purchased. But when his rights become nonforfeitable, the value of the annuity at that time is treated as a payment by the organization as of that time and is subject to the 20% limitation detailed above with respect to nonforfeitable contracts.

If a forfeitable annuity is purchased by an exempt organization other than one exempt under Section 501(c)(3), or a public school, the value of the annuity as of the date it becomes nonforfeitable is fully taxable to the employee to the extent attributable to employer contributions made after 1957. See generally Regulations 1.403(d)-1. If an annuity, forfeitable or nonforfeitable, is purchased by such organization under a plan which otherwise qualifies under the rules of Section 401 pertaining to coverage, discrimination, etc., the employee is not taxable until he is entitled to benefits under the qualified plan.

SUPPLEMENTARY COMPENSATION—SALARY REDUCTION

For taxable years beginning before January 1, 1958, the purchase of an annuity for an employee of a Section 501(c)(3) organization or a public school had to qualify under the test that the purchase of the annuity contract was merely a "supplement to past or current compensation," to be determined by all the surrounding facts and circumstances. For taxable years beginning after December 31, 1957, there is no requirement that it be merely a "supplement to past or current compensation" in order for the exclusion to apply.

The exclusion is also applicable to amounts contributed by an employer for an annuity contract as the result of an agreement with an employee to take a reduction in salary, or to forgo an increase in salary, but only to the extent that such amounts are earned by the employee after the agreement becomes effective. Such an agreement must be legally binding and irrevocable with respect to amounts earned while the agreement is in effect. The employee is not permitted to make more than one agreement with the same employer during any taxable year of such employee beginning after December 31, 1963. Furthermore, the exclusion is not to apply to any amounts which are contributed under any further agreement made by such employee during the same taxable year beginning after such date. However, the employee may be permitted to terminate the entire agreement with respect to amounts not yet earned. [Regs. 1.403(b)-1(b)(3)(i).]

The regulations clearly indicate that the employee has a choice each year of taking his pay in cash or in a tax-deferred annuity, up to the extent of the exclusion allowance. This freedom makes the annuity selection more attractive to employees who otherwise would not wish to irrevocably commit portions of their annual pay in this manner. They can make this decision on the basis of their forecasted cash needs for the coming year. If during a year the employee's financial situation forces him to terminate the agreement, the termination does not prevent him from entering into another annuity arrangement beginning next year, if he so desires.

Part-time employees are also covered under this provision. [Regs. 1.403(b)-1(f)(5).]

TRUSTEED PLANS AND EMPLOYEE CONTRIBUTIONS

The rules outlined above do not apply to employer contributions made to a trust or used to provide retirement benefits other than through the purchase of annuities. Neither are they applicable to employee contributions of any kind. [T.I.R. 372.]

INSURANCE COMPANIES' RESERVES

For years beginning after December 31, 1963, the same tax exemption is given to income on reserves for Section 403(b) annuity contracts for employees of public schools and colleges as is given to Section 403(b) annuities for employees of tax-exempt educational institutions. This exemption applies to the investment income of life insurance companies attributable to reserves for retirement annuities for employees of public school systems. [Sec. 803(d)(1)(D).]

(c) TAXABILITY OF BENEFICIARY UNDER NONQUALIFIED ANNUITY

If an annuity is purchased under a nonqualified plan and the employee's rights under his annuity contract are nonforfeitable except for failure to pay future premiums, the amounts contributed by the employer for the contract are taxable to the employee at the time of contribution. Such amounts, plus the employee's own contributions, are treated as his consideration paid for purposes of determining his investment in the contract under the life expectancy rules.

(d) TAXABILITY OF BENEFICIARY UNDER CERTAIN FORFEITABLE CONTRACTS PURCHASED BY EXEMPT ORGANIZATIONS

This subsection relates, in part, to subsection (b) above and provides rules under which certain employees are currently taxed when their forfeitable rights under an annuity contract become nonforfeitable.

Deduction for Contributions of an Employer to an Employees' Trust or Annuity Plan and Compensation Under Deferred-Payment Plan

(b) ABSENCE OF FORMAL PLAN

(c) CERTAIN NEGOTIATED PLANS

(d) CARRYOVER OF UNUSED DEDUCTIONS

(e) SPECIAL LIMITATIONS FOR SELF-EMPLOYED INDIVIDUALS

(f) LOAN REPAYMENTS CONSIDERED AS CONTRIBUTIONS

(a) GENERAL RULE

As a general rule, amounts contributed by an employer under a qualified plan are deductible. The general rule is modified, however, by a number of underlying rules relating principally to annual limitations, carryovers, reorganizations, time and method of making contributions, and information requirements. These rules are discussed below, together with a consideration of the deduction of amounts contributed under a nonqualified plan.

ANNUAL LIMITATIONS—PENSION PLANS

LIMITATION UNDER SECTION 404(a)(1)(A). The deduction for contributions to a pension trust for any taxable year is initially limited to an amount not in excess of 5% of the compensation otherwise paid or accrued to all employees who are participants under the plan, except to the extent that Section 404(a)(1)(B) is applicable. This initial limitation applies to the first year for which a contribution deduction is claimed by the taxpayer. It also applies to any subsequent year for which the percentage is not reduced by the Commissioner. The amount which is deductible may not be more than the amount which is reasonable and necessary to fund the cost of the plan. In view of this basic principle, it is provided that the Commissioner may review the actuarial data relating to the plan at intervals of not less than five years to determine whether the 5% (or lesser percentage then used) is proper for the timely funding of the plan. [Regs. 1.404(a)-4(b).] He may then adjust the percentage limitation. The new percentage is used until the next evaluation by the Commissioner. The Commissioner will not disturb the 5% limitation in the initial year.

LIMITATION UNDER SECTION 404(a)(1)(B). It may be found that the 5%-of-compensation limitation is not sufficient to fund the cost of past and current service credits when such credits are distributed as a level amount or a level percentage of compensation over the remaining service of each employee under the plan. In such a case the required amount in excess of 5% of compensation is also deductible. An exception to this rule is that if the unfunded cost attributable to any three individuals is greater than 50% of the total unfunded cost of all participants, the unfunded cost of those three individuals must be spread evenly over a period of at least five taxable years. This rule applies also to an annuity plan.

Example: An employer provides retirement benefits for his employees through an exempt pension trust. The third year of the pension plan reveals the following data:

(1)	Total payroll of participants for current year .	$ 842,000
(2)	5% thereof	$ 42,100
(3)	Value of all benefits expected to be paid after the beginning of the year for benefit of all beneficiaries	$ 1,136,700
(4)	Value of all funds in the plan at the beginning of the year	$ 70,000
(5)	Amount to be distributed as a level percentage: item (3) minus item (4)	$ 1,066,700
(6)	Maximum amount attributable to any three employees	$ 400,000
(7)	Value of all compensation to be paid to covered employees after the beginning of the year	$12,630,000
(8)	Accrual rate for level percentage computation: item (5) ÷ item (7)	8.44576%
(9)	Excess percentage over 5%	3.44576%
(10)	Excess over 5% of payroll; item (9) × item (1)	$ 29,013

Since item (6) is less than 50% of item (5), that factor is ineffective. The deduction, therefore, is $71,113 of which $42,100 is deductible under Section 404(a)(1)(A) and $29,013 is deductible under Section 404(a)(1)(B).

A lump-sum contribution to a pension plan to fully fund newly granted supplemental benefits to retired employees and the future service credits to normal retirement of active employees cannot be deducted in the year of the contribution even though the employer ceases business. The deduction is allowed under Section 404(a)(1)(A) and (B) by distributing the past and current service credits over the period remaining until the normal commencement of retirement benefits to the employee. Query: Is the deduction ever obtainable? [Rev. Rul. 60-132.] If the employer continues in business and there are no active employees who are participants in the plan, it would seem that the contribution should be deductible under Section 404(a)(1)(C) at the rate of 10% per year.

LIMITATION UNDER SECTION 404(a)(1)(C). A taxpayer may claim a deduction for the normal cost of the plan plus 10% of the past service cost of the plan. The "normal cost" of the plan for any year is the amount, actuarially determined, which would be required as a contribution to maintain the plan if the plan had been in effect from the beginning of service of each then-included employee and if the costs for prior years had been paid and all assumptions as to interest, mortality, time of payment, etc. had been fulfilled. The "past service cost" is the amount which would be required to completely fund or purchase the pension or annuity credits as of the date when they are included in the plan, and which would be required at such time to meet all the future benefits provided under the plan which would not be met by future normal costs and employee contributions. "Past service cost" is deductible at a rate not in excess of 10% each year. [Regs. 1.404(a)-6(a).]

If a plan is subjected to substantial amendment to provide increased past service credits, the 10% limitation applies separately to the additional funding from the time of amendment. Interest on unfunded past service cost is not included in the 10% limitation base, but increases in cost due to unfavorable experience or underestimation of cost or changes in insurance company annuity rates are included. [Rev. Rul. 55-411.]

If an employer fails to contribute all, or a portion of, the normal cost of a plan for any year, the unpaid normal cost becomes unfunded past service cost. [Rev. Rul. 55-480.] There is disagreement regarding the period over which the additional past service cost (i.e., the unpaid normal cost) may be amortized. Part III(B) of Bureau Bulletin on Section 23(p), issued in 1945, suggests that a "special 10% base" may be used in lieu of the standard past service cost base. The term "special 10% base" is defined in the Bulletin to include unpaid normal costs. Under this approach, the unpaid normal cost is added to the initial past service cost for purposes of computing the 10%-of-past-service-cost limitation. As a result, the additional past service cost may be amortized over substantially the same period as the initial past service cost.

Example 1:

1.	Initial past service cost		$1,000,000
2.	Normal cost each year*		80,000
3.	Contribution each year for first 8 years		150,000
4.	No contribution in 9th year on either normal cost ($80,000) or past service cost		0
5.	Aggregate interest for the 9 years on unfunded past service cost		200,000
6.	Unfunded past service cost at beginning of 10th year		640,000
7.	Contribution in 10th year		
	Normal cost for 10th year $80,000		
	Normal cost for 9th year 80,000		
	Additional amount 100,000		260,000
8.	Deduction under 404(a)(1)(C)		
	Normal cost for current year 80,000		
	10% of special past service base** ... 108,000		$188,000

See Part III(B) of Bureau Bulletin on Section 23(p), issued in 1945, and Illustration D-1, First Year.

*Assumed to be a constant figure for simplification.

**Special or supplementary past service cost base:

Unfunded past service cost at beginning of 10th year	$	640,000
Excess of past service cost contributions over interest on unfunded past service costs		360,000
Normal cost unpaid for 9th year		80,000
Special base	$1,080,000	

Informal discussions with officials of the Internal Revenue Service, however, indicate that they consider that unpaid normal cost should be treated as a separate past service cost base. A separate 10% limitation on deductibility would apply beginning with the year of payment.

Example 2: In the example above, the $80,000 normal cost for the ninth year becomes a separate past service cost base. In the tenth year the deduction under Section 404(a) (1) (C) will be:

Normal cost for current year	$	80,000
10% of past service base		100,000
10% of additional past service base		8,000
		$188,000

While this example produces the same deduction for the tenth year as Example 1, the difference will become evident in subsequent years. Ignoring additional interest accumulations, a comparison of future deductions appears as follows:

Year	Example 1	Example 2 Initial base	Example 2 Additional base
11	$108,000	$100,000	$ 8,000
12	108,000	100,000	8,000
13	108,000	100,000	8,000
14	108,000	100,000	8,000
15	108,000	100,000	8,000
16	108,000	100,000	8,000
17	72,000	40,000	8,000
18	—	—	8,000
19	—	—	8,000
20	—	—	8,000
Total	$720,000	$640,000	$80,000

LIMITATION UNDER SECTION 404(a)(2). If a pension plan is in the form of an annuity plan, the annual payment to the insurance company is limited in the same manner as are payments to an exempt trust. In the case of an annuity plan, refunds of premiums must be applied within the taxable year or the next succeeding taxable year toward the purchase of such retirement annuities.

LIMITATIONS—GENERAL. The taxpayer is entitled to deduct in full the amount paid to an employees' pension trust which is actuarially necessary to provide with respect to all employees under the trust the remaining unfunded cost of their past and current service credits distributed as a level amount over the remaining future service of each such employee, even though such amount exceeds the amount deductible under Section 404(a)(1)(C)—that is, normal or current cost plus 10% of past service cost. In other words, Section 404(a)(1)(C) does not represent a ceiling on the amount deductible. [Saalfield Publishing Co., 11 T.C. 756 (1948).] Nor does Section 404(a)(1)(C) limit the deduction under Section 404(a)(1)(A). [Rev. Rul. 57-89.] The Section 404(a)(1)(C) limitation is in lieu of the (A) and (B) limitation. Consequently, the employer is not permitted to compute the limitation in part (for example, the purchase of individual level premium ordinary whole life policies) under (A) and (B) and in part (contributions to an auxiliary fund) under (C). [Rev. Rul. 67-427.]

The regulations provide in substance that whatever method is adopted by the taxpayer to determine the amount deductible for any taxable year, if the return for such year has been filed, is binding on the taxpayer for such year. For subsequent years, however, the taxpayer is free to change to any other proper method without prior approval of the Commissioner. [Regs. 1.404(a)-3(c).]

Example: The Commissioner determines upon examination of a return that incorrect methods and other factors were used to compute normal and past service costs under the unit credit method and the limitation under Section 404(a)(1)(C). The Commissioner may correct the actuarial assumptions. The taxpayer may not change from the unit credit method or the (C) limitation for that return. He may, however, change for tax returns not yet filed. [Rev. Rul. 67-365.]

An employer will be allowed a deduction for a pro rata part of the annual contribution necessary to meet the current cost of an employees' pension plan for a short taxable year resulting from a change in accounting period [Rev. Rul. 55-428] as well as a pro rata part of the annual 10% of past service cost deduction. [Rev. Rul. 56-672.]

A qualified trust may accumulate dividends from insurance and annuity contracts without danger of disqualification of the plan under Section 401. The dividends and interest thereon credited by the insurance company must be used to reduce employer contributions. [Rev. Rul. 60-33.]

Any expenses incurred by the employer in connection with the plan, such as fees and compensation of a trustee or actuary, which are not provided for by contributions under the plan, are not subject to the limitations of Section 404(a), but are deductible to the extent they are ordinary and necessary business expenses or expenses for the production of income. [Regs. 1.404(a)-3(d).]

FINANCIAL ACCOUNTING. In 1966, the American Institute of Certified Public Accountants issued Accounting Principles Board Opinion No. 8. This landmark document established generally acceptable accounting principles for providing for the cost of pensions. APB Opinion No. 8 relates only to the reporting of pension costs in the financial statements and does not relate to the actual funding of such costs. The principles set forth in APB Opinion No. 8 do not in all instances follow the funding methods outlined in the Internal

Revenue Code. Consequently, a taxpayer may have a charge to income for financial reporting purposes which differs from the deduction allowed by Section 404. It must be noted that the deductibility of an employer's contribution to a qualified pension plan is governed by Section 404 irrespective of its treatment by the employer for book and financial purposes. [Rev. Rul. 68-34.]

ANNUAL LIMITATIONS—PROFIT-SHARING AND STOCK BONUS PLANS

The deduction for contributions to qualified profit-sharing trust or stock bonus trust is limited to an amount equal to 15% of the compensation otherwise paid or accrued during the taxable year to the employees covered by the plan. This is the primary limitation. A secondary limitation is operative in the case of a credit carryover. [Sec. 404(a)(3).] A credit carryover arises when less than the maximum amount deductible has been contributed in prior years. A contribution carryover arises when more than the maximum amount deductible has been contributed in prior years. (See page 84.)

Where a corporation loans a participating employee to a joint venture of which it is a member, the wages paid to the participating employee by the joint venture may be included in the corporation's wages for purposes of computing the 15% limitation. [Rev. Rul. 60-379.]

A profit-sharing trust must not be one which is designed to provide retirement benefits for which the contributions can be determined actuarially. In other words, the trust must not be one providing pensions. Of course, payments out of a profit-sharing trust can be postponed until after retirement.

ANNUAL LIMITATIONS—MORE THAN ONE PLAN

If an employer has at least one employee who is covered under a pension or annuity plan and is also covered under a profit-sharing or stock bonus plan, there is a special annual limitation on contributions. [Sec. 404(a)(7).] In any taxable year the total allowable deduction for contributions under all plans cannot exceed 25% of the total compensation otherwise paid or accrued to all participants under all plans. The 25% limitation applies only to "overlapping" trusts or plans—i.e., trusts or plans which cover the same individual. [Regs. 1.404(a)-13.]

Example: An employer establishes pension trust A and pension trust B. He also establishes a profit-sharing plan and a stock bonus plan. Employee Smith participates in pension trust A and also in the profit-sharing plan. He is the only employee who participates in more than one plan or trust. The 25% limitation applies only to the contributions made to pension trust A and the profit-sharing plan. Pension trust B and the stock bonus plan do not overlap with each other or with pension trust A or the profit-sharing plan.

The 25% limitation is an overall limitation only. The individual trusts or plans must first meet the separate limitations applicable to them. The 25% limitation becomes effective only if the aggregate of the separate limitations exceeds 25% of the total compensation of the participants.

If the 25% limitation operates, any amount contributed in excess of that limitation may be deducted in later years as a contribution carryover. [Regs. 1.404(a)-12(b).]

ANNUAL LIMITATIONS—OTHER

Where an employee is shifted from one participating employer to another, either may make contributions to fund his past service credits. [Rev. Rul. 55-629 and Rev. Rul. 58-165.]

An employees' trust which is not created or organized in the United States cannot qualify for exemption. However, if a stock bonus, pension, or profit-sharing trust would qualify for exemption except for the fact that it was created or organized outside of the United States, contributions to the trust by an employer who is a resident, or a corporation, or other entity of the United States, are deductible in accordance with the rules relating to exempt trusts. [Sec. 404(a)(4).]

Contributions to qualified plans are deductible only to the extent that the contributions, considered along with other compensation paid to the covered employee, are reasonable. [*Bardahl Manufacturing Corp.*, TCM 1960-223.] The reasonableness of compensation for any year is determined by reference to services rendered and compensation paid in prior years as well as in the current year. [Regs. 1.404(a)-1(b).] (See chapter on "Reasonable Executive Compensation," beginning at page 305. See also Rev. Rul. 67-341, page 315.)

In considering the requirements for qualifying the plan, the Wage-Hour laws should not be overlooked. In order to avoid having contributions to the plan included in the base on which overtime is computed, the Wage-Hour laws (which differ in some respects from the Revenue Service rules) must be complied with. For example, a profit-sharing plan must have a contribution formula for a FLSA exemption. [Opinion Letter of Wage-Hour Administration, December 29, 1966.]

AFFILIATED GROUP

An affiliated group which has a common profit-sharing plan (and in some instances a stock bonus plan) may shift contributions and deductions between members. [Sec. 404(a)(3)(B).]

The affiliated group must have a qualified plan under which contributions are determined by reference to profits. The term "affiliated group" has the same meaning for this provision as it has for purposes of filing consolidated tax returns. Each member of the affiliated group need not participate in the plan. [Regs. 1.404(a)-10(a)(1).]

If a participating member is prevented from making a required contribution because it has neither current nor accumulated earnings or profits, the contribution may be made on its behalf by other participating members of the affiliated group. A participating member must have sufficient earnings or profits, after its own contribution, from which to pay the "make-up" contribution. [Regs. 1.404(a)-10(a)(3).]

The affiliated group does not have to file a consolidated return to receive the benefits of this provision. If a consolidated return is filed, it is immaterial which of the participating members makes the contribution and takes the deduction or how the contribution or deduction is allocated between members. If a consolidated return is not filed, the participating members must divide the contribution so that each member bears the proportion of the "make-up" contribution which its current and accumulated earnings or profits bear to the total current and accumulated earnings or profits of all members which have such. Special rules are provided for the computation of current and accumulated earnings or profits. [Regs. 1.404(a)-10(c).]

Each participating member is allowed to deduct that portion of the "make-up" contribution which is allocated to it, provided such portion would have been deductible by the loss corporation if it had made it. The total amount of "make-up" contribution which is deductible is determined by applying the regular limitations as though the contribution had actually been made by the loss corporation. For example, the 15%-of-compensation limitation is determined by reference to the compensation paid or accrued to the employees of the loss corporation. The participating corporation which makes the contribution does not consider the contribution when it determines its own limitations. For purposes of the credit and contribution carryovers, the loss corporation treats the "make-up" contribution as having been made by itself. [Regs. 1.404(a)-10(b).]

The same rules apply where a participating member is prevented from making a full contribution because of insufficient profits. In such a case, the member makes its contribution to the extent of its profits. The excess of the total contribution over the portion contributed by the member becomes a "make-up" contribution. [Regs. 1.404(a)-2.] These rules also apply to the affiliated corporations, even though unrelated corporations adopt the same plan and trust. [Rev. Rul. 57-388.]

The terms of a plan may prevent a member from making a contribution even though sufficient profits exist.

Example: Under an affiliated group plan, the group contributes 5% of its combined net income after first deducting 10% of its total invested capital. The affiliated group does not file a consolidated return. The total required contribution is allocated to the members under a formula based upon participants' wages and service. Dugan Company, one of the members, is allocated $50,000 of the total contribution. Dugan has no accumulated earnings and its current earnings ($40,000) are less than 10% of its invested capital. Under the plan, Dugan is not required to make a contribution.

In this example, only $10,000 may be considered as a "make-up" contribution and shifted to other members of the group. Dugan has earnings of $40,000. Dugan was prevented from making its contribution of $50,000 by the terms of the plan, but of that amount only $10,000 was prevented by the absence of earnings. The contributing members may deduct only $10,000. [Rev. Rul. 67-214.]

CARRYOVERS

PENSION PLANS. When an employer contribution paid under a pension plan in a taxable year exceeds the deduction limitation for that year, the excess of the amount paid over the limitation may be carried forward to a later year. The amount of the deduction in the year to which carried is subject to the regular limitations. [Sec. 404(a)(1)(D).]

Example: In the taxable year 1968 the employer makes a contribution of $100,000. The limitation applicable to that year is $60,000. The employer may deduct $60,000 in 1968 and carry over $40,000 to 1969. In the calendar year 1969 the employer makes a contribution of $25,000. The limitation and amount deductible for 1969 is $50,000. Of the $40,000 carryover from 1968, $25,000 is absorbed in 1969 and $15,000 is carried over to 1970.

Excess contributions under a qualified pension plan may be carried over whether or not the trust or plan is qualified in the year in which the excess contributions are deducted. [Regs. 1.404(a)-3.] If an amount is deductible as an excess-contribution carryover and is deducted in a year in which the pension trust or annuity plan is not qualified, or which ends after the trust or plan has terminated, the normal limitations on contributions set forth in Section 404(a) (1) and (2)—i.e., the 5% limitation, the "level amount" limitation, and the "normal cost" limitation—are not applicable. The excess contributions are allowed only to the extent of the limitation based upon past service costs under Section 404(a)(1)(C)—i.e., 10% of past service or supplementary costs. [Regs. 1.404(a)-6 and 7.]

PROFIT-SHARING AND STOCK BONUS PLANS. If an employer contribution paid in a taxable year exceeds the 15%-of-compensation limitation, the excess may be carried forward to a later year. In the later year the contribution carryover is added to the actual contribution of that year to the extent the actual contribution is less than the 15% limitation. If the employer pays less than 15% in one year the resulting credit may be carried forward and added to the maximum amount otherwise deductible; but the amount so added cannot exceed 15% of the compensation paid during the succeeding year, subject to the limitation explained in the next paragraph. [Sec. 404(a)(3)(A).]

The operation of the credit carryover is subject to a secondary limitation for any given year equal to the lesser of (1) an amount equal to twice the primary limitation for such year, or (2) any excess of (*a*) the aggregate of the primary limitations for such year and for all prior years over (*b*) the aggregate of the deductions allowed or allowable under the limitations provided in Section 404(a)(3)(A) for all prior years. [Regs. 1.404(a)-9(d).] The regulations illustrate the operation of the primary and secondary limitations as in Illustration 1 on page 86.

When an excess contribution to a profit-sharing or stock bonus trust is carried forward to a taxable year in which the trust is not exempt or has been terminated, the primary limitation is based upon 15% of compensation otherwise paid or accrued during such year to employees who, at any time during the one-year period ending on the last day of the last calendar month during which the trust was exempt, were covered by the plan. [Regs. 1.404 (a)-9.] The secondary limitation does not apply in such a situation. The allowable deduction due to the contribution is the lesser of the primary limitation or the excess contribution.

If excess payments are made into a profit-sharing or stock bonus trust, and also into a pension trust or under an annuity plan, the excess may be carried forward but the total deduction in any one year including the carryover cannot exceed 30% of the compensation paid or accrued during the taxable year to all beneficiaries. [Sec. 404(a)(7).]

The limitations under Section 404(a)(7) apply only if at least one employee is a common beneficiary under a pension or annuity plan *and* a profit-sharing or stock bonus plan.

The regulations illustrate the application of Section 404 (a)(7) and the treatment of carryovers in the case of an overlapping pension trust and profit-sharing plan as in Illustration 2 on page 88.

REORGANIZATIONS

Under Section 381 an acquiring corporation in certain business transfers steps into the shoes of the transferor corporation insofar as the determination of amounts deductible under Section 404 is concerned. The business transfers contemplated are tax-free

ILLUSTRATION 1

Illustration of provisions of Section 404(a)(3)(A) for a plan put into effect in the taxable (calendar) year 1954, before giving effect to Section 404 (a)(7). (All figures represent thousands of dollars.)

	Taxable (calendar) years						
	1954	1955	1956	1957	1958	1959	1960
1. Amount of contributions:							
a. In taxable year	$ 65	$ 10	$ 15	$100	$ 70	$ 40	$ 30
b. Carried over from prior taxable years	0	8	0	0	4	5	3
2. Primary limitation applicable to year: 15% of covered compensation in year[1]	57	54	51	48	45	42	39
3. Secondary limitation applicable to year:							
a. Twice primary limitation				96	90	84	
b. (i) Aggregate primary limitations (see item 2)				210	255	297	
(ii) Aggregate prior deductions (see item 4c)				90	186	255	
(iii) Excess of (i) over (ii)				120	69	42	
c. Lesser of (a) or (b)				96	69	42	
4. Amount deductible for year on account of:							
a. Contributions in year	57	10	15	96	69	40	30
b. Contributions carried over	0	8	0	0	0	2	3
c. Total	57	18	15	96	69	42	33
5. Excess contributions carried over to succeeding years	8	0	0	4	5	3	0

[1] Compensation otherwise paid or accrued during the year to the employees who are beneficiaries of trust funds accumulated under the plan in the year.

liquidations of subsidiaries and type A, C, D and F reorganizations under Section 368(a)(1).

Excess contributions under a pension plan and excess contributions and unused credits of a profit-sharing or stock bonus plan may be carried forward to the acquiring corporation. The acquiring corporation is considered to be the transferor corporation for all Section 404 purposes. [Regs. 1.381(c)(11).]

The following requirements for deductions are set forth:

1. In order for the acquiring corporation to obtain a deduction for contributions made by it to the transferor's plan, the plan must retain its qualified status. The transferor's plan must maintain its own status unless it becomes part of a single plan for the acquiring corporation.
2. Excess contributions may be carried over and deducted by the acquiring corporation regardless of whether the exempt status is maintained in the year of the deduction. For purposes of the special limitations which are applicable when deductions are claimed in a year when the exempt status is not maintained, the transferor's plan shall be considered continued by the acquiring corporation provided the plan is:
   a. Continued as a separate qualified plan;
   b. Consolidated with another qualified plan; or
   c. Replaced with a comparable plan.
3. Unused credits may be carried over and used by the acquiring corporation, if such corporation continues the plan as a separate plan, consolidates it, or replaces it with a comparable plan. The separate, consolidated, or replacement plan must be qualified in the year the excess credit is used.
4. A pension trust and an annuity plan are "comparable." Neither is comparable with a profit-sharing or stock bonus plan, but a profit-sharing trust and a stock bonus trust are comparable.
5. All excess contributions and unused credits must be separate and distinct and properly identified by transferor and plan.
6. If, after the Section 381 transaction, the acquiring corporation makes contributions to two or more profit-sharing or stock bonus trusts, one or more of which was inherited

from a transferor, all the trusts are considered to be a single trust for purposes of determining the primary limitations and the secondary limitations on the acquiring corporation.

This subject is treated in greater detail in a subsequent chapter entitled "Business Combinations."

ILLUSTRATION 2

Illustration of application of provisions of Section 404(a)(7) and of treatment of carryovers for overlapping pension and profit-sharing trusts put into effect in 1954 and covering the same employees. (All figures represent thousands of dollars.)

	Taxable (calendar) years			
BEFORE GIVING EFFECT TO SECTION 404(a)(7)	1954	1955	1956	1957
Pension trust contributions and limitations, deductions, and carryovers under Section 404(a)(1):				
1. Contributions paid in year	$215	$ 85	$140	$ 60
2. Contributions carried over from prior years	0	5	0	20
3. Total deductible for year subject to limitation	215	90	140	80
4. Limitation applicable to year	210	175	120	85
5. Amount deductible for year	210	90	120	80
6. Contributions carried over to succeeding years	5	0	20	0
Profit-sharing trust contributions and limitations, deductions, and carryovers under Section 404(a)(3):				
7. Contributions paid in year	200	125	105	65
8. Contributions carried over from prior years	0	35	10	0
9. Total deductible for year subject to limitation	200	160	115	65
10. Limitation applicable to year	165	150	135	110
11. Amount deductible for year	165	150	115	65
12. Contributions carried over to succeeding years	35	10	0	0

APPLICATION OF SECTION 404(a)(7)

Totals for pension and profit-sharing trust:
13. Amount deductible for year under Section 404(a)(7):
 a. 30% of compensation covered in year[2] .... —[3] 300 270 180

b. (i) (A) 25% of compensation covered in year[2] 275 250 225 150

(B) Total amount otherwise deductible for year(item 5 plus item 11) 375 240 235 145

(C) Smaller of (A) or (B)... 275 240 225 145

(ii) Carryover from prior years under Section 404(a)(7) 0 100 40 10

(iii) Sum of (i)(C) and (ii) 275 340 265 155

c. Amount deductible: lesser of a or b (iii) 275 300 265 155

14. Carryover to succeeding years under Section 404(a)(7): item 13b (ii) plus item 13b (i)(B) minus item 13c .. 100 40 10 0

[1] Includes carryover of 20 from 1956.
[2] Compensation otherwise paid or accrued during the year to the employees who are beneficiaries under the trusts in the year.
[3] 30% limitation not applicable to first year of plan.

TIME AND METHOD OF CONTRIBUTION

TIME OF PAYMENT. A contribution by an employer under a qualified retirement plan is generally deductible only in the taxable year in which paid. An important exception to this rule exists for the accrual-basis taxpayer. A contribution accrued within a taxable year may be deducted within such year provided it is paid not later than the time prescribed by law (including extensions) for filing the tax return for the accrual year. [Sec. 404(a)(6).]

Example: The Ajax Corporation is an accrual-basis taxpayer which reports on the calendar-year basis. During 1968 Ajax makes no contributions to its exempt pension trust. On May 16, 1969 it pays over to the trust the amount of $100,000 to fund its 1968 normal costs. It files its 1968 tax return on June 2, 1969 under an extension to June 15, 1969. The $100,000 is deductible for the year 1968.

The employer's contribution may be made any time up to the last date (including extensions) for filing the tax return, regardless of when the tax return is actually filed. [Rev. Rul. 66-144.]

It appears that contributions paid after the end of the accrual year but before the filing of the tax return must be taken as a deduction in the accrual year to the extent they are within the limits of deductibility used by the taxpayer in computing the deduction—e.g., normal cost plus 10% of past service cost. The deduction may not be postponed until year of payment; in other words, there is no option as to the year in which the deduction may be claimed. [*Time Oil Co. v. Com.*, 294 F.2d 667 (9th Cir. 1961).]

The above rules with respect to deductibility for the year of accrual of payments made after the end of such year apply to payments applicable to any self-employed. [Regs. 1.404(e)-1(b)(3)(ii).]

Query whether (in the case of a pension plan) the employer must have recorded the liability on its books at the end of the year in order to deduct for such year a payment made within the grace period after year-end. Depending upon the terms of the particular plan, a liability (unenforceable by the beneficiaries whether recorded on the books or not, because under most plans the employer may discontinue contributions at any time) exists at the end of the year which would appear to be sufficient to support a deduction for payment made within the grace period even though not recorded on the books at year-end.

Where a profit-sharing plan does not contain a contribution formula, or where the contribution exceeds the amount determined under a formula, a written commitment must be made and communicated to the employees prior to the end of the taxable year in order to create an accrual. [Rev. Rul. 63-117.]

Usually this means that before the end of the taxable year, the board of directors must determine the amount that will be contributed to the profit-sharing trust and advise the employees of its action. It might also be necessary for each employee to be advised of the portion allocated for his benefit. In establishing these requirements, the Internal Revenue Service is attempting to force the employer to create a real liability to the trust. If the employee does not know that a contribution has been agreed upon, the employee is not in a position to enforce the liability.

A deduction is not barred merely because a contribution is refundable if the Internal Revenue Service does not approve the plan. [Mim. 5985.] In order to get the deduction, however, the trust must be in existence as determined under local law during the year of the deduction. In addition, the trust must be created under a written trust agreement. If these conditions are met, the trust will be recognized and the deduction allowed even though the trust has no corpus, provided the contribution is made in the succeeding year within the time limits prescribed by Section 404(a)(6). [Rev. Rul. 57-419.]

No deduction is allowed in a year prior to the year in which the plan becomes effective. [*West Virginia Steel Corp.*, 34 T.C. 851 (1960).] Under a nontrusteed annuity plan, a deduction may be taken in the year that the plan is adopted even though the group annuity contract is not issued during that year, provided that before the end of the year all other steps have been taken and provided that the contract is issued and paid for prior to the filing date of the tax return. [Rev. Rul. 59-402.]

If a payment to a trust can be withdrawn unless shareholder approval is obtained, it does not give rise to a deduction. It is not an unconditional payment. It represents no more than a provisional deposit. [*Dejay Stores, Inc. v. Ryan*, 229 F.2d 867 (2nd Cir. 1956).]

METHOD OF PAYMENT. If an employer transfers tangible property to a qualified employees' trust, the employer may deduct the fair market value of the property as a contribution under Section 404. If the property has a fair market value in excess of the employer's tax basis in the property, the employer will realize gain in the amount of such excess. [*U.S. v. General Shoe Corp.*, 282 F.2d 9 (6th Cir. 1960).] If, however, a loss is sustained on the transfer because the fair maket value is less than the tax basis to the employer, the loss is denied under Section 267 because the transaction is between the exempt trust and its grantor. [Rev. Rul. 61-163 and *Dillard Paper Co.*, 42 T.C. 588 (1964), aff'd (4th Cir. 1965).] In the case of a prospective loss upon the transfer of property, it would appear prudent to sell the property to an unrelated party, realize the loss, and contribute the proceeds to the exempt trust.

The contribution of stock or securities of a corporation which is not the employer will result in the same tax consequences as set forth above relating to tangible property.

If a corporation's own stock is contributed, the tax consequences are not clear. Under Section 1032 a corporation does not realize gain or loss on the exchange of its own stock for money or other property. Whether or not Section 1032 will prevent the realization of gain under the *General Shoe* theory has not been settled.

The tax consequences of a corporation contributing its own notes payable to a trust is also unsettled. The Internal Revenue Service tends to the position that the contribution of a note does not give rise to a tax deduction. The courts usually take a more liberal position; for example, the delivery by an employer to a profit-sharing trust of the employer's unsecured, interest-bearing promissory notes with stated maturity dates was held to be payment and the employer was permitted to take the value of the notes as deduction for the year of delivery. [*Wasatch Chemical Co. v. Com.*, 313 F.2d 843 (10th Cir. 1963).] The delivery of non-interest-bearing demand notes has also entitled the taxpayer to a deduction. [*Time Oil Co. v. Com.*, 294 F.2d 667 (9th Cir. 1961).] The delivery of a secured interest-bearing note, payable at a specific date, with a fair market value equal to face value constituted payment. [*Steele Wholesale Builders Supply Co. v. U.S.*, 226 F. Supp. 82 (D.C. Tex., 1963).] In *Van Products, Inc.*, 40 T.C. 1018 (1963), however, the employer made a cash contribution to the trust and immediately borrowed back the cash on an unsecured, interest-bearing note. The trust lost its exemption for making loans without adequate security and the contribution deduction was lost to the employer.

INFORMATION REQUIREMENTS

Neither the Code nor the regulations require that, as a condition precedent to obtaining the tax benefits incident and pertaining to a qualified plan, an advance ruling as to initial qualification be obtained. An advance ruling, or determination letter, is issued only at the request of the taxpayer and is never initiated by the Revenue Service. It is a matter of convenience to the taxpayer. The careful tax practitioner, however, will obtain a determination letter before effecting an employees' plan in order to insure deductibility of contributions by the employer and nontaxability of contributions to the employees. The procedures for obtaining a determination letter for plans seeking qualification are set forth in Revenue Procedure 67-4.

An employer claiming a deduction for a contribution to a qualified plan is required to furnish certain information in support of the deduction. [Regs. 1.404(a)-2(a).] The required information includes the following:

1. Copies of instruments.
2. Description of plan.
3. Information relating to 25 highest-paid employees covered by the plan.

4. Nondeferred compensation for covered employees and all employees, and amounts allocated to benefit of employees.
5. Breakdown of eligible and ineligible employees.
6. Financial statements or other statements for trusteed and nontrusteed plans.
7. If a pension or annuity plan, a description of all methods, factors, and assumptions used in determining costs and in adjusting costs for actual experience; and, in the case of a trust, a description of the basis used in valuing the investments held.
8. A statement of the annual limitations on deductions and an explanation of the method of determining such limitations, a summary of the data, and a statement of computations necessary to determine the allowable deduction for the taxable year. Also, in the case of a pension or annuity plan, a summary of the costs or liabilities and adjustments for the year under the plan based on the application of the methods, factors, and assumptions used under the plan, in sufficient detail to permit ready verification of the reasonableness thereof.
9. A statement of the date and amount of each payment of contribution during the year and a statement of the computation of carryover deductions.

All of the above information is required for the first year in which a deduction is claimed under the plan. In subsequent years, items 1, 2, and 7 need be filed only in the event of a change in the plan, instruments, methods, factors, or assumptions upon which the data and information in items 1, 2, and 7 are based. Absent changes in the plan and the method and basis of allocation, and unless otherwise requested by the District Director, item 3 need be furnished for subsequent years only to the extent of employees owning more than 5% of the voting stock. Items 4, 5, 6, 8, and 9 must be furnished each year a deduction is claimed. [Regs. 1.404(a)-2(b).]

Form 2950, "Statement in Support of Deduction," is provided by the Treasury Department to enable a taxpayer to file the necessary annual information. All taxpayers who have qualified plans for their employees must file Form 2950 or, if the plan covers self-employed persons, Form 2950E (see page 121). Form 2950 is usually filed as a part of the employer's Federal income tax return. A portion of the information required to be filed annually under the Welfare and Pension Plans Disclosure Act, such as financial statements, may be submitted to satisfy similar requirements under Regulations 1.404(a)-2. [Rev. Proc. 60-14.]

All information required by Regulations 1.404(a)-2 should be filed with the tax return in which the deduction for the contribution is claimed. With the exception of parts of item 4 (relating to total non-deferred compensation paid or accrued during the year to all employees and to covered employees) and item 9, the information may be filed within 12 months after the close of the taxable year in which the deduction is claimed, provided the tax return contains a statement setting forth reasons why the information cannot reasonably be filed with the return. [Regs. 1.404(a)-2(d).]

Refer to page 203 for information required from the trustee of an exempt trust.

CONTRIBUTIONS UNDER NONQUALIFIED PLAN

In the case of a qualified plan, the deductibility of a contribution does not depend upon whether the rights of the employees are forfeitable or nonforfeitable. The rights of the employees are important, however, if the plan is not qualified.

NONFORFEITABLE RIGHTS. Contributions made under non-qualified pension, profit-sharing, stock bonus, annuity, or other deferred compensation plans are allowable as deductions if the employees' rights in the contributions are nonforfeitable at the time the contributions are paid. [Sec. 404(a)(5).] The deduction is allowed in the year in which the contribution is paid and only to the extent that it constitutes an ordinary and necessary business expense — i.e., to the extent that it constitutes reasonable compensation (see page 315).

The special payment period after the close of the taxable year for accrual basis taxpapers (see page 89) does not apply to contributions under nonqualified plans. Consequently, no deduction is permitted for direct pensions to former employees or for death benefits to employees' beneficiaries until the amounts are paid. [Regs. 1.404(a)-12.]

The nonforfeitability of employees' rights is tested by reference to individual employees rather than by reference to the employees as a class. [Regs. 1.404(a)-12.]

Example: In 1968 an employer makes an irrevocable contribution to a trust under a deferred compensation plan for the benefit of a class of employees. The specified class of employees has a nonforfeitable right to the contribution. No individual member of the class has a nonforfeitable right. Under Section 404(a)(5) no deduction is allowed to the employer in 1968. [*Bailey Co. v. Com.,* 192 F.2d 574 (3rd Cir. 1951).]

FORFEITABLE RIGHTS. The regulations provide that if the employees' rights are forfeitable in the year in which the contribution is paid, the employer is allowed no deduction in the year of payment. Furthermore, it is the Commissioner's position that no deduction is allowable in any subsequent year in which the employees' rights become nonforfeitable. In the subsequent year the payment test is not met—i.e., the employer has not made a payment. [Regs. 1.404(a)-12.] Contrary to the regulations are *Russell Manufacturing Co. v. U.S.,* 175 F. Supp. 159 (Ct. Cl. 1959); Revenue Ruling 59-383; *Mississippi River Fuel Corp. v. U.S.,* 314 F.2d 953 (Ct. Cl. 1963); and *Buttrey Stores, Inc.,* 375 F.2d 799 (Ct. Cl. 1967). See also page 287.

(b) ABSENCE OF FORMAL PLAN

If there is no formal plan but a method of employer contributions or compensation has the effect of a pension, profit-sharing, stock bonus, or annuity plan, or of a similar plan deferring the receipt of compensation, such contributions or compensation will be treated as if they had been made under such a plan.

Example: The Carter Company is on the accrual basis. It contracts with Jones, an executive, to employ him for a period of five years as president at an annual salary of $50,000, payable for ten years. After five years Jones retires but continues to receive $50,000 each year for five years. The amounts paid by Carter Company have the effect of a plan of deferred compensation and are governed by the rules of Section 404(a). The company receives the deductions in the years in which the amounts are paid.

An employer's direct payments to retired employees of monthly benefits based on compensation and service are deductible only under Section 404(a)(5). [Rev. Rul. 68-180.]

If an arrangement does not involve deferment of compensation, it is not subject to the restrictions of Section 404(a), and deductions for payments are allowed as necessary business expenses.

Example: Company G made regular annual contributions to an employees' association organized to provide sickness and disability benefits, medical aid, burial expenses, group life, accident, and hospital insurance, and other benefits for dues-paying members. In the taxable year, an extra $12,000 was contributed by the company to help put the association on an actuarially sound basis. It was held that this was for a business purpose and, since it involved an amount which was only 6½% of the annual payroll, it could not be considered a capital investment. It was therefore held to be deductible as an ordinary and necessary business expense. [*Weil Clothing Co.*, 13 T.C. 873 (1949).]

(c) CERTAIN NEGOTIATED PLANS

There are certain unqualified union-negotiated pension and medical plans to which Section 404(a) does not apply. A contribution to a trust under such a plan is deductible, if at all, as an ordinary and necessary business expense under Section 162. The United Mine Workers welfare fund is an example of such a plan.

In order to fall within this provision the plan must have been established prior to 1954 as a result of negotiations between a union and the U. S. Government during a period of Government operation, under seizure powers, of a major portion of the employer's facilities.

The special provision does not apply after the trust qualifies for exemption.

(d) CARRYOVER OF UNUSED DEDUCTIONS

This provision acts as a bridge between the 1939 Code and the 1954 Code. It provides that unused carryovers which arose under the 1939 Code will be allowed as a deduction under the 1954 Code as though the 1939 Code applied in the 1954 Code years.

The transition rule does not allow a double deduction for carryovers—i.e., once under the 1939 Code and once under the 1954 Code.

Example: A pension plan, effective January 1, 1953, has a past service cost of $1,000,000. In 1953 the employer contributes $500,000 toward past service costs. Under the 1939 Code $100,000 is deductible in 1953 and $400,000 is available as a carryover. In 1954 the remaining $500,000 is funded. The past service cost deduction is limited to $100,000 in 1954, with $800,000 as a carryover to 1955.

(e) SPECIAL LIMITATIONS FOR SELF-EMPLOYED INDIVIDUALS

(f) LOAN REPAYMENTS CONSIDERED AS CONTRIBUTIONS

The above subsections relate to retirement plans of self-employed individuals. This subject is treated in summary in the chapter beginning on page 115.

Qualified Bond Purchase Plans

GENERAL STATEMENT
REQUIREMENTS FOR QUALIFICATION
DEDUCTION OF CONTRIBUTION
TAXATION OF RETIREMENT BONDS
BASIS OF BONDS
RETIREMENT BONDS

GENERAL STATEMENT

Since 1962 it has been possible for retirement plans qualified under Section 401 to be funded, in whole or in part, through the acquisition of a special series of United States bonds. Also, a specially constructed qualified bond purchase plan may purchase such bonds and provide the benefits of a plan qualified under Section 401. In either case, the plan under which the bonds are purchased may cover only common-law employees, self-employed persons, or both. [Regs. 1.405-1(a).]

REQUIREMENTS FOR QUALIFICATION

Pension and profit-sharing plans are qualified under Section 401 (see page 15). A bond purchase plan is qualified under Section 405, although the basic requirements of Section 401 must also be met. [Regs. 1.405-1(b).] If the plan covers a self-employed person, it must also meet the special requirements applicable to such persons (see page 115).

A bond purchase plan is a simplified method of providing

tax-favored retirement benefits to employees without the benefit of a trust. It must be established and maintained by an employer for the sole purpose of purchasing and distributing the retirement bonds. The conventional pension or profit-sharing plan may invest a portion of its funds in the retirement bonds, but the bond purchase plan must invest all of its funds in the bonds. The plan must be a definite written plan; it must be communicated to the employees; it must be a permanent plan. [Regs. 1.405-1(b)(1).]

The bonds are purchased in the name of the employee, and the plan must provide that the employee's rights to the bonds so purchased are nonforfeitable. The employer can never recover in any way his contribution on behalf of the employee. [Regs. 1.405-1(b)(2).] Rules are provided to gear the employer contribution to an amount that can be readily invested in the bonds. [Reg. 1.405-1(d).]

The bond purchase plan must have the characteristics of either a pension plan or a profit-sharing plan. If it is a profit-sharing plan, for example, it must have a definite allocation formula (see page 20), and if it covers an owner-employee it must have a definite contribution formula. [Regs. 1.401-12(d).] Some of the traditional characteristics of pension and profit-sharing plans are changed, however, to meet the special needs of the bond retirement plan. If the plan is a pension plan, for example, it need not provide systematically for the payment of definitely determinable benefits (see page 17). The bonds may be distributed at any time (they are restricted as to redemption), so long as the distribution is nondiscriminatory. In addition, the plan may not contain a formula for contributions or benefits which might require the reallocation of amounts to an employee's credit or provide for the reversion of amounts to the employer. [Regs. 1.405-1(c).] Because of the nonforfeitability of the bonds, the plan must also restrict the contribution for any employee's benefit to an amount which would not result in discrimination in the event of an early termination of the plan. [Regs. 1.405-1(d).]

DEDUCTION OF CONTRIBUTION

The time and amount of the employer's deduction under a bond purchase plan are governed by the rules which apply to contributions to exempt trusts (see page 89).

The deduction is allowed in the year the contribution is paid. As in the case of conventional plans (see page 89), if an accrual-basis taxpayer incurs a liability to make a contribution during a taxable year and records such a liability at its year-end, the deduction may be taken in the year of the accrual if the contribution is actually paid prior to the filing of the tax return for such year. [Regs. 1.405-2(c).] For the purposes of this section, a contribution is deemed paid at the time the application for the bond is made and the full purchase price is paid. [Regs. 1.405-2(a).]

The limitations on the amount of the deduction under a bond purchase plan are similar to those applicable to pension plans and profit-sharing plans (see page 74). In other words, if a bond purchase plan has the characteristics of a pension plan, the deduction limitations applicable to pension plans are applicable. [Regs. 1.405-2(b).]

TAXATION OF RETIREMENT BONDS

Generally, the employer's contribution under a bond purchase plan does not result in taxable income to the employee. The distribution of a retirement bond, either under a qualified bond purchase plan or from an exempt employees' trust, does not produce taxable income to the employee. [Regs. 1.405-3(a)(1).] Usually a distribution to an employee under a qualified retirement plan results in taxable income to the employee. In this case, however, the distribution to an employee under a qualified retirement plan does not result in taxable income to the employee. He cannot redeem the bond until the attainment of a certain age or the occurrence of a certain event.

Taxable income (ordinary) arises when the employee redeems the bond to the extent of the excess of the redemption proceeds over the employee's basis in the bond.

The taxable income resulting from the redemption is entitled to neither the special five-year averaging device available to self-employed persons (see page 121) nor the capital gain treatment available for total distributions (see page 47). In the latter case, however, retirement bonds are not taken into consideration in determining whether a distribution is a total distribution. [Regs. 1.405-3(a)(1) and (4).]

Example: Jones has no cost basis for his interest in the XYZ Company pension trust. In 1968 he receives a total distribution of $60,000. The severance distribution includes cash of $50,000 and retirement bonds of $10,000. Jones is taxed at capital gains rates on the $50,000 in 1968 and at ordinary income rates on the $10,000 at such time as the bonds are cashed.

Example: Smith has no cost basis for his interest in the XYZ Company pension trust. In 1967 he receives a severance distribution of $50,000 in cash which represents the total amount standing to his credit in the trust except for $10,000 in retirement bonds. The trust distributes the bonds to him in 1968. Smith is taxed at capital gains rates on the $50,000 in 1967 and at ordinary income rates on the $10,000 at such time as the bonds are cashed.

If a bond is redeemed in part and reissued for the unredeemed part, the original bond is considered to have been issued as two separate bonds. [Regs. 1.405-3(a)(2).]

Example: Carter has a retirement bond of $1,000 denomination. His basis in the bond is $200. He surrenders the bond for partial redemption and receives $800 in cash and a new bond for $200. The $200 basis is prorated between the cash proceeds ($160) and the new bond ($40). Carter's present gain on the partial redemption is $640. His future gain on the new bond will be $160.

If a bond is redeemed after the death of the registered owner (the employee), the gain is income in respect of a decedent under Section 691. [Regs. 1.405-3(a)(3).]

BASIS OF BONDS

In the case of a common-law employee participating in a bond purchase plan or covered by an exempt trust, the term "basis" means his contribution to the total purchase price of the retirement bond. [Regs. 1.405-3(b)(1).]

Example: The bond cost $1,000. The employer contributed $800 and the employee contributed $200. The latter figure is the employee's basis.

If the person for whom the bond is purchased is a self-employed person, the term "basis" has a more complex definition. [Regs. 1.405-3(b)(3).]

In a situation where the bonds are redeemed by a self-employed person, all bonds redeemed during a taxable year are considered in the aggregate as a single bond. The basis of the "single" bond is the difference between its face amount and the lesser of the following [Regs. 1.405-3(b)(3)(i)]:

1. One-half the face amount; *or*
2. The aggregate of the unused amounts allowed as a deduction at the end of the taxable year in which the redemptions are made.

The phrase "aggregate of the unused amounts allowed as a deduction" means an amount equal to the following [Regs. 1.405-3(b)(4)(i)]:

1. The total amounts allowable for all years (current and prior) as a deduction for contributions to bond purchase plans to purchase bonds on behalf of the individual while a self-employed person;

less

2. The portion of the face amounts of such bonds redeemed in prior years and included in the individual's gross income.

Example: Miller, a self-employed person, participates in a bond purchase plan during 1967 and until his retirement on June 30, 1968. In 1967, $2,000 of bonds were purchased for him; in 1968, $500 of bonds were so purchased. His deduction for 1967 was $400 (he overestimated his income) and for 1968 was $250. In July 1968 he redeemed a $500 bond; in August 1968 he redeemed another $500 bond. The two redeemed bonds are treated as a single bond with $1,000 face amount. The basis for the bond is $500, computed as follows:

1. One-half of face amount		$ 500
2. Aggregate of unused amounts allowed as a deduction:		
1967		$ 400
1968		250
Total		$ 650
3. Face amount		$1,000
Lesser of 1 or 2 above		500
Basis		$ 500

In 1969 Miller redeems another $500 bond. His basis for this bond is $350, computed as follows:

1. One-half of face amount		$ 250

2. Aggregate of unused amounts allowed as a deduction:
   1967 ....$ 400
   1968 250
   Total ....$ 650
   Less portion included in income in 1968 500
   Lesser of 1 or 2 above ....$ 150
3. Face amount ....$ 500
   Net 150
   Basis ....$ 350

In 1970 Miller redeems the remaining $1,000 bond. The basis of this bond is $1,000 because the aggregate of the unused amounts allowed as a deduction was reduced to zero in 1969.

Over the three-year period, Miller has received proceeds of $2,500 and had included in gross income $650, an amount equal to his tax deductions in 1967 and 1968. Interest is included in gross income in the year received.

A special basis computation must be made where a bond is redeemed after the death of the self-employed person. [Regs. 1.405-3(b)(3)(ii).]

If a retirement bond is purchased by an exempt trust for a self-employed person, there is allocated to it that portion of the contribution used to purchase the bond which resulted in a deduction for the self-employed person and which is used in computing the unused amounts allowed as a deduction. Such portion does not constitute basis for assets distributed from the trust. [Regs. 1.405-3(b)(4)(ii).]

RETIREMENT BONDS

U.S. Retirement Plan Bonds have the following characteristics:

1. The bonds may be purchased only in the name of an individual. Ownership is nontransferable.
2. Interest of 3.75% to 4.15%, compounded semiannually, is paid only upon redemption.
3. Interest accrues only until the earlier of redemption date or maturity date. Interest stops within five years after the death of the owner.
4. The bonds may not be redeemed until the owner reaches

age 59½, becomes disabled, or dies, whichever event is earliest.

5. The bonds are subject to estate, inheritance, or other excise taxes, whether Federal or state, but are exempt from all taxation now or hereafter imposed on the principal or interest thereof by any state, municipality, or local taxing authority. [Regs. 341.13.] To the extent that an employer's contribution to a qualified pension or profit-sharing plan is invested in such bonds, the foregoing provision regarding Federal estate taxes would appear to be contra to Section 2039(c)(1), and the exemption from state and municipal income taxes differs from the tax treatment accorded other qualified plan distributions.

6. No more than $5,000 face value of the bonds may be purchased in the name of any one person as registered owner during any one taxable year.

The bonds are described in detail in Regs. 341.0-341.15, Department Circular, Public Debt Series No. 1-63.

Employee Savings or Thrift Plans

GENERAL TRENDS
THE MECHANICS
    The employee's contribution
    The employer's contribution
    The trust
    The distribution
    Status under Federal securities laws

GENERAL TRENDS

Employee savings and thrift plans have grown at a remarkably rapid rate in recent years. Quite a number of large companies and an increasing number of medium-size and smaller companies are adopting employee savings plans. Recent surveys have attributed the fast growth to a number of factors: low cost to the company, employee satisfaction, tax advantages, employee stock ownership features, and conditions that encourage thrift.

The savings plan was originally developed by the oil industry but spread rapidly to other industries until at present it is employed by a substantial number of companies. The plans provide additional current security for the employee and in many cases a proprietary interest in the business of the employer. The employer benefits through an improvement in employee morale and a reduction in employee turnover. In one sense, every contributory pension plan is a thrift plan, since an incentive to save is usually present.

The amount of the company contribution, the liberality of

vesting provisions, and the freedom of choice of investment media seem to have a great deal of influence as to the extent of employee participation in a savings plan. The more generous the company contribution, the more encouragement there is for employees to join the plan. Early vesting makes plan benefits seem more tangible and thus more attractive to employees. Plans that allow employees to have a choice in the investment of their funds also seem to have greater employee participation.

If the plan qualifies under Section 401, the trust is exempt from taxation under Section 501(a) as an exempt employees' trust.

Some plans provide for elective current cash payments to participants and deferment for others. [Rev. Rul. 65-178, Part 2(h), but see *Hicks* case on pages 45 and 47.] Qualification of such a plan will depend largely on whether enough employees elect deferment rather than current cash payments, so that the plan annually meets the percentage coverage or nondiscriminatory classification requirements of the law. [Rev. Rul. 65-178, part 4(d); Regs. 1.401-3 (c).] If employees are allowed to take part of their share in cash and leave the balance in the profit-sharing trust, they are counted as participants only to the extent of their shares paid into the trust. For example, if an employee elects to receive one-half and defer one-half, he is counted as a one-half participant. The Revenue Service will not rule on qualification until coverage requirements are satisfied. Coverage sufficient for qualification initially must also be satisfied annually thereafter, to maintain qualification. [Rev. Rul. 56-497.]

A formula for employers' contributions may be based upon the combination of annual salary and years of service of the employees and may be related to the employee's contribution. However, the resulting benefits must be free of discrimination. Whether a weighted allocation and distribution formula has a discriminatory effect will depend upon the actual operation of the plan. If such weighting favors the higher-paid over the lower-paid employees, the plan may be disqualified. In this respect, to give effect to a length-of-service formula, employees are grouped by salary brackets and a determination is made of the ratio which employer contributions allocated to each group bear to the compensation. If the ratio determined for employees in the lower brackets is substantially lower than the ratio for those in the higher brackets as the result of giving credit for length of service, the allocation formula is considered discriminatory even though the method of crediting length of service is the same for all employees, regardless of salary [I.T. 3685; I.T. 3686.]

When using formulas based on length of service, it may be necessary for a ceiling to be placed upon certain employees' salaries for purposes of determining the allocation of the employer's contribution to the participants in order to avoid discrimination.

One District Office has refused to issue a favorable determination letter where the plan provided for the employer to contribute 50% of the employee's contribution and the employee could contribute an increasing percentage of current compensation as his length of service increased — e.g., 4% for up to 7 years of service, 5% for 7 to 17 years, and 6% for more than 17 years. Since the contribution percentage did not exceed 6% as a maximum, the refusal to issue a ruling seems contrary to the provisions of Part 4(g) of Revenue Ruling 65-178.

THE MECHANICS

Although the details of the plans differ considerably, the basic mechanics are identical for all. The employee contributes a portion of his income on a regular basis. The employer makes a contribution at the same time. The combined funds are turned over to a trustee who invests them in securities which are held in the name of the employee. The trustee distributes the assets of the trust to the employee upon termination of employment or at some other date in the future. The broad facets and their tax effects are discussed below in the following sections:

1. The employee's contribution.
2. The employer's contribution.
3. The trust.
4. The distribution.
5. Status under Federal securities laws.

THE EMPLOYEE'S CONTRIBUTION. The employee is permitted to "save" a portion of his periodic pay by making a contribution under the plan. The percentage of his pay check which he may contribute may vary from 1% to 10%, depending upon the type of plan, and may vary within a particular plan depending upon years of service. The employee makes an election as to the amount of his contribution when he first qualifies under the plan and generally has a right to increase or decrease his contribution periodically. However, if he drops out of the plan he will have to wait a stated length of time before reinstatement. The contribution is usually made by means of a payroll deduction.

Some plans require the employee to contribute a stated percentage of compensation before he may participate in the plan. If the requirement of contributions by employee-participants is so burdensome as to make the plan acceptable only to highly paid employees, discrimination may occur in favor of highly paid employees, with the result that the plan may not qualify. [Regs. 1.401-3(d).] If, for example, a plan requires employee contributions of 10% and lower-paid employees do not participate because of the contribution requirement, the plan may be held to be discriminatory in favor of highly paid employees and therefore fail to qualify. As a general rule, employee contributions of 6% or less are deemed not to be burdensome. [Rev. Rul. 65-178, Part 4(g).]

Where employees are permitted to make voluntary contributions to which employer contributions are not geared, a potential disproportionate allocation of employer contributions is absent. Such voluntary contributions, however, must be kept within reasonable bounds. Accordingly, provision may be made for voluntary employee contributions of amounts up to 10% of compensation, provided that employer contributions, or the benefits derived therefrom, are not geared to employee contributions. The employee contributions must be used to provide additional benefits only for the individual contributing employee. [Rev. Rul. 59-185; Rev. Rul. 65-178, Part 4(h).] It is possible under a set of circumstances that an employee could contribute as much as 16% of his compensation, where the plan requirement is 6% and the additional voluntary amount is 10%. (See page 35 for an even higher limit if the employee is a participant in more than one plan.)

The employee's contribution is made from his after-tax earnings. It has, therefore, no tax effect other than to give him a basis for his investment in the plan and a vehicle in which the accumulation of earnings is free from tax until a later date and then possibly at the more favorable capital gains rate.

A number of thrift plans permit an employee to withdraw his own contributions at any time. Usually, he then suffers some penalty such as forfeiture of his rights to employer contributions or termination of participation in the plan for six months or so. Other plans allow the employee to withdraw vesting portions of the employer contributions concurrently with his own contributions. [Rev. Rul. 58-230.]

The significance of the penalty for withdrawal is that it insulates the employee from having constructive receipt and maintains the savings concept of a thrift plan. If the employee has an unrestricted right of withdrawal, the amounts might be considered constructively received and thus includable in the employee's income. [Rev. Rul. 63-180.]

THE EMPLOYER'S CONTRIBUTION. Although the employer's contribution may run as high as 100% of that of the employee, a majority of the plans require the employer make a contribution equal to 50% of the employee's contribution. A few plans compute the employer's contribution in terms of annual earnings and at least one employer bases its contribution on the relationship of earnings to invested capital. Generally the employer's contribution is in cash, although sometimes it is in stock.

If the savings plan meets the requirements of a qualified pension, profit-sharing, or stock bonus plan as outlined in Section 401, the employer's contribution is deductible as a business expense under Section 404.

THE TRUST. The funds of the employee and employer are turned over to a trust for investment. The terms of the plan dictate the nature of the investments which are to be made by the trustee. The following investment patterns are found:

1. Stock of the employer.
2. U.S. Government bonds and employer stock.
3. Listed securities.
4. Combination of employer stock, U.S. Government bonds, and listed securities.

The trustee generally makes his investments by purchasing the securities on the open market, although in the case of employer stock some plans require the trustee to invest in unissued stock, thereby providing a source of financing for the employer. As the trustee makes investments, the securities are credited to the individual accounts of the participants. When dividends and interest are received by the trustee, these amounts are credited to the participants' accounts and are usually reinvested in accordance with the investment pattern. Stock rights, stock splits, and stock dividends are also administered for the participant's account. Insofar as employer stock voting rights are concerned, the plan may provide that the trusteed stock is "sterile," that it is voted by the trustee, or that it is voted by the participant if he is possessed of a vested right.

There may be more than one trust created, depending upon whether the plan is noncycle or cycle. The principal purpose of the noncycle plan is to provide benefits for employees upon their retirement or other termination of employment. One trust serves during the entire life of the plan. The employee's right to the employer's contribution becomes vested after a prescribed period (usually five years) or at retirement, disability, or death, if earlier. The cycle plan creates a trust at the beginning of each year, to which contributions are made during that year. After a stated period (usually three years), the assets of the trust are distributed and the trust is terminated. As the plan operates, a new trust is born each year and an old trust dies each year. The employee's right to the employer's contribution is vested at the end of the cycle, or at retirement or death, if earlier. Both plans permit an employee to withdraw prior to vesting, in which case he receives his contributions plus increases attributable to them. The advantage of the cycle plan is that it permits the employee to realize the benefits of his savings program at an early date. It has a disadvantage, however, in that the distribution during an employment year will be taxed (to the extent taxable) as ordinary income.

The terms of the plan may authorize the trustee to invest the amounts credited to the employee at the employee's direction. Earmarked investments may be made in common stocks, employer securities, insurance contracts, or government obligations. The trustee is required to invest all employees' interest under the plan in the same proportion unless each participant has the right to direct the trustee to select the types of investment with respect to amounts credited to his account. [Rev. Rul. 65-178, Part 5(r).]

Some plans have separate funds administered by the trustee which the employee can select by electing the specific funds in which his credits are to be invested. For example, the employee may choose Fund A, with a portfolio of only common stocks, Fund B, common stocks and government bonds, or Fund C, government bonds only. The employee may annually elect the fund into which his and the company's distributions are to be made.

THE DISTRIBUTION. A distribution by the trust is taxed to the beneficiary under the rules of Section 402(a) explained previously. Under the general rule of that section the excess of the market value of securities received over the employee's cost basis is taxed as ordinary income (distributions prior to termination of service) or capital gain (distributions after termination). If the distribution includes securities of the employer, the unrealized appreciation in such securities is excluded from the distributee's income in the year of such distribution to the following extent:

1. In the case of a voluntary or normal distribution (as in the case of a cycle plan) occurring in a service year, the unrealized appreciation attributable to the employee contribution. [Regs. 1.402(a)-1(b)(1)(i)(b).]
2. In the case of a termination-of-service distribution, the unrealized appreciation attributable to both employee and employer contributions. [Regs. 1.402(a)-1(b)(1)(i)(a).]

See example on page 53.

STATUS UNDER FEDERAL SECURITIES LAWS. Plans which provide for the investment of employee contributions in stock of the employer, even though such stock may be issued and outstanding stock purchased by a trustee on the open market, may require registration, under the Securities Act of 1933, of the employee participations in the plan and the related stock of the company. Exemption from full registration may be available under the provisions of Regulation A of the Securities Act of 1933 if, among other things, the employee contributions under the plan do not exceed $300,000 during specified periods. The filing of certain information, including an offering circular, with a regional office of the SEC is, however, required in such cases. Since the provisions of the Federal securities law relating to the determination of whether an issue of securities must be registered are highly technical, it is essential that this aspect be reviewed with legal counsel.

Form S-8 may be used in certain circumstances to register the participations in the plan and related stock of the employer. This form requires, among other things, information as to the tax aspects of the plan. Until the registration statement becomes "effective" (usually from three to six weeks after the date of the initial filing), no subscriptions to the plan may be accepted from employees. If a determination as to the tax status of the plan is to be obtained from the Internal Revenue Service prior to the effective date of the registration statement, an estimate must be made of the number of employees who will participate. It does not appear, however, to be a requirement that such a determination letter be secured prior to the time the registration statement becomes effective. The registration statement may indicate (1) that a determination letter is to be secured and (2) what the consequences will be if the determination is favorable. After the registration statement is effective and the applications of the participants have been received, a determination letter can be requested from the Internal Revenue Service.

If the prospectus included in the Form S-8 registration statement is to be used more than nine months after the effective date and contains information as of a date more than 16 months prior to the time of use, the Securities Act requires that it be brought up to date.

Retirement Plans for the Self-Employed

GENERAL STATEMENT

For years beginning after 1962, self-employed persons are given some of the tax benefits previously available only to common-law employees [see Regs. 31.3401(c)-1(b)] covered by qualified plans. The 1962 amendments to the Code treat the self-employed as both employers and employees for retirement plan purposes. This makes applicable to them, but with modification, most of the pre-existing laws, regulations, and rulings relating to benefits, diversion of funds, coverage, and discrimination with respect to qualified retirement plans.

This chapter covers the major provisions of the Self-Employed Individuals Tax Retirement Act of 1962 insofar as they modify, supplant, and conflict with pre-existing retirement plan principles.

DEFINITIONS

EMPLOYEE. In order to participate, a self-employed person must qualify as an "employee," as that term is defined in the statute. [Sec. 401(c)(1) and Regs. 1.401-10(b)(3).] In general, the term includes all individuals who are subject to the social security self-employment tax. Specifically, an individual who qualifies as an employee is one who:

1. Had "earned income" during the year; *or*
2. Would have had "earned income" during the year if his business had been profitable; *or*
3. Qualified as an "employee" under either 1 or 2 above in a prior year.

The individual may be a sole proprietor or a partner.

EARNED INCOME. The term "earned income" has considerable importance, for it is the touchstone by which both eligibility and amount of contribution are determined. "Earned income" means the net income from a trade or business which is attributable to personal services rendered by the self-employed person. [Regs. 1.401-10(c).] Inactive owners who obtain their income entirely from investments cannot participate. Certain individuals who are not presently covered by social security (doctors, certain ministers, etc.) may nevertheless compute their earned income as though they were covered and become eligible as "employees."

Prior to 1968, in a business in which both capital and personal services were material income-producing factors, earned income could not exceed 30% of the net profits of the business. After 1967, earned income is defined to include the entire income of the business if personal services are a material income-producing factor. [Sec. 401(c)(2).]

OWNER-EMPLOYEE. Self-employed persons are divided into two general classes. The first class, "owner-employees," includes any individual who (1) owns the entire interest in an unincorporated trade or business or (2) is a partner who owns more than 10% of either the capital interest or the profits interest in a partnership. [Regs. 1.401-10(d).] The second class is made up entirely of partners who have an interest of 10% or less in a partnership. Most of the special rules apply only to the sole proprietorship and to the partnership which has one or more owner-employee partners. Each provision must be examined to determine its application to a plan not covering an owner-employee.

EMPLOYER. In order to qualify, a retirement plan must be created by an "employer." A sole proprietor is considered to be his own employer as well as his own employee. A partnership is considered to be the employer of all of its partners. The partnership must set up the plan in which the partners will participate. An individual partner is not an employer who may set up a qualified plan with respect to only his services to the partnership. [Regs. 1.401-10(e).]

COVERAGE

For a retirement plan which covers an owner-employee, the coverage rules (see page 28) are modified to require that the plan include all employees who have at least three years' service. An exception exists for employees who customarily work for not more than 20 hours each week or not more than five months in any calendar year. [Regs. 1.401-12(e).]

This modification represents two important changes. In the first place, the length-of-service requirement under the regular rules is five years, as compared with the three-year requirement under the special rule. In the second place, the special rule requires all employees (except the 20-hour or five-month employees) to be brought into the plan. In the traditional retirement plan, the employer has considerable latitude in classifying his employees as to coverage, so long as he does not discriminate in favor of officers, shareholders, supervisory personnel, or highly compensated employees. These two changes may cause a substantial increase in the number of actual employees who are eligible for coverage and thereby increase the cost of providing retirement benefits.

If a sole proprietor has two or more businesses, he is required to group such businesses together and coalesce them for purposes of determining whether employee coverage is complete. [Regs. 1.401-12(1)(2).]

Example: Smith owns and operates a grocery store in one location and a printing plant in another location. These are separate businesses with separate employees. He cannot have a qualified plan in which he participates at the grocery store unless the employees at the printing plant are also covered by a qualified plan. The requirement does not mean that the two businesses must be covered by the same plan, but rather that when the two plans are theoretically combined into a single plan, such single plan will meet the coverage requirement.

An individual who is an owner-employee in a business (whether or not he controls it) and who is also an owner-employee of another business which he controls must establish a retirement plan in his controlled business which will be at least as favorable as to contributions and benefits as the plan under which he is covered in the first business if he wishes to be so covered. [Regs. 1.401-12(1)(1).]

Example: Carter is a 60% partner in a law partnership which has a self-employed individual retirement plan under which he is covered. He is also the sole proprietor of a bookshop. A retirement plan must be provided for the employees of the bookshop which qualifies under Section 401 and the contributions and benefits of which are at least comparable to those of the plan in the law partnership.

The term "control" in this instance means (1) complete ownership of an unincorporated business or (2) ownership of more than 50% of either the capital interest or the profits interest of a partnership by an owner-employee or by two or more owner-employees. [Regs. 1.401-12(1)(3).] Indirect ownership may constitute control

VESTING

Under the standard rules, there may be complete vesting, partial vesting, or no vesting (see page 36). If an owner-employee participates in a plan, contributions for employees must be nonforfeitable at the time the contributions are made under the plan. This provision for full vesting must be included as one of the terms of the plan. [Regs. 1.401-12(g).]

A partnership in which no partner has more than a 10% interest is not required to vest, except upon termination or discontinuance of contributions and unless the lack of vesting results in discrimination — e.g., where there is a high rate of turnover among common-law employees other than highly compensated employees.

DISCRIMINATION

A qualified plan must not discriminate in favor of officers, shareholders, supervisory personnel, or highly compensated employees (see page 33). This rule continues except that, for purposes of applying the compensation test, the total compensation of a self-employed person is his earned income. His basic or regular rate of compensation is that portion of his earned income which bears the same ratio to his total earned income as the basic or regular compensation of the common-law employees under the plan bears to their total compensation. [Regs. 1.401-11(d)(2).] A plan is not discriminatory under certain circumstances merely because excessive contributions are permitted for the purchase of annuity, endowment, or life insurance contracts on the life of an owner-employee. [Regs. 1.401-12(f)(3).]

Plans covering self-employed persons may be integrated with social security. [Regs. 1.401-12(h).]

CONTRIBUTIONS

Contributions to a qualified plan by an employer on behalf of an owner-employee are limited to 10% of earned income or $2,500, whichever is the lesser, per year. Contributions on behalf of others participating in the plan are governed by traditional principles.

A plan may not provide that an employee, other than an owner-employee, is ineligible to participate because he does not consent to be a participant or because he does not consent to make reasonable contributions under the plan. [Regs. 1.401-12(e)(1).]

The plan may provide for voluntary contributions. Voluntary contributions are not deductible for tax purposes. They represent a cost contribution on the part of the participant and are taken into account under the rules governing the taxability of benefits.

The owner-employee may not assume a relatively better position, insofar as nondeductible voluntary contributions are concerned, than that of the other participants. If the owner-employee may make voluntary contributions, the other participants must also be permitted to do so. For example, if the plan permits the owner-employee to make voluntary contributions of up to 7% of his earned income, the other participants must be permitted to make voluntary contributions of up to 7% of their total compensation. [Regs. 1.401-13(b)(3)(ii).] If the owner-employee has no employees, he cannot establish a plan which permits voluntary contributions. [Sec. 401 (d)(5)(B).]

The amount of a voluntary contribution is limited. The owner-employee cannot contribute more than 10% of his earned income or $2,500, whichever is the lesser. [Regs. 1.401-13(b)(3) (iii).] The other participants, including the partner who is not an owner-employee, are limited to 10% of their total compensation.

Penalties are provided for excess contributions. [Regs. 1.401-13.]

DEDUCTION FOR CONTRIBUTION

The self-employed person may deduct 100% of the amount which he contributes as his own employer to an annual maximum of $2,500. Prior to 1968, a deduction was allowed only to the extent of 50% of the contribution with a $1,250 maximum. (See Rev. Rul. 68-138 for fiscal-year partnerships.) The self-employed person can deduct the full amount contributed under the plan on behalf of his common-law employees if that amount is within the statutory limits (see page 74). The partnership, which may in reality make the contribution on behalf of the partner, does not take the deduction on its partnership tax return. It passes the amount through to the partner as a separate item under Section 702, and the partner claims the deduction on his individual tax return. [Regs. 1.404(e)-1(e).] The partnership does, however, claim the deduction for the contribution made on behalf of the common-law employees.

All deductions for contributions under qualified plans must be within the statutory limits. Because the self-employed person and the common-law employees under the same plan have two separate and distinct limitations, the statute provides that two computations are to be made. [Regs. 1.404(e)-1(b).] One is for the self-employed person(s) only, without regard to the common-law employees. Another is for the common-law employees after the computation for the self-employed person(s) has been carved out of the plan.

Both the sole proprietor and the partner file Form 2950SE to support their deductions. The partnership also files Form 2950SE relating to its common-law employees and its partners.

DISTRIBUTIONS

An owner-employee may begin to receive retirement benefits when he reaches age 59½; he *must* begin to receive the benefits no later than age 70½. If he becomes permanently disabled, his benefits may begin immediately. In the event he dies before retirement, his beneficiaries may receive his full share in the plan which has accumulated to the date of his death. [Regs. 1.401-12(m).] A common-law employee or a partner other than an owner-employee must start receiving distributions in the year in which he retires or the year in which he reaches 70½, whichever is later. [Regs. 1.401-11(e)(2).]

Any self-employed person is taxed under the annuity rules of Section 72 if the retirement payout is in the form of installment payments. Section 72(m) provides that a self-employed person does not obtain a basis under the annuity rules as an investment in the contract to the extent of the portion of the contribution which has resulted in a tax deduction at the time contributed (see page 58). If a lump-sum distribution is made, any self-employed person is denied the capital gain treatment which is available to the common-law employee. [Regs. 1.403(a)-2(c).] A special five-year averaging device is provided for the self-employed person so that a lump-sum distribution will not be too burdensome. [Regs. 1.72-18.]

No employee, common-law or self-employed, can receive the benefit of the capital-gain treatment on a total distribution insofar as the distribution includes U.S. bonds of the new nontransferable series. Such portion of the total distribution which does not include the bonds may qualify for the capital gain treatment with respect to common-law employees if the other requirements of severance or death are met (see page 47). [Regs. 1.405-3.]

Premature distribution may incur penalties. [Regs. 1.72-17 and 1.401-12(m).]

TYPE OF PLAN

The plan covering the self-employed person may be (1) a profit-sharing plan if the contributions for common-law employees are geared to the income of the self-employed person or (2) a pension plan if the contributions for common-law employees are based upon a percentage of their compensation, regardless of the income of the self-employed person. [Regs. 1.401-11(b).]

METHODS OF FUNDING

Self-employed retirement plans may be funded through conventional methods — i.e., by contributions to a trust or by purchase of annuity contracts (see page 233). The traditional rules of funding, however, are modified to a considerable degree.

If a trust is used for an owner-employee plan and the funds of the trust are invested in stock, bonds, or any property other than annuity, endowment, or life insurance contracts, the trustee must be a bank, a trust company, a domestic building and loan association, or corporation subject to the supervision and examination of a state banking authority. [Regs. 1.401-12(c)(1).] The trust instrument, nevertheless, can grant to a person other than the trustee the power to control the investment of the trust funds. [Regs. 1.401-12(c)(3).] The other person may be the owner-employee. The power to control may include the power to direct the investment of the trust funds or to disapprove investments proposed by the trustee. The power may apply not only to the initial investment but also to reinvestments, disposals, and exchanges. A bank-type trustee is not required for a trust which was created and determined to be exempt prior to October 10, 1962. [Regs. 1.401-12(c)(1)(ii).]

If the trust invests solely in annuity, endowment, or life insurance contracts, a bank-type trustee is not required. [Regs. 1.401-12(c)(4).] In such a case, the insurance company must supply annually certain information concerning the trust transactions which affect the owner-employee covered under the plan.

A retirement plan may be funded by the direct purchase of annuity contracts. It may be funded by direct purchase of non-transferable face-amount certificates. A special series of non-transferable U.S. bonds may be acquired (see page 99). Funding may be through a custodial account (see page 37).

PROHIBITED TRANSACTIONS

The traditional prohibited transaction rules (see page 207) apply to exempt trusts which cover only common-law employees and/or partners who are not owner-employees. If the trust is a part of a plan which extends to owner-employees, an owner-employee may not engage in any of the following transactions [Regs. 1.503(j)-1]:

1. Borrow from the trust, regardless of the interest rate and the security.
2. Charge any fees for services rendered to the trust.
3. Buy from or sell property to the trust, regardless of the adequacy of the consideration involved.
4. Make any part of the services of the trust available on a preferential basis.

The prohibition on these specific transactions extends to certain family members and controlled corporations.

Tax Planning for the Professional Person

H.R. 10 AMENDMENTS

When H.R. 10 first became law in 1962, the limit on tax benefits discouraged most self-employed persons from using this method of providing for their retirement income. The principal reason for the lack of enthusiasm was because only one-half the amount contributed by a self-employed person could be deducted, up to a maximum of $1,250. However, the law was amended and beginning in 1968 the self-employed person can set aside and deduct 10% of his earned income up to a maximum of $2,500 per year. A calendar-year partner who is a member of a fiscal-year partnership with a taxable year beginning in 1967 and ending in 1968 which makes a contribution for the partner, can deduct only one-half of the contribution during that fiscal year in his calendar-year 1968. [Rev. Rul. 68-138]. Funds so set aside earn income tax-free during the

Tax Planning for the Professional Person 125

period of accumulation to retirement and are then taxed to the person when distributed either before or at retirement.

If plans previously approved are amended only to make the plan conform to the liberal provisions of the new law, the previous approval will apply to the amended plan. There is no need to resubmit the plan for approval. [Rev. Proc. 67-26].

The combination of the tax deduction and the exemption from income tax on earnings of the fund make self-employed retirement plans an attractive investment opportunity for the self-employed. Although created primarily for purposes relating to retirement, there is sufficient flexibility in the law to allow a self-employed individual a choice of investment opportunities suited to his personal needs and purposes. Self-employed persons in the medium to high income tax bracket should have an interest in a plan in which amounts paid are fully deductible and the earnings are free from tax until they are distributed.

POINTS TO CONSIDER

FORECASTING TAX BRACKETS. No one can accurately forecast the exact tax saving of any particular retirement plan. Satisfactory results will depend ultimately on a number of factors. Some will vary from year to year because of business conditions and circumstances beyond the individual's control. The points to consider are the tax bracket and rates at date of retirement or distribution, the self-employed individual's current tax bracket, the fact that unrealized appreciation when realized is treated as ordinary income rather than as capital gain, and the general requirement that all employees with three years of service must be covered.

TAX BRACKET AT RETIREMENT OR DISTRIBUTION. If a self-employed person is now in the 70% tax bracket and expects to be in the 25% bracket when the funds are paid out, he can expect to save 45 cents on each $1 of deductible contributions made to the retirement fund. If a person now in the 50% bracket expects to be in the 25% bracket when he receives his retirement fund, he can expect to save 25 cents on each $1 of deductible contributions.

If a person in the 50% bracket expects to be in the 25% bracket on retirement at, say, age 62, but finds himself for some reason in the 50% bracket at that age, the expected tax saving might not be realized because of the unpredictable event. If the estimated tax difference is large enough in the beginning, however, the self-employed person should be more inclined to adopt a plan on the basis of reasonably expecting to be in a lower bracket at the date of distribution.

Divorce, death of a spouse without remarriage, and other income and/or deductions are factors beyond the control of the self-employed tending to increase the tax bracket. Where the circumstances are expected to be of relatively short duration, their effect can be minimized by electing an annuity distribution whereby a substantial portion of the individual's benefits are received when the tax bracket may have declined to some lower level. [Sec. 72.]

EXAMPLES OF TAX SAVINGS. Assume a self-employed person in the 50% tax bracket who has no employees and has earned income of $25,000 annually.

He adopts a profit-sharing plan for himself, under which annually he will contribute 10% of his earned income up to the maximum of $2,500 each year. He expects his income tax bracket during his working years to remain at about 50%. Thus, while the contribution to the fund is at the rate of $2,500 a year, he is really out of pocket only $1,250 each year. If he is now 50 years old and the fund earns 5%, it will total about $54,000 in 15 years at age 65. Assuming the average tax bracket at retirement to be 25%, income tax on the $54,000 will be approximately $13,500. Net, after tax, will be $40,500.

Without a plan, he will have had only $1,250 a year to invest. Assuming a 5% rate of return, the accumulation in 15 years after tax will have been $22,500. Thus, the retirement plan is $18,000 better—$40,500 compared to $22,500.

In a lower tax bracket the benefits of a qualified retirement plan are less but still attractive.

Assume a married, self-employed person in the 28% bracket who has $16,000 to $20,000 of taxable income and contributes $1,800 a year to a retirement fund earning 5%. Annual tax saving is $504. In 15 years the accumulation is about $39,000. If at the end of 15 years his tax bracket is 19%, $4,000 to $8,000 taxable income, the income tax is $7,410. A net of about $31,600 is left.

Without a qualified retirement plan, only $1,296 after tax annually is left to invest. In 15 years this accumulates to about $25,100. The overall saving is approximately $6,500 under the plan.

TABLES OF TAX SAVINGS. The following tables illustrate the tax savings annually and the accumulation of tax-free earnings and capital appreciation. Table I assumes that the self-employed person files a joint return and that his net earnings from his business are equal to his taxable income. His other income is equal to his exemptions and deductions.

The examples above assumed that there were no real employees with three years or more of service who had to be covered under the plan. Where employees are covered, the tax savings are reduced because the after-tax cost of employee retirement funds must be considered.

Assume a self-employed person in the 50% tax bracket, with earned income of $25,000 or more, who has one employee with a salary of $8,000. A plan could be created under which a contribution of $1,700 could be made without incurring additional out-of-pocket cost to cover the employee.

Contribution	$2,500
Less contribution for employee 10% of $8,000....	800
	$1,700

$1,700 per year for 15 years at 5% will accumulate to $36,700. Assume the bracket at age 65 is 25%, net after tax is $27,525. Without a plan the net after tax is $22,500. Thus, there is a $5,000 advantage with a plan.

TABLE I
ANNUAL TAX SAVINGS

A	B	C	D	
Net income from business	Maximum contribution for employer	Tax savings on contribution for employer	Tax savings after contributions made for employees in the following amounts: $500	$1,000
$15,000	$1,500	$ 375	$ 0	$(375)*
20,000	2,000	560	200	(160)*
30,000	2,500	960	640	320
40,000	2,500	1,125	850	575
60,000	2,500	1,325	1,090	855
90,000	2,500	1,490	1,280	1,070

*Amounts in parentheses represent annual after-tax cost.

Table II below shows the accumulating power of a tax-free trust. Column B assumes that $1,000 is added to the trust at the end of each year and earnings are compounded at the rate of 4% per year. Column C accounts for appreciation in capital and assumes that total earnings and appreciation will compound at a rate of 7% per year. Column D assumes that earnings are compounded at a rate of 4% without the intervention of a qualified plan by individuals in various tax brackets after income taxes.

TABLE II

ACCUMULATION TABLE

A	B	C	D		
		Principal,	After-tax accumulation		
	Principal and	income, and	of principal and income		
Years	income com-	appreciation	compounded at 4% by		
of	pounded at	compounded at	individuals in the		
accumu-	4% in a tax-	4% in a tax-	following tax brackets:		
lation	free trust	free trust	60%	50%	36%
5	$ 5,416	$ 5,750	$ 2,065	$ 2,602	$ 3,368
10	12,006	13,816	4,300	5,474	7,189
14	18,291	22,550	6,221	7,986	10,614
18	25,645	33,999	8,268	10,706	14,404
20	29,778	40,995	9,341	12,148	16,447
25	41,645	63,249	12,177	16,015	22,031
30	56,084	94,460	15,248	20,284	28,367

Note: The above table can be used when other amounts are contributed. For example, if the annual contribution is $2,500, an approximate comparison can be made by multiplying the amounts in the table by 2½.

For the young self-employed person, the decision to adopt a self-employed retirement fund should take into consideration the fact that the funds contributed are virtually locked in until he reaches age 60 or becomes disabled except as noted later in this chapter. For the young professional person who is at the beginning of his career, this might be a problem. Consequently, a self-employed retirement plan generally will have a greater attraction for those persons who are at or around their peak earning years and possibly in the 35 to 50 age group.

PRESENT TAX BRACKET. The higher the individual's present tax bracket, the more his before-tax income is invested in the fund. Without a plan, a person in the 70% bracket retains $30 of each $100 of income earned. If the before-tax $100, however, is a deductible contribution, under a plan, he has in effect retained $100 to invest under the terms of the plan. In addition, the higher the tax bracket, the greater the worth of the tax deduction and the tax exemption on the income from the funds invested.

For example, an individual in the 70% bracket retains only $30 of each $100 of income earned on his investments owned outside of a plan, while an individual in the 50% bracket retains $50 of each $100. But, if a $100 is earned tax-free in a qualified retirement fund, the 70% bracket person in effect is able to reinvest the entire $100 and earns income on that amount rather than on $30. For the 50% bracket person, the additional free reinvestment is $50.

CAPITAL GAINS. Capital gains, unrealized appreciation, and other income, though currently tax-exempt when earned by the qualified fund under a plan, are taxed as ordinary income when distributed from the fund to the self-employed individual. Since capital appreciation is usually important in the accumulation of a retirement fund, this is an important factor in any decision to adopt a self-employed retirement plan.

For example, where a bank is trustee and invests the funds in equity securities, there is a likelihood in today's economy of a realization of substantial appreciation. Normally, a sale of securities at a gain by an individual is subject to the lower capital gains tax, whereas if distributed out of a self-employed retirement fund it is subjected to rates applied to ordinary income. [Regs. 1.402(a)-1(a)(7).]

COVERAGE OF EMPLOYEES. Employees who work for the self-employed person for three years or more must be included in the plan if the self-employed person adopts a plan. [Sec. 401 (d)(3); Regs. 1.401-12(e).] If a self-employed person also controls another unincorporated business, then the employees of that other business must also be covered under a plan providing comparable benefits. [Sec. 401(d)(10); Regs. 1.401-12(1).]

The added expense of covering other employees may often cost more than the tax benefits to the self-employed person. However, this might be offset by important personnel and other nontax reasons for adopting a plan.

The cost of covering employees can be reduced by using a contribution percentage of earned income of less than 10%. A self-employed person who expects his earned income, for example, to be at a consistent level of $50,000 or more, can make a maximum contribution of $2,500 under a formula calling for only 5% of earned income. Applying this percentage to the compensation of his regular employees, the cost to the self-employed is reduced by 50%. See Table II above at page 129.

The Treasury prohibits reducing the wages of an employee at or about the time a plan is adopted as a means of financing the cost of covering other employees under a plan. [Regs. 1.401-11 (b)(2).] However, instead of granting a pay raise, the adoption of plan contributions may be used as a substitute.

VOLUNTARY CONTRIBUTIONS. The law allows the self-employed individual to also make voluntary nondeductible contributions under certain conditions. Voluntary contributions are permitted by the self-employed if he also has employees or minor partners who are covered under the plan, if they are also permitted to make voluntary contributions for themselves within certain limits. The self-employed's voluntary contribution cannot be at a higher level than that permitted for employees and minor partners. Voluntary nondeductible contributions are in addition to the regular deductible contributions which the self-employed makes for himself.

However, there is a limit on the amount of the voluntary contribution. It cannot exceed 10% of the self-employed's earned income up to a maximum of $2,500. When this is added to the amount of the deductible contributions, voluntary contributions enable the self-employed person to put as much as 20% of his earned income into the fund up to $5,000 annually. [Sec. 401(e)(1)(B); Regs. 1.401-13(a)(2) and (b)(3).]

The advantage of making voluntary contributions is that earnings on such contributed amounts can be accumulated tax-free, since they are part of the self-employed retirement fund. Later withdrawal of the voluntary contribution is not taxable, since it was not deductible at the time of the contribution. Only the earnings and the deductible portion of the contribution are taxed at the time they are withdrawn.

WITHDRAWAL OF RETIREMENT BENEFITS

Generally speaking, benefits under a plan cannot be withdrawn before age 59½ without incurring a penalty. Benefits must be distributed starting with the year in which the self-employed person reaches age 70½. Early withdrawal of benefits is permitted if the self-employed person has a disability severe enough to prevent him from performing his professional activities. [Sec. 401(d)(4)(B); Regs. 1.401-12(m).]

If a withdrawal is made before age 59½ or disability, a 10% penalty is added to the tax payable on receiving the early distribution. [Sec. 72(m)(5)(A), (B), (C) and (D).] The self-employed person, in addition, is disqualified for five years from participating any further in the plan. [Sec. 401(d)(5)(C).]

The penalty is not as severe as it may seem. For example, if the self-employed person had contributed over a period of ten years into a retirement fund, and suddenly, because of circumstances beyond his control, he lost his practice or his income dwindled down to nothing, he could still withdraw his entire interest from the retirement fund. The penalty in such circumstances might be minimal. If he had no other income in the year of withdrawal, he might be in a low income tax bracket and could thus realize more after tax than he otherwise would have realized if he had other income.

In any event, if the self-employed person makes additional voluntary contributions over and above the amounts permitted to be deducted, these funds can earn income free from income tax, and, if circumstances later make it necessary to withdraw the self-employed person's own voluntary contributions, the withdrawals are not subject to income tax (since they were not deductible in the first place) nor does the 10% penalty apply. In such cases, earnings in the fund accumulate tax-free until the date of retirement.

On death, the self-employed individual's entire interest must generally be distributed or converted to an annuity for his beneficiary within five years. [Sec. 401(d)(7); Regs. 1.401-12(m)(3).]

Foreign Operations

GENERAL STATEMENT

U.S. entrepreneurs have continually enlarged their commercial beachheads on foreign soil since World War II. The multinational, migratory corporation is personified by the expatriate — the U.S. citizen who carries the technical, the professional, the business know-how from his homeland to the foreign arena of commerce — and also carries the responsibility of returning for taxation his worldwide income unless protected by exemption or exclusion.

The employer and the expatriate are not lacking for compensation and tax problems: salary, bonuses, overseas differentials, cost-of-living indices, retirement benefits, travel allowances, and taxes. Many of the problems of the compensation package can be satisfactorily solved by intelligent use of three basic tax tools:

> Section 911. The exemption from U.S. taxation of income earned abroad in cases where the U.S. citizen is a bona fide resident of a foreign country or is physically present in a foreign country for 17 months.
> Section 901. The foreign tax credit.
> Section 894. Tax treaties.

During his pre-repatriation employment, the U.S. citizen is a participant in the domestic employer's retirement program. In most instances the U.S. citizen will not agree to work overseas unless his retirement benefits are continued. Providing retirement benefits for foreign employees through qualified pension, profit-sharing, and stock bonus plans demands careful planning.

This chapter is intended to serve as a primer on the tax aspects of retirement income planning for foreign-service employees, with emphasis on the trusteed pension plan.

The two chapters which follow examine Sections 406 and 407 of the Code, which provide special relief for certain U.S. citizens who are affiliated with corporate subsidiaries operating overseas. (See pages 141 and 147.)

FORMS OF BUSINESS

The legal form in which the overseas business is operated produces varying tax consequences to the employee and the employer. In general, the U.S. corporation uses one or more of three forms.

BRANCH. The U.S. corporation establishes a branch operation in a foreign country.

DOMESTIC SUBSIDIARY. A domestic subsidiary of the U.S. parent is organized under the laws of a state within the United States. The domestic subsidiary then establishes a branch in a foreign country. The "Western Hemisphere trade corporation" may operate in this manner.

FOREIGN SUBSIDIARY. The U.S. parent organizes a subsidiary under the laws of a foreign country.

QUALIFICATION OF THE PLAN

In order to achieve preferential tax treatment, a retirement plan must meet the qualification requirements of Section 401 as to benefits, diversion of funds, coverage, and discrimination (see page 16). In providing pension benefits for the U.S. citizen in foreign service, perhaps the most pressing problem concerns the matters of coverage and discrimination The qualification rules do not distinguish between domestic and foreign employees, between residents and nonresidents, or between citizens of the United States and citizens of other countries. Employees are employees — and the foreign operation in most instances will employ foreign nationals. The question is: Should the foreign nationals be covered by the retirement plan which provides for the expatriate?

BRANCH. If the U.S. employer conducts his foreign operations through the medium of a foreign branch which is operated by resident U.S. citizens abroad, nonresident U.S. citizens abroad, and foreign nationals, he faces one overriding problem: The U.S. citizens, if previously covered by the retirement plan in the United States, continue to be covered while on foreign duty. The employer-employee relationship does not change. The foreign nationals, however, are also employees and must be considered as to coverage and discrimination in light of the whole plan. In order to retain qualification after the foreign nationals become employees, the employer must reevaluate the coverage and discrimination requirements of Section 401(a)(3) and (4), including the foreign nationals as though they were U.S. citizens. It may be possible to exclude the foreign nationals, at least temporarily, on the basis of age, length of service, wage level, or type of work. The plan might be amended to provide a classification exclusion on the basis of residence, but in this event the nonresident U.S. citizens would be excluded. The plan might also be changed to require each participant to serve a minimum period of employment within the United States or to be a U.S. citizen.

In excluding the foreign nationals reference may be made to the 70%–80% tests of Section 401(a)(1)(A) or the classification test of Section 401(a)(1)(B). (See page 28.) In either event, care must be exercised to insure that the exclusion does not discriminate in favor of officers, shareholders, supervisory personnel, or highly paid employees. (See page 33.) While not covered by the statute, it has been found that a plan covering foreign employees can be integrated with social security systems which are established along lines similar to the U.S. system.

In any event, the employer cannot ignore his foreign national employees in the branch operation; he must find a method, acceptable to the Internal Revenue Service, for excluding them.

DOMESTIC SUBSIDIARY. The foreign operation may be conducted through a domestic subsidiary, with the U.S. citizen moving his employment from the U.S. parent to the subsidiary. In order to provide a retirement program for the expatriate, several avenues are available.

First, the U.S. parent may avail itself of the relief offered under Section 407. For years after 1963, Section 407 permits certain U.S. citizens who are affiliated with domestic subsidiaries operating overseas to be covered by qualified retirement plans of domestic parent corporations. This relief provision is treated in detail in a subsequent chapter. (See page 147.) The situations to which the relief provision may be applied are limited. Many domestic subsidiaries will not meet the statutory requirements.

Second, the retirement plan of the U.S. parent may be amended to cover the employees of the domestic subsidiary. Basically, this approach is similar to that of the branch operation. There is no change of employment for purposes of the qualified plan. No transfer is required of the credits of the former U.S. employee. The foreign nationals become eligible for coverage unless an acceptable exclusion is found for them. The same problems of coverage and discrimination exist here as under the branch operation approach.

Third, the subsidiary corporation may set up a separate plan, funding through the exempt trust of the parent, and giving the participants (i.e., the expatriate) credit for past service with the parent company. This avenue is not greatly different from the two above.

Foreign nationals must be considered for purposes of satisfying the coverage and discrimination requirements.

FOREIGN SUBSIDIARY. If the overseas business is carried out through a foreign subsidiary, relief may be found in Section 406, the counterpart of Section 407 applicable to foreign subsidiaries. (See page 141.) As with Section 407, the relief is limited.

Alternatively, the foreign corporation may follow avenues available to the domestic subsidiaries by seeking coverage under the U.S. parent's plan or by creating its own plan. The problems for the foreign subsidiary are at least as great as those of the domestic subsidiary.

OTHER FORMS. In some instances, the various methods discussed above for continuing the retirement benefits of the expatriate are not acceptable to the U.S. parent and/or the expatriate himself. Other arrangements which have been used are noted below. This is not intended to be a complete listing nor is it intended to indicate approval or disapproval by the Internal Revenue Service. Any arrangement which is outside the pretraveled avenues should be approached cautiously.

1. It has been suggested that if an employer wishes to exclude the foreign nationals, he might employ only foreign nationals in the overseas subsidiary. All U.S. citizen employees will be retained in the U.S. parent and covered by the U.S. plan. Services rendered by the U.S. citizens to the foreign subsidiary will be billed to that company on a contractual basis. While the employee may like this plan, the employer may experience some dismay when the contractual reimbursement encounters the problems of foreign country deduction, foreign withholding taxes, foreign legal liabilities, foreign tax credits, Code Section 482, and other hazards.

2. Additional wages are paid to the expatriate to compensate for the loss of retirement benefits. While the additional wages may escape U.S. taxation through Section 911, foreign income taxes may seriously erode the wages. Another

weakness is that current income is substituted for retirement income.

3. A nonqualified retirement plan may be created for the U.S. citizen in foreign service. The tax aspects of nonqualified plans are discussed elsewhere in this book. (See, for example, page 285.)

4. All the rules may be disregarded. The U.S. parent may continue to contribute under its plan for the expatriate who works for a domestic or foreign subsidiary. There are, however, dangers in ignoring the rules, one of which is the disqualification of the plan.

THE PENSION TRUST

A domestic-situs employees' trust which is qualified under Section 401 is exempt from taxation [Sec. 501.] Income earned by the domestic-situs trust is not subject to taxation except such income as may be derived from a business lease or an unrelated trade or business. Contributions to the trust under a qualified plan are deductible by the employer when paid. [Sec. 404(a).] Benefits payable by the trust are not taxed to the employee until actually received. [Sec. 402(a).]

An employees' trust which is not created or organized in the United States is not exempt from U.S. taxation. [Sec. 501.] Nevertheless, if a trust is qualified for exemption in every way except for the fact that it is a foreign-situs trust, then contributions by a U.S. employer are deductible under the same rules as apply to contributions to a domestic-situs trust. [Sec. 404(a)(4).] Benefits payable by the foreign-situs trust are not taxed to the employee until actually received. [Sec. 402(c).]

If the foreign-situs trust derives all of its income from foreign sources and the income is not effectively connected with the conduct of a trade or business in the United States, the fact that it is not exempt under Section 501 is immaterial because the United States cannot tax such foreign-source income of a foreign entity. Such trust income may be subject, however, to the taxing jurisdiction of a foreign country. If the foreign-situs trust receives income from U.S. sources (it might, for example, own securities of a U.S. corporation), the lack of exemption under Section 501 may be quite important. Under such circumstances the foreign-situs trust is taxed on its fixed or determinable annual or periodic income from U.S. sources. [Sec. 871.] The trust will be subject to withholding (usually 30% under Section 1441). Subjecting the trust to foreign tax or U.S. tax will tend to increase the cost of providing the retirement benefits.

While an explicit definition of a foreign-situs trust is difficult to state, it would appear that certain attributes are necessary: i.e., the trust instrument must be executed in a foreign jurisdiction, the trustee must be a foreigner, and the trust assets must be kept in a foreign country.

Both domestic- and foreign-situs trusts which form a part of a qualified plan may include U.S. citizens, resident or nonresident, and aliens, resident or nonresident.

One trust may serve the plans of several employers provided all the plans are qualified. [Regs. 1.401-1(d).]

TAXATION OF EMPLOYEES

RESIDENT U.S. CITIZEN — DOMESTIC TRUST. A U.S. citizen, resident in the United States, working abroad, is taxed on distributions from a domestic-situs trust. [Sec. 402.] A relief provision exists, however, if the citizen qualifies under the "510-day rule" [Sec. 911(a)(2)] and thereby is not taxed on income earned abroad up to $20,000 per year. Pension contributions are considered to be earned income. Section 72(f) provides with respect to contributions made before January 1, 1963 that an employer's contribution will be considered to be an employee's contribution if, when the contribution was made, the contribution would not have been taxable income to the employee if the contribution had been made directly to the employee. [Regs. 1.72-8(a)(2).] When Section 911 (a)(2) and Section 72(f) are considered together, it means that the distribution from a domestic-situs trust may be taxed to the beneficiary only to the extent of the employee's pro rata share of the trust's earnings because the employee has a cost basis equal to his own contribution and his employer's contribution.

The above rule relating to Section 72(f) applies only to amounts contributed on or before December 31, 1962 for services performed on or before such date. Subsequent employer contributions will not increase the employee's basis, unless pursuant to the provisions of a plan in existence on March 12, 1962 in which the employee had a vested interest and contributions to which were for services rendered before January 1, 1963. [Regs. 1.72-8(a)(3).] An example of this would be a 1965 contribution to fund 1958 past service costs.

RESIDENT U.S. CITIZEN — FOREIGN TRUST. The distributions from a foreign-situs trust are taxed in exactly the same manner as distributions from a domestic-situs trust.

NONRESIDENT U.S. CITIZEN — DOMESTIC TRUST. A U.S. citizen, not a resident of the United States, working abroad, is taxed on distributions from a domestic-situs trust according to the rules of Section 402. This citizen is entitled also to preferential tax treatment beyond that contained in Section 402. He can convert his employer's contribution into his own contribution by relying upon a combination of the "510-day rule" and Section 72(f) or a combination of the foreign-residence rule [Sec. 911(a)(1)] and Section 72(f). As in the case of resident U.S. citizens, Section 72(f) does not apply to certain employer contributions after December 31, 1962. [Sec. 72(f)(2).]

NONRESIDENT U.S. CITIZEN — FOREIGN TRUST. Distributions from a foreign-situs trust are taxed in exactly the same manner as distributions from a domestic-situs trust.

NONRESIDENT ALIEN — DOMESTIC TRUST. The nonresident alien who receives a distribution from a domestic-situs trust is taxable on income received by him to the extent it is U.S.-source income. The capital gain treatment of lump-sum severance distributions [Sec. 402(a)(2)] is not available to a nonresident alien [Sec. 871.] Tax at the rate of 30% is withheld [Sec. 1441] on the income arising from any distribution unless such tax is prohibited or reduced by an international tax treaty. The nonresident alien is permitted the use of Section 72(f) to convert the employer's contribution into his own contribution.

NONRESIDENT ALIEN — FOREIGN TRUST. Distributions to a nonresident alien from a foreign-situs trust are not subject to U.S. taxation.

Employees of Foreign Subsidiaries

(a) TREATMENT AS EMPLOYEES OF DOMESTIC CORPORATION
    REQUIREMENTS FOR QUALIFICATION
(b) SPECIAL RULES FOR APPLICATION OF SECTION 401 (a)
(c) TERMINATION OF STATUS AS DEEMED EMPLOYEE
(d) DEDUCTIBILITY OF CONTRIBUTIONS
(e) TREATMENT AS EMPLOYEE UNDER RELATED PROVISIONS

(a) TREATMENT AS EMPLOYEES OF DOMESTIC CORPORATION

Prior to 1964 a U.S. employer which operated outside the United States through the medium of a foreign or domestic subsidiary found it difficult to provide retirement benefits for U.S. citizens employed by such subsidiaries. The overseas subsidiary was seldom able to design a plan which met the standard requirements for qualification and still covered only its U.S. citizen employees. The U.S. citizen employed by the overseas subsidiary could not be covered by the plan of the U.S. parent because the necessary employee-employer relationship was not present (see page 24).

Section 406, added to the Code by the Revenue Act of 1964, offers a solution to the problem for foreign corporations. If certain requirements are met, U.S. citizens who are employed by a foreign corporation are considered to be employees of the U.S. domestic parent corporation for retirement plan purposes.

Section 406(a) covers the requirements which must be met. Section 406(b) discusses the rules for integrating the U.S. citizen employees with the domestic U.S. employees for purposes of avoiding discrimination within the plan of the U.S. parent. Section 406 (c) presents a special rule for capital gain distributions. Section 406 (d) deals with the deductibility of contributions. Section 406 (e) extends the special status of the U.S. citizen employees to other provisions of the Code. Commissioner's regulations have not been issued under Section 406.

REQUIREMENTS FOR QUALIFICATION

The foreign subsidiary which may qualify is defined in Section 3121(1)(8). At least 20% of its voting stock must be owned by the domestic parent corporation. If the foreign corporation seeking qualification is a second-tier foreign subsidiary, 50% of its voting stock must be owned by a first-tier subsidiary which in turn meets the 20% ownership test.

The domestic parent first must enter into a Section 3121(1) agreement with the Revenue Service relating to social security taxes. Under such an agreement, social security benefits are provided for U.S. citizens who are employed by foreign subsidiaries. The social security agreement must cover the foreign subsidiary which employs the U.S. citizens to whom the retirement plan will be extended. [Sec. 406(a)(1).]

The retirement plan extended to the U.S. citizen employees must be (1) a plan established and maintained by a domestic corporation and (2) a qualified pension, profit-sharing, or stock bonus plan [Sec. 401(a)], an annuity plan [Sec. 403], or a bond purchase plan [Sec. 405(a).]

The retirement plan must expressly provide coverage for U.S. citizen employees in all foreign subsidiaries covered by the Section 3121(1) agreement. All U.S. citizen employees in each qualified foreign corporation need not be covered if exclusion of some is within the provisions of the plan of the domestic parent. If, for example, the plan excludes from coverage any employees who have less than five years' service (see page 28), U.S. citizen employees of the foreign subsidiary with less than five years' service may also be excluded. [Sec. 406(a)(2).]

The U.S. citizen employees must not be covered by another funded plan of deferred compensation, whether or not qualified, insofar as the same compensation is concerned. If, for example, the foreign subsidiary has a pension plan of its own in which the U.S. citizen employees participate, they cannot be treated as employees of the domestic parent. [Sec. 406(a)(3).]

(b) SPECIAL RULES FOR APPLICATION OF SECTION 401(a)

In order for the plan to be qualified, there must be no discrimination in favor of officers, stockholders, supervisory personnel, or highly compensated employees (see page 33). The qualified plan of the domestic parent corporation presumably is free from discrimination before it is extended to the U.S. citizen employees of the foreign subsidiary. However, it must be reexamined by the taxpayer to determine whether the new participants cause a condition of discrimination not previously present. For purposes of measuring discrimination, if a U.S. citizen employee is an officer, shareholder, or supervisory employee of the foreign subsidiary, he will be treated as having that same status with the domestic parent. If, for example, an individual is president of the foreign subsidiary, he will be considered to be a president of the domestic corporation. [Sec. 406 (b)(1)(A).]

The determination of whether the U.S. citizen employee is highly compensated is made by treating his total compensation as having been paid by the domestic parent and by considering his simulated status with the domestic parent. [Sec. 406(b)(1)(B).]

The term "total compensation," as used above and for all purposes of determining qualification under Section 401(a), means the remuneration paid to the U.S. citizen employee by the foreign corporation which would constitute his total compensation if the services had been performed for the domestic parent. The portion of total compensation which constitutes the basic or regular rate of compensation is left to the Commissioner's regulations. [Sec. 406(b) (2)(A).]

A plan which treats a U.S. citizen employee as an employee of the domestic parent may be integrated with social security (see page 257). Presumably, the U.S. citizen employee is considered to have paid the amount of tax paid by the domestic parent which is equivalent to the social security tax imposed by Section 3101. [Sec. 406(b)(2)(B).]

(c) TERMINATION OF STATUS AS DEEMED EMPLOYEE NOT TO BE TREATED AS SEPARATION FROM SERVICE FOR PURPOSES OF CAPITAL GAIN PROVISION

Section 402(a)(2) and Section 403(a)(2) provide that if a total distribution is made to an employee within one taxable year because of separation from service, the amount of such distribution is treated as the proceeds from the sale of a capital asset held over six months (see pages 47 and 65). In addition to the separation-from-service rules which apply to a domestic employee, however, the U.S. citizen employee of a foreign corporation is subject to special rules. The required separation from service does *not* exist if any of the following events occur:

1. The Section 3121(1) agreement is terminated. [Sec. 406 (c)(1).]
2. The U.S. citizen employee becomes an employee of a foreign subsidiary corporation which is not covered by the Section 3121(1) agreement. [Sec. 406(c)(2).]
3. The U.S. citizen employee ceases to be an employee of the foreign subsidiary corporation and becomes an employee of another corporation controlled by the domestic parent. [Sec. 406(c)(3).] For purposes of this provision, a domestic corporation controls another corporation if it owns, directly or indirectly, 50% or more of the voting stock of the corporation.
4. The plan is changed to exclude the U.S. citizen employee. [Sec. 406(c)(4).]

(d) DEDUCTIBILITY OF CONTRIBUTIONS

The domestic parent does not receive a deduction for contributions to a qualified plan on behalf of the U.S. citizen employee. In most cases an unreimbursed contribution will be treated as a contribution to the capital of the foreign subsidiary. The statute does not say whether a reimbursement of the contribution will result in an inclusion in the income of the domestic corporation, an adjustment in the basis of the foreign corporation's stock, or otherwise.

The regulations under Section 482 may assist in answering the question. The matter of reimbursement here differs from that involving social security contributions under a Section 3121(1) agreement. Section 176 allows a deduction for the social security payment and calls for taxable income if reimbursed. The foreign subsidiary will be allowed a deduction for the contribution made by its domestic parent. The questions of whether the contribution constitutes income and whether a deduction is allowable in computing a foreign income tax liability must be answered by reference to foreign tax law. The deduction is available, however, only to the extent it is otherwise allowed as a deduction under other provisions of the Code. (See, for example, Section 863.) The amount of the deduction reduces the earnings and profits of the corporation. If a deduction is claimed, it is deductible for the taxable year of the subsidiary with or within which the taxable year of the domestic parent ends.

(e) TREATMENT AS EMPLOYEE UNDER RELATED PROVISIONS

The U.S. citizen employee is treated as an employee of the domestic parent with respect to other sections of the Code relating to qualified retirement plans. This extension gives to the employee and his beneficiary the same tax benefits as are enjoyed by his domestic employee counterpart in regard to the annuity rules, death benefit exclusion, and estate and gift tax exemptions. The Code sections specifically designated are as follows:

Section 72(d) — Taxation of employee's annuities.
Section 72(f) — Special rules for computing employee's contributions with respect to annuities.
Section 101(b) — The $5,000 exemption for employee's death benefits.
Section 2039 — Annuities for estate tax purposes.
Section 2517 — Annuities for gift tax purposes.

Employees of Domestic Subsidiaries
Engaged in Business Outside the United States

(a) TREATMENT AS EMPLOYEES OF DOMESTIC PARENT
CORPORATION

REQUIREMENTS FOR QUALIFICATION

DEFINITIONS

(b) SPECIAL RULES FOR APPLICATION OF SECTION 401 (a)

(c) TERMINATION OF STATUS AS DEEMED EMPLOYEE

(d) DEDUCTIBILITY OF CONTRIBUTIONS

(e) TREATMENT AS EMPLOYEE UNDER RELATED PROVISIONS

(a) **TREATMENT AS EMPLOYEES OF DOMESTIC PARENT
CORPORATION**

Section 407 is the counterpart of Section 406. It provides that U.S. citizen employees of a domestic subsidiary of a domestic parent corporation may be covered under the qualified plan of the domestic parent if the subsidiary's business is conducted largely through foreign branches.

Section 407(a) covers the requirements to be met and offers certain definitions. Section 407(b) discusses the rules for integrating the U.S. citizen employee with the domestic U.S. employees for purposes of avoiding discrimination within the plan of the U.S. parent. Section 407(c) presents a special rule for capital gain distributions. Section 407(d) deals with the deductibility of contributions. Section 407(e) extends the special status of the U.S. citizen employee to other provisions of the Code. Commissioner's regulations have not been issued under Section 407.

REQUIREMENTS FOR QUALIFICATION

The retirement plan extended to the U.S. citizen employee must be (1) a plan established and maintained by a domestic corporation and (2) a qualified pension, profit-sharing, or stock bonus plan [Sec. 401(a)], an annuity plan [Sec. 403], or a bond purchase plan [Sec. 405(a)].

The plan of the domestic parent must expressly provide coverage for all of its domestic subsidiaries as that term is defined for the purposes of this section. [Sec. 407(a)(1)(A).]

The U.S. citizen employees must not be covered by another funded plan of deferred compensation, whether or not qualified, insofar as compensation received from the domestic subsidiary is concerned. [Sec. 407(a)(1)(B).] Neither the U.S. social security system nor a foreign-government-sponsored retirement system of the same nature as the U.S. social security system are considered to be plans of deferred compensation. [Rev. Rul. 67-389.]

DEFINITIONS

The term "domestic subsidiary" as used in this section means a corporation which meets all of the following standards [Sec. 407(a)(2)(A)]:

1. Eighty percent or more of its outstanding voting stock is owned by another domestic corporation.
2. Ninety-five percent or more of its gross income for a three-year period including the taxable year was derived from sources outside the United States. If the domestic subsidiary does not have a three-year experience period, it uses such portion of the three-year period as it was in existence.
3. Ninety percent or more of its gross income for the three-

year period (or that portion when it was in existence) was derived from the active conduct of a trade or business.

The term "domestic parent" means a domestic corporation which owns 80% or more of the outstanding voting stock of a "domestic subsidiary". [Sec. 407(a)(2)(B).]

Example: Company XYZ, a domestic corporation, owns 100% of Company A and Company B, both of which are also domestic corporations. Assume that Company A qualifies as a "domestic subsidiary," as that term is defined in Section 407 and that Company B does not so qualify. For purposes of Section 407, Company XYZ is the domestic parent of Company A but not of Company B.

(b) SPECIAL RULES FOR APPLICATION OF SECTION 401(a)

The special rules are the same as the special rules which apply to foreign corporations (see page 143).

(c) TERMINATION OF STATUS AS DEEMED EMPLOYEE NOT TO BE TREATED AS SEPARATION FROM SERVICE FOR PURPOSES OF CAPITAL GAIN PROVISION

Section 402(a)(2) and Section 403(a)(2) provide that if a total distribution is made to an employee within one taxable year because of separation from service, the amount of such distribution is treated as the proceeds from the sale of a capital asset held over six months. (See pages 47 and 65). In addition to the separation-from-service rules which apply to a domestic employee, however, the U.S. citizen employee of a domestic subsidiary is subject to special rules. The required separation from service does *not* exist if any of the following events occur:

1. The domestic subsidiary ceases to qualify as a domestic subsidiary. [Sec. 407(c)(1).]

Example: Eighty percent of the outstanding voting stock of Company A is owned by Company XYZ, a domestic parent, at December 31, 1968. Company A qualifies as a domestic subsidiary at that date. During 1969, with Company A at all times qualifying as to income, Company XYZ disposes of a portion of its Company A stock so as to bring its ownership down to 63%. Company A is disqualified as a domestic subsidiary and Company XYZ is disqualified as its domestic parent. The U.S. citizen employees of Company A can no longer be covered by the qualified plan of Company XYZ. Such employees, however, have not been separated from service.

2. The U.S. citizen employee ceases to be an employee of the domestic subsidiary and becomes an employee of another corporation controlled by the domestic parent. [Sec. 407(c)(2).] For purposes of this provision, a domestic corporation controls another corporation if it owns, directly or indirectly, 50% or more of the voting stock of the corporation.

3. The qualified plan of the domestic parent is changed to exclude the U.S. citizen employees of its domestic subsidiaries. [Sec. 407(c)(3).]

(d) DEDUCTIBILITY OF CONTRIBUTIONS

The rules relating to the deductibility of the contributions made by a domestic parent on behalf of U.S. citizen employees of domestic subsidiaries are the same as those which apply to foreign corporations (see page 144).

(e) TREATMENT AS EMPLOYEE UNDER RELATED PROVISIONS

As in the case of foreign corporations, the deemed-employee status of the U.S. citizen employee of a domestic subsidiary is extended to other sections of the Code (see page 145).

Stock Options — General

GENERAL STATEMENT

Stock options are frequently used by corporations as incentive devices to attract new management, to retain executives who might otherwise leave, or to give executives or other employees a direct interest in the success of the corporation by making them, in effect, "partners" in the business. Stock options are also used occasionally to pay for current services from nonemployees, such as underwriters, without diluting working capital.

The acquisition of stock through the exercise of an employer-granted option is inherently a bargain purchase. Gain from a bargain purchase is taxed as compensatory income. To circumvent the bargain purchase rule, and thereby provide the desired incentive to employees, preferential tax treatment is given to certain stock options.

Employee stock options generally fall within the following categories:

1. Qualified stock options — covered by Section 422. (See page 165.)
2. Employee stock purchase plans — covered by Section 423. (See page 173.)
3. Restricted stock options — covered by Section 424. (See page 177.)
4. Stock options not specifically provided for in the statute but subject to the rules contained in Regulations 1.421-6. (See page 191.)

Section 421 sets forth general rules which are applicable to the employee stock options provided for in Sections 422 to 424.

DEFINITIONS

OPTION. Under the definition of this term, an "option" must give to the individual the right to purchase a stated number of shares of stock from the corporation within a specific period of time at a determinable price. The optionee must be under no compulsion to exercise the option. The option may be revocable by the corporation. The option must be in writing and its terms must be clearly stated. It may be a part of an employee stock purchase plan or subscription contract. [Regs. 1.421-7(a).]

STATUTORY OPTIONS. The term "statutory options" applies to qualified stock options, options under an employee stock purchase plan, and restricted stock options. It does not apply to those stock options which are subject to the rules of Regulations 1.421-6. [Regs. 1.421-7(b)(1).]

The option by its terms cannot be transferred by the optionee other than by will or by the laws of descent and distribution. Neither can the option be exercised by anyone other than the optionee. Notwithstanding this rule, the optionee may be permitted to designate during his lifetime the person who can exercise the option after his death. [Regs. 1.421-7(a)(2).]

Whether an option is a statutory option is determined as of the date on which it is granted. The character of the option is established on the date of grant. Subsequent events do not change its character but may change the tax treatment of the transaction. [Regs. 1.421-7(b)(3).]

TIME AND DATE OF GRANT. This and similar terms refer to the date on which the corporation completes the corporate action constituting the offer to sell the stock. The corporation generally stipulates the date on which the offer is to be made, but if there is an unreasonable delay in communicating the offer to the employee, the later notification date might constitute the grant date. A distinction is drawn between a condition which affects the granting of the option and a condition which governs the exercise of the option. The former is recognized if recognition is in accordance with the intent of the corporation. For example, if the option requires approval of the SEC, the grant date is delayed until such approval is received if the corporation clearly intends that no grant be made without SEC approval. If no such intent exists, the approval is considered a condition upon exercise, and the date of the grant is determined as though the approval is not required. If an option is granted upon the condition that an individual become an employee, the condition affects the date of the grant and the option is not granted until the condition is met. [Regs. 1.421-7(c)(2).] Section 425(i) provides a special rule for options subject to stockholder approval under which the date of the grant is determined as though the option had not been subject to that approval. A condition which governs the exercise of an option does not affect the grant of the option. [Regs. 1.421-7(c)(3).]

The time and date of grant is important in determining the exercise period.

STOCK. The term "stock" means capital stock of any class. It includes common and preferred, voting and nonvoting, treasury stock and stock of original issue. It includes a special class of stock created especially for the stock option plan so long as it has the rights and characteristics of capital stock. [Regs. 1.421-7(d).]

OPTION PRICE. This and related terms mean the consideration which the optionee must pay (in money or property) to purchase the stock upon exercise of the option. The option price does not include any amounts paid as interest under a deferred-payment arrangement or treated as interest under Section 483. [Regs. 1.421-7(e).] Relief from imputed interest is provided for options granted prior to January 31, 1965.

Any reasonable valuation method may be used to determine whether the option price requirement is met, including the methods described in the Estate Tax Regulations. [Regs. 1.421(e).]

Example: In 1966, Carr received a qualified stock option at $100 under a plan which permits the optionee to pay for the stock in 24 monthly installments. The fair market value of the stock at the grant date was $100. In January 1968, Carr exercises the option and receives the stock. He pays for the stock subsequently by 24 monthly payroll deductions. No interest was paid on the outstanding debt. Due to the imputing of interest under Section 483, the option price does not meet the requirement of Section 422.

Example: In the above example, the stock is not transferred to Carr until the end of the payment period. He had a withdrawal refund right prior to the final payment date. Section 483 does not apply. The sale does not occur until after the payments are completed.

EXERCISE. The term "exercise" refers to the acceptance by the optionee of the corporation's offer to sell. It is the time when there is a sale or a contract to sell between the two parties. It does not include an agreement by the optionee to make payments under a stock purchase plan while the optionee has the right to withdraw the payments. [Regs. 1.421-7(f).]

TRANSFER. "Transfer" means the transfer of ownership or of substantially all the rights of ownership. A transfer must be recorded on the books of the corporation within a reasonable time. [Regs. 1.421-7(g).]

EMPLOYMENT RELATIONSHIP. An employee-employer relationship must exist, at the time the option is granted, between the optionee and the optionor (or a qualified related corporation). In defining such a relationship, the regulations relating to withholding taxes are controlling. [Regs. 1.421-7(h).] The option must be granted for a reason connected with the optionee's employment, such as an inducement for employment or an incentive for continued employment, even though the optionor reserves the right to revoke the option arrangement. [Rev. Rul. 54-467.] The option may not, however, be granted before employment or after the employee has terminated his employment.

RELATED CORPORATION. See Section 425 (page 183) for the definition of this and additional terms.

REPORTING REQUIREMENTS

A corporate employer is required to report annually to the Commissioner the occurrence of either or both of two events within the taxable year [Sec. 6039]:

1. The transfer of stock to an employee under a qualified stock option plan or a restricted stock option plan. This requirement applies to all transfers made after December 31, 1963.
2. The transfer of stock from an employee to another party if the stock was acquired through the exercise of an

option after December 31, 1963 under one of the following:

a. A stock purchase plan where the option price is between 85% and 100% of the stock value on the date of grant; or

b. A restricted stock option plan where the option price is between 85% and 95% of the stock value on the date of grant.

Form 3921 is used to report the transfer from the corporation to the employee. Form 3922 is used to report the transfer from the employee to the third party. Both forms, together with Form 4067, a summary report, are due on February 28 following the close of the taxable year of the corporate employer. On or before January 31 preceding the February 28 due date, the employee must be furnished with copies of Forms 3921 and 3922. Form 3922 may be filed by a transfer agent in lieu of the employer corporation.

In the case of a transfer of stock by an employee, the employer is not expected to follow the ownership of the stock beyond the first transfer. For example, if the employee transfers stock to a street name and later sells the stock, the employer need report only the transfer to street name. A return is required, however, when an optionee transfers stock from himself to himself and another person as joint tenants, tenants by the entireties, or tenants in common. [Regs. 1.6039-1(b)(4).]

STATUS UNDER FEDERAL SECURITIES LAWS

In formulating an option plan, the employer company should seek the advice of its legal counsel as to whether the stock to be offered must be registered under the Securities Act of 1933. Generally, the stock must be registered unless the plan is limited to executive or management personnel who are acquainted with and have access to the type of business and financial information concerning the company which would be otherwise available in a registration statement, and providing such personnel intend to hold the stock for investment purposes.

If the stock must be registered, a registration statement, generally on the SEC's Form S-8, should be prepared and filed before the options are granted. This form requires, among other things, a brief description of "the tax advantages which may accrue to employees as a result of participation in the plan and the tax effect, if any, upon the registrant."

The prospectus filed in the initial Form S-8 registration statement must be kept current by the annual filing with the SEC of a post-effective amendment including a prospectus which updates all information in the original prospectus. If the particular class of stock is also registered under the Securities Exchange Act of 1934, upon exercise of options thereon, officers and directors must also take into consideration the provisions of Section 16 of that Act. That section provides, in general, for (a) the reporting of changes in beneficial ownership of securities of the employer corporation by officers and directors and (b) the recapture by the employer corporation of any profit accruing to an officer or director as a result of a purchase and sale, or sale and purchase, of an equity security within a period of less than six months.

FINANCING TECHNIQUES

RESTRICTED STOCK OPTIONS. The restricted stock option, with its ten-year option, its two-year no-disposition-from-date-of-grant rule and its six-month stock holding period, permits a long, large buildup of capital gain during the holding period, followed by exercise of the option and sale of the stock six months later.

The optionee who is interested primarily in a cash profit can finance the acquisition of the stock with a short-term bank loan of six months, secured by high-value, low-cost stock.

The optionee who is interested primarily in retaining as much equity as possible can use the same method for a portion of his stock — i.e., finance, acquire, and sell enough stock to produce sufficient after-tax cash to repay the loan and to exercise the remaining options.

QUALIFIED STOCK OPTIONS. The five-year option term of the qualified stock option permits less time for the capital buildup. Under the three-year holding period, a comparatively long period must elapse before the profits from the first stock acquisition can be used to finance the exercise of the remaining options. A three-year bank loan might be possible, but it will be shadowed by the risk of collateral decline during its term. The optionee may look to new financing techniques under one of the following plans:

1. *Installment exercise of the options.* This plan spreads out the payment period so that self-financing may be possible. It also spreads out the expiration of the three-year holding periods and reduces the risks of declining values.
2. *Installment payment for total or partial exercise of the options.* The corporation may be willing and permitted by state law and its by-laws to grant the loan. The loan must carry at least 4% interest in order to avoid the imputed-interest problem of Section 483 (see page 155). The stock, whether or not used as collateral for the loan, must be owned by the optionee in order to start the running of the three-year holding period. [Regs. 1.421-7(g).]
3. *Bank loan blessed by corporation.* A bank loan may be arranged for the executive with the corporation's bank, with the corporation extending some type of assurance of repayment.
4. *Sale during holding period.* The optionee may sell part of his stock during the three-year holding period in order to obtain cash to pay for the stock. Only a portion of his total gain will be taxed as compensatory income. That portion is measured by the spread between the option price and the market value at the time the option is exercised. Any gain in excess of the compensatory income is capital gain. (See page 161.)

QUALIFIED VS. NONSTATUTORY STOCK OPTIONS

A comparison is difficult to make between the statutory stock option and the nonstatutory stock option as compensation devices. The timing elements are different. Stock received under a qualified stock option must be held for three years; stock received under a nonstatutory stock option need be held only for six months in order to achieve long-term capital gain status. The qualified optionee may be tempted to withhold action for the full five-year exercise term to watch the movement of the stock. The nonstatutory optionee may exercise the option early in the hope of limiting his compensatory income. The former pays tax when he disposes of the stock; the latter pays both when he exercises the option and when he sells the stock. Financing techniques also differ. (See page 157.)

Nevertheless, a comparison may be reached if the favorable and unfavorable effects of the time element are eliminated.

Example: Smith has taxable income of $50,000 before the stock option transaction. He is granted qualified stock options at 100% of fair market value and nonstatutory stock options at 80% of fair market value of the stock at the grant date.

	Qualified stock option	Nonstatutory stock option
Fair market value of stock at grant date	$60,000	$60,000
Appreciation	25,000	25,000
Sales price	85,000	85,000
Cost of stock	60,000	48,000
Total cash gain	25,000	37,000
Less—tax on gain:		
Ordinary income	———	6,300
Capital gain	6,250	6,250
Total tax	6,250	12,550
Net cash gain	$18,750	$24,450

The example above, which ignores the time element, is used to demonstrate the possibility that the nonstatutory stock option may be a superior compensation tool under certain circumstances. It may give the employee more stock for the same cash outlay or the same amount of stock for less cash outlay.

The position of the employer should be considered in the comparison.

Example: Under the qualified stock option, the employer receives $60,000 for its stock. Under the nonstatutory stock option the employer receives $48,000 for its stock and a deduction of $12,000 for compensation paid. Assuming a 50% tax rate, its total cash benefit is $54,000.

(a) EFFECT OF QUALIFYING TRANSFER

An employee does not realize compensatory income (with a single exception, discussed below) upon exercise of a statutory stock option provided the following conditions are met [Regs. 1.421-8(a)]:

1. The stock is transferred under a qualified stock option plan, an employee stock purchase plan, or a restricted stock option plan.

2. The employee does not dispose of the stock within the statutory holding period prescribed for the type of plan under which the stock was transferred to him.

3. The person who exercises the option qualifies as an employee of the grantor-corporation, or a related corporation, as prescribed for the type of plan under which the transfer is made.

If these conditions are met, no tax deduction is allowed to the corporation with respect to the issuance of the stock. In addition, the amount considered received by the corporation for the stock is limited to the amount paid under the terms of the option agreement. These two facets round out the position that there is no compensatory income inherent in the exercise of the tax-favored option.

Example: On January 1, 1967, XYZ Corporation grants to Jones, an employee, a qualified stock option to purchase one share of its stock at $100. The market value is $100 on that date. On January 1, 1968, while Jones is still an employee and when the fair market value is $125, Jones exercises the option. On June 30, 1971, Jones sells the stock for $145. Upon exercise of the option Jones realizes no income for the difference between $100 and $125. The corporation is allowed no deduction for the difference. Jones's basis for the stock is $100. Upon sale, Jones realizes a long-term capital gain of $45.

There is an important exception to the general rule that no compensatory income is realized at the exercise date. A qualified stock option with a defective option price can be redeemed by recognizing a measure of compensatory income in the year in which the option is exercised. This relief provision is discussed on page 168.

SURRENDER OF OPTION. Gain realized from a stock option is a form of compensation. It may be taxed wholly or partially as capital gain through legislative grace, provided the full statutory cycle is completed — grant, exercise, and disposition. If a statutory option is surrendered or sold to an employer, any resulting gain is taxed as ordinary income. [*Rank v. U.S.*, 345 F.2d 337 (5th Cir. 1965.]

(b) EFFECT OF DISQUALIFYING DISPOSITION

The preferential tax treatment is available if the stock is not disposed of within the statutory holding period. If the disposition takes place prematurely, the stock option is disqualified. In the case of a disqualifying disposition, the optionee realizes compensatory income and the corporation receives a deduction measured by the excess of the fair market value of the stock at the date it is transferred to him over the option price. [Regs. 1.421-6(f).] See page 186 for the definition of "disposition."

The income is taxed to the employee and the deduction is allowed to the corporation in the year that the qualifying dispositon takes place, regardless of the year of the transfer. The extent to which the deduction is allowed to the corporation is determined, however, by reference to the extent it would have been allowable had it been claimed in the year of the transfer. [Regs. 1.421-8(b).] Each share of stock is considered separately for purposes of determining the holding period. [Regs. 1.421-8(a).] The fact that one share is disposed of prematurely does not disqualify the remaining shares.

Example 1: White is granted an option on January 1, 1967 to acquire one share of XYZ Corporation at $100. The value on the date of grant is $100. On June 30, 1967 he exercises the option. The value on the date of exercise is $120. On February 1, 1968 he sells the share for $140, thereby violating the three-year holding requirement. In 1968 he realizes compensatory income of $20 ($120 minus $100). The corporation receives a deduction of $20 in 1968. White's basis becomes $120, and he realizes a long-term capital gain in 1968 of $20 ($140 minus $120).

Example 2: Assume in Example 1 above that White is paid a salary of $10,000 in 1967 and $8,000 in 1968, and the Revenue Service successfully contends that reasonable compensation for 1967 is $9,000. The deduction of $20 is not allowable in 1968 because it would not have been allowed in 1967 as compensation.

(c) EXERCISE BY ESTATE

In a situation where the optionee dies before the option is exercised, the estate or individual who receives by bequest, inheritance, or death obtains the full benefits of Section 421 if the optionee was qualified at his death. In addition, the employment requirement and the holding requirement need not be met. The estate or individual is placed in the position of the deceased optionee except that these two limitations are removed. [Regs. 1.421-8(c)(1).] The option acquires a new basis equal to the difference between the option price and the value of the stock on the estate valuation date.

When an estate or individual exercises a qualified stock option or a 95%-or-more restricted stock option or a 100% purchase plan option and disposes of the stock, any gain or loss is capital gain or loss. When an estate or individual exercises an 85%-95% restricted stock option or a less-than-100% purchase plan option and disposes of the stock, compensatory income is included in the gross income of the estate or individual in the same manner as it would have been included in the gross income of the optionee.

Example: Jones receives an employee purchase plan stock option on January 1, 1966 to purchase one share of XYZ Corporation at $85. The value on that date is $100. On March 1, 1967 Jones dies without exercising the option. The value of the stock is then $130. The option is transferred to his estate. On June 30, 1967, when the stock is worth $135, the estate exercises the option. The estate sells the stock on June 30, 1968 for $150. The estate realizes $15 ordinary income ($100 minus $85) and $20 capital gain ($150 minus $130 basis).

Insofar as the estate is concerned, a disposition occurs when the stock is sold or distributed to a beneficiary. A disposition occurs when an individual who acquired the option through the death of the optionee sells, exchanges, or transfers the stock or when he dies owning the stock. [Regs. 1.421-8(c)(2).]

Example: In the preceding example, a disposition would have occurred if the estate had distributed the stock to the beneficiaries instead of selling it.

If compensatory income is included in the gross income of the estate or the heir, a deduction is allowed for the estate tax attributable to the inclusion of the option in the taxable estate. The deduction is computed under Section 691(c) by including the option as a Section 691 gross-income item and treating the compensatory income as an amount included in gross income under Section 691 in respect of such item of gross income [Regs. 1.421-8(c)(3).]

Example: In the preceding example, assume that the estate valuation of the option is $45 ($130 minus $85) and there are no other Section 691 items. The estate tax on the option is $15. The compensatory income is $15. The deduction allowable under Section 691(c) is $5 (15/45 times $15).

The tentative cost basis of the optioned shares is computed by adding to the value of the option for estate tax purposes the option price. The tentative basis is reduced to the extent that the compensatory income taxed to the estate is less than what it would have been if the optionee had exercised the option and held the stock at death. The tentative basis is increased by the amount by which the compensatory income exceeds the option value for estate tax purposes. [Sec. 421(c)(3).]

Example: In the preceding example, the basis is computed as follows:

Estate tax valuation of option	$ 45
Option price	85
Tentative basis	130
Reduction (below)	(—)
Addition (below)	—
Basis	$130

Reduction:	
Income to Jones ($100 − 85)	$ 15
Income to estate ($100 − 85)	15
Excess	$ —

Addition:	
Income to estate	$ 15
Estate tax valuation of option	45
Excess	$ —

Example: On January 1, 1963 Smith receives a restricted stock option to purchase one share of ABC Company at $85. The value on that date is $100. On March 1, 1967 Smith dies without exercising the option; the value of the stock is then $110. On March 1, 1968 the estate exercises the option; the value is then $95. On October 1, 1968 the stock is sold for $90. The basis is computed as follows:

Value of option (optional date)	$10
Option price	85
Tentative basis	95
Reduction (below)	(10)
Addition (below)	—
Basis	$85

Reduction:

Income to Smith ($100 − 85)	$15
Income to estate ($90 − 85)	5
Excess	$10

Addition:

Income to estate	$ 5
Value of option	10
Excess	$—

Qualified Stock Options

(a) GENERAL RULE
(b) QUALIFIED STOCK OPTION
 Option plan
 Duration of plan
 Exercise period
 Option price
 Prior outstanding options
 Transferability
 Ownership limitations
(c) SPECIAL RULES
 Option price less than value of stock
 Small-corporation ownership
 Ownership rules
 Certain disqualifying dispositions

(a) GENERAL RULE

In general, the preferential tax treatment of Section 421 is extended to qualified stock options provided two conditions are met:

1. The individual must not dispose of the stock within three years of the date on which the stock is transferred to him; *and*
2. The individual must be an employee of the grantor-corporation, its parent or subsidiary, or of a corporation,

its parent or subsidiary, which issued or assumed the option, at all times during the period beginning with the option grant date and ending within three months prior to the exercise date. Military leave and sick leave count as employment time.

This general rule is subject to a number of exceptions and definitions. See particularly the following references:

Definition of "disposition" — page 186.
Circumstances under which options may be assumed — page 183.
Exception to holding and employment periods for estates — page 162.
Exception to holding period for insolvent persons — page 171.

(b) QUALIFIED STOCK OPTION

The term "qualified stock option" means an option which is granted to an individual after 1963, and which meets each of the requirements set forth below (except in the case of options granted in calendar-year 1964, which had less stringent requirements).

OPTION PLAN. The option must be granted under a plan which is approved by the shareholders. Such approval must be granted within 12 months before or after the date on which the plan is adopted. Approval must conform to the requirements of the corporate charter and by-laws and the laws of the state of incorporation, and must be approved by a majority of shareholders. If the corporate charter or by-laws or the laws of the state of incorporation specifically require a greater percentage of approving shareholders for approval of a stock option plan, such greater percentage must be met. [Regs. 1.422-2(b)(1).]

The plan must set forth the aggregate number of shares which may be issued under option. It must also indicate the employees or class of employees who are eligible for options. The plan may provide, however, that the board of directors, a stock option committee, or other group may select the specific individuals from an approved class to receive the options. The aggregate number of shares and the employees or class of employees are the only features of the plan requiring shareholder approval. If there is any change in either of these two features (barring a mere change in capitalization due to a stock split, stock dividend, etc.), the shareholders must approve the amended plan. [Regs. 1.422-2(b)(3).]

DURATION OF PLAN. The option must be granted within ten years of the date on which the plan is adopted or the date on which the plan receives shareholder approval, whichever date is earlier. [Regs. 1.422-2(c).]

EXERCISE PERIOD. The option must be exercisable only within five years of the date of grant. This limitation must be a condition of the option itself. [Regs. 1.422-2(d).]

OPTION PRICE. The option price must be at least 100% of the fair market value of the underlying stock at the date of grant. [Regs. 1.422-2(e).] There is an exception to the 100% rule for certain corporations, as discussed on page 168.

PRIOR OUTSTANDING OPTIONS. In order to avoid option price resetting, a qualified stock option, by its terms, must not be exercisable while there is outstanding to the same individual any earlier qualified or restricted stock option. [Regs. 1.422-2(f).] The terms of an option need not contain this limitation if the optionee holds no prior outstanding options. [Rev. Rul. 67-166.] If two options are granted on the same day, neither option is considered to have been previously granted. [Rev. Rul. 67-462.] An option is treated as outstanding until it is exercised in full or until it expires by reason of the lapse of its exercise period. [Regs. 1.422-2(f)(1).] Consequently, the rule cannot be avoided by terminating an earlier option; even though terminated, it will be treated as still in existence for its exercise period.

Several relief provisions exist. A restricted stock option granted before 1964 is not treated as outstanding for any period before the first day on which by its terms it may be exercised. [Sec. 422 (c)(2).] The rule against overlapping options does not apply unless any one of the earlier qualified or restricted stock options has a higher option price than the later option, and provided all qualified or restricted stock options held by the individual relate to the same class of stock. [Sec. 422(c)(6).]

Example: Wolfe is an employee of Horne Corporation. He has been granted but has not exercised statutory options to purchase Class A common stock as follows:

Type	Grant	Expiration	Price
Restricted	1960	1969	$100
Qualified	1966	1971	90
Qualified	1967	1972	85
Qualified	1968	1973	95

Wolfe terminated the 1960 restricted stock option in 1967. In this situation Wolfe cannot exercise any options until after the 1969 expiration date of the terminated restricted stock option. After such expiration in 1969 he may exercise the 1966 option at $90. He may not, however, exercise the 1967 option at $85 until either (a) the $90 option has been exercised or (b) 1971, when it expires. He may exercise the 1968 option at $95 any time after the 1969 expiration of the restricted stock option.

TRANSFERABILITY. The option by its terms must not be transferable by the optionee other than by will or the laws of descent and distribution. It must be exercisable, during the lifetime of the optionee, only by him. [Regs. 1.422-2(g).] See also page 155.

OWNERSHIP LIMITATIONS. The optionee, immediately after the option is granted, may not own stock possessing more than 5% of the combined voting power or value of all classes of the stock of the employer corporation, its parent or subsidiary. [Regs. 1.422-2(h).] This condition, with its important exception for small corporations, is discussed in detail on page 169.

(C) SPECIAL RULES

OPTION PRICE LESS THAN VALUE OF STOCK. The option price must be at least 100% of the value of the stock on the date of grant. The burden of valuing the stock rests with the taxpayer. The Revenue Service will accept any reasonable method of valuation, including the methods described in the Estate Tax Regulations. [Regs. 1.421-7(e)(2).]

It is difficult to place a precise value on the stock of a closely-held corporation. In order to make the qualified stock option feasible for the closely-held corporation, a relief provision will save the qualified status of the option even though the option price is less than 100% of the value of the stock. If there is an attempt made in good faith to price the option at the market value of the stock at the date of grant, but the attempt is unsuccessful, the qualified stock option will not fail to qualify because of this fact alone. However, as a penalty, 150% of the excess of the actual value of the stock at the grant date over the option price is taxed to the optionee as compensatory income in the year in which the option is exercised. [Regs. 1.422-2(e)(2).]

Example:

Actual fair market value at date of grant	$87
Option price	77
Excess	$10
Compensatory income at 150%	$15

If the difference between the option price and the market value of the stock at the date on which the option is exercised is less than the penalty computed under the 150% rule, such lesser amount becomes the penalty.

Example: If, in the example above, the value of the stock on the exercise date was $80, the compensatory income penalty becomes $3.

The basis of the stock acquired is increased by the amount of the compensatory income penalty. No deduction is allowed to the corporation for the income taxed to the optionee.

What constitutes an attempt made in good faith to arrive at an accurate value depends upon the facts and circumstances in each case. The regulations suggest that the taxpayer use an average of the values set by completely independent and well qualified experts. Imputed interest under Section 483 is not included as a part of the purchase price for this purpose. [Regs. 1.422-2(e)(2).]

SMALL-CORPORATION OWNERSHIP. The general ownership rule limits the optionee to 5% of the stock of a corporation. An exception to the general rule is provided for small corporations. [Regs. 1.422-2(h)(3).]

If a corporation has equity capital of $2,000,000 or more, the ownership limitation is 5%. If its equity capital is $1,000,000 or less, the limitation is 10%. If the equity capital is between $2,000,000 and $1,000,000, the 5% limitation is increased by an amount which bears the same ratio to 5% as the difference between the equity capital and $2,000,000 bears to $1,000,000.

Example: Sigma, Inc. has equity capital of $1,600,000 at the date on which options are granted to Boyd. The ownership limitation which applies to Boyd is 7% ($400,000 is ⅖ths of $1,000,000; ⅖ths of 5% is 2%; 2% plus 5% is 7%).

For the purposes of this provision, the term "equity capital" means assets (computed on adjusted basis for determining gain) less indebtedness other than shareholder indebtedness. In the case of a group of corporations consisting of a parent and its subsidiaries, the total equity capital of the group must be adjusted for intercompany profits, indebtedness, and stock ownership. [Regs. 1.422-2(h)(3)(b).]

OWNERSHIP RULES. In determining ownership for the 5% (or 5%-to-10%) rule, the ownership attribution rules of Section 425 (d) apply (see page 187). The percentage of ownership is computed by comparing the stock owned by the optionee with the total stock actually issued and outstanding immediately after the grant of the option. In arriving at the total stock actually issued and outstanding, neither treasury shares nor shares authorized for issue under outstanding options held by anyone are counted. However, in computing the shares held by the optionee, stock which the optionee may purchase under outstanding options is counted, whether or not the options are statutory options. Options which may be exercised only in installments, or after a fixed period of time, are also treated as outstanding. [Regs. 1.422-2(h)(1).]

Example: Repsa Corporation has equity capital in excess of $2,000,000 and 200,000 shares of stock issued and outstanding. Wayland is granted an option to purchase 10,000 shares. After the grant, Wayland is treated as owning 5% of Repsa Corporation.

If an optionee is granted an option to purchase shares in excess of the 5% (or 5%-to-10%) limitation, the option is treated as a qualified option only to the extent that the optionee could, if the option were exercised in full at the date of grant, purchase stock without exceeding the limit. The shares in excess of such limit are treated as nonstatutory options regardless of stock ownership when the excess shares are actually acquired. The first shares purchased are considered to be qualified stock option shares to the extent of the limitation. [Regs. 1.422-2(h)(2).]

Example: In the example above, assume that Wayland is granted an option to purchase 10,400 shares. Wayland exercises options for 10,000 shares. These are qualified stock option shares (5% of $200,000). Later he exercises options for the remaining 400 shares. The latter shares are not eligible for the special tax treatment, since the option was not qualified when granted even though at the date of exercise the limitation was not exceeded (5% of 200,000 plus 10,000 is 10,500 shares).

CERTAIN DISQUALIFYING DISPOSITIONS. If stock is disposed of within the three-year holding period and the disposition is a sale or exchange on which a loss, if sustained, would be recognized, the amount includable in the optionee's income and deductible by the corporation shall not exceed the excess of the proceeds of the sale or exchange over the adjusted basis of the stock. This limitation does not apply to a wash sale, a sale between related parties, or a gift where loss would not be recognized. [Regs. 1.422-1(b).]

If an insolvent optionee transfers a share of stock acquired under a qualified stock option to a trustee, receiver, or similar fiduciary in a proceeding under the Bankruptcy Act or similar insolvency proceeding, the transfer will not constitute a disqualifying disposition. [Regs. 1.422-1(a)(2).]

Employee Stock Purchase Plans

(a) GENERAL RULE
(b) EMPLOYEE STOCK PURCHASE PLAN
(c) SPECIAL RULE WHERE OPTION PRICE IS BETWEEN
    85% AND 100% OF VALUE OF STOCK

(a) GENERAL RULE

Although prior to 1964 the restricted stock option was regarded and used primarily as an incentive compensation device for key executives, some companies made options available to employees in general. While such employee plans were constructed within the statutory framework of the restricted stock option, they were generally referred to as "employee stock purchase plans." In most cases, the employee stock purchase plan was designed to raise capital. (The option discount generally equalled the cost which would have been incurred in floating a new stock issue.) Specific provision for this type of stock option was made in the Revenue Act of 1964. In general, the rules for employee stock purchase plans in the 1964 Act correspond to the rules for restricted stock options.

The provisions of Section 423 are applicable to options granted after December 31, 1963 under an employee stock purchase plan, if three conditions are met:

1. No disposition is made of the stock within two years of the date on which the option was granted; *and*

2. No disposition is made of the stock within six months of the date on which the stock was transferred to the individual; *and*
3. The person, other than an estate, who exercises the option must be an employee of the grantor-corporation, its parent or subsidiary, or of a corporation, its parent or subsidiary, which issued or assumed the option, at all times during the period beginning with the option grant date and ending within three months prior to the exercise date.

(b) EMPLOYEE STOCK PURCHASE PLAN

As in the case of a qualified stock option, the plan under which the option is granted must be approved by shareholders within 12 months before or after its adoption; an employee-employer relationship must exist; and the option by its terms must be non-transferable other than at death and must be exercisable during the optionee's lifetime only by him. The optionee may not own more than 5% of the stock of the corporation, but (unlike the qualified stock option) there is no exception to this 5% rule for small corporations. The definitions under these rules are substantially the same as those contained in the rules for qualified stock options (see page 151).

An employee stock purchase plan must avoid discrimination by making the options available to all employees, except that the following categories may be excluded [Sec. 423(b)(4)]:

1. Employees who have been employed for less than two years.
2. Employees who are part-time and have been employed 20 hours or less per week.
3. Employees whose customary employment is for not more than five months a year.
4. Officers, supervisory personnel, or highly compensated employees.

In addition, all employees granted options must have the same rights and privileges. However, the amount of stock which may be purchased by any employee may be a uniform percentage of total compensation or regular or basic compensation. The plan may provide for the maximum amount of shares to be purchased. [Regs. 1.423-2(f).]

The option price may not be less than the lesser of (*a*) 85% of the market value of the stock at the option grant date, or (*b*) 85% of the market value of the stock at the option exercise date. [Regs. 1.423-2(g).]

If under the terms of the plan the option price is to be not less than 85% of the market value of the stock at the option exercise date, the exercise period cannot exceed five years from the date of grant. In all other cases the option exercise period cannot exceed 27 months from the date of grant. [Regs. 1.423-2(h).]

In order to assure broad employee coverage, no employee may have the right to purchase more than $25,000 of stock in any one year. [Regs. 1.423-2(i).]

(c) SPECIAL RULE WHERE OPTION PRICE IS BETWEEN 85% AND 100% OF VALUE OF STOCK

If the two-year and six-month holding periods are satisfied (unless excused by death), but the option price was less than 100% of the value of the stock on the date of grant, the disposition of the stock gives rise to compensatory income to the individual. The amount of ordinary income is the excess of the market value of the stock on the date of grant over the option price. However, if the market value of the stock at the date of its disposition is lower than its value at the date of grant, such lower figure is substituted. The date of death is used in lieu of the date of disposition in the case of a deceased holder of stock. The employer does not receive a deduction at any time for the compensatory income taxed to the individual. The individual is taxed in the year of disposition of the stock or the year of death, whichever is appropriate. [Regs. 1.423-2(k).] Compensatory income is added to the basis of the stock.

Restricted Stock Options

(a) GENERAL RULE

(b) RESTRICTED STOCK OPTION

(c) SPECIAL RULES
    Where option price is between 85% and 95%
      of value of stock
    Variable-price option
    Certain options granted after December 31, 1963

(a) GENERAL RULE

In general, Section 421 is applicable to restricted stock options provided the following conditions are met:

1. The individual does not dispose of the stock within two years of the date on which the option was granted; *and*

2. The individual does not dispose of the stock within six months of the date on which the stock was transferred to him; *and*

3. The person, other than an estate, who exercises the option must be an employee of the grantor-corporation, its parent or subsidiary (see page 188), or of a corporation, its parent or subsidiary, which issued or assumed the option (page 183) at the exercise date or was an employee within three months prior to the exercise date.

(b) RESTRICTED STOCK OPTION

The term "restricted stock option" means an option which was granted to an individual after February 26, 1945 and before January 1, 1964 (with limited exceptions discussed below), provided:

1. It was issued in connection with the employment of the individual by the corporation, its parent or subsidiary, to purchase stock of such corporation(s); *and*
2. It is by its terms not transferable by the individual otherwise than by will or by the laws of descent and distribution; *and*
3. It is exercisable, during the individual's lifetime, only by him; *and*
4. The option price qualifies; *and*
5. The option term qualifies; *and*
6. The individual meets the stock ownership test.

"Option price" and related terms mean the consideration which the optionee must pay (in money or property) to purchase the stock upon exercise of the option. At the time the restricted stock option is granted, the option price must be at least 85% of the fair market value of the stock as of the same date or, in the case of a variable-price option, must be 85% of the fair market value on the grant date computed under the formula as if the option had been exercised when granted.

The burden of valuing the stock for the 85% rule (and the 95% rule) is on the taxpayer. The Revenue Service will accept any reasonable method of valuation, including the methods described in the Estate Tax Regulations. Because the qualification of an option as "restricted" may hinge upon an accurate valuation of the option stock at the grant date, many plans contain a price determination provision which states that if the Commissioner finds that the option price is less than the 85% of fair market value, the optionee shall pay to the employer an amount sufficient to bring the option price up to 85% of the fair market value as determined by the Commissioner. The burden cannot be so shifted to the Commissioner by a price determination provision. A plan containing such a provision does not provide a fixed or determinable price on the grant date, and therefore the options cannot qualify as restricted stock options. [Rev. Rul. 59-243.] The foregoing ruling will not be applied retroactively for options granted prior to July 20, 1959. [Rev. Rul. 60-242.]

An option must not be exercisable after the expiration of ten years from the grant date if the option date was later than June 21, 1954. If the grant date is later than December 31, 1963, certain additional requirements must be met.

At the time the option is granted, except as noted below, the optionee cannot own more than 10% of the total combined voting power of all classes of stock of either the employer corporation or its parent or subsidiary. Attribution rules apply in determining the percentage of ownership. Stock owned directly or indirectly by or for brothers and sisters (whole- or half-blood), spouse, ancestors, and lineal descendants is attributed to him. Stock owned directly or indirectly by or for a domestic or foreign corporation, partnership, estate, or trust is attributed to the stockholders, partners, and/or beneficiaries. The 10% rule does not apply if, other requirements being met, the option price at the grant date is at least 110% of the fair market value of the stock *and* the option is not exercisable after five years from the grant date.

(c) SPECIAL RULES

SPECIAL RULE WHERE OPTION PRICE IS BETWEEN 85% AND 95% OF VALUE OF STOCK. If the option price at the grant date is 95% or more of the value of the stock, gain or loss on the disposition of the stock acquired under a restricted stock option is taxed as capital gain or loss, provided the holding periods are met. A special rule applies, however, if the option price is between 85% and 95%, under which gain may be taxed in part as compensatory income.

Unless the option is a variable-price option, the amount which is taxed as ordinary income is the amount by which the option price is exceeded by the lesser of the fair market value of the stock (1) at the time of disposition or (2) at the time the option was granted. If the special rule applies, the ordinary income is taxed in the year of disposition and the optionee's basis is increased by the amount of compensatory income. The corporation does not receive a deduction for the compensatory income.

Example: On January 1, 1963, XYZ Corporation grants to Jones, an employee, an option to purchase one share of its stock at $85. The value of the stock is $100 on the grant date. Jones exercises the option on January 1, 1964, when the stock has a value of $125. On June 30, 1965, Jones sells the stock for $145. The option is a restricted stock option. Jones is taxed in 1965 as follows:

Value at disposition	$145
Value at grant	$100
Option price	85
Excess—ordinary income	$ 15
Purchase price	$ 85
Ordinary income	15
Total basis	100
Proceeds	145
Capital gain	$ 45

In the above example, assume that the value at disposition is $80. The option price is not exceeded by the value at disposition and no compensatory income exists. Jones has a $5 long-term capital loss.

In the above example, assume that Jones gives the stock to his son on June 30, 1965. This is a disposition, and Jones includes $15 in gross income. The son's basis is $100 plus the gift tax paid (if any). The gift tax value is $145.

If the option is a variable-price option the compensatory income is the lesser of (1) the excess of the value at disposition over the price paid under the option or (2) the excess of the value at the grant date over the option price computed as if the option had been exercised at the grant date.

Example: In the above example, assume that the option provides that the option price is to be 90% of the value on the date of exercise. On January 1, 1964 (date of exercise) the value is $125 and Jones pays $113. Jones is taxed as follows:

Value at disposition	$145
Price paid under option	113
Excess	$ 32
Value at grant	$100
Option price (90% of $100)	90
Excess	$ 10
Compensatory income	$ 10

Purchase price	$113
Ordinary income	10
Total basis	123
Proceeds	145
Capital gain	$ 22

The special rule also applies in the event the optionee dies while owning the stock. In this case, the date of death becomes the date of disposition. The two-year and six-month holding periods do not apply. The compensatory income is included in the gross income of the year of death. The basis determined under Section 1014 of the stock in the hands of the estate or person receiving it by bequest or inheritance is not increased by the compensatory income, nor is the basis of the stock in the hands of a surviving joint owner increased. [Regs. 1.424-2(b)(2).]

If the optionee exercises the option but dies before the stock is transferred to him, and the stock is transferred by the corporation directly to the estate or beneficiary, the special rule also applies.

VARIABLE-PRICE OPTION. The term "variable-price option" means an option under which the option price of the stock is fixed or determinable by a formula in which the only variable is the value of the stock at any time during a period of six months which includes the day the option is exercised. The formula may determine the price by reference to a specific day in the six-month period or by any combination or average of days. Other non-variable factors may be contained in the formula.

Example 1: An arrangement provides that the option price shall be 90% of the average value of the stock during the month following the month in which the option is exercised.

Example 2: An arrangement provides that the option price shall be $20 below the average market price for the month in which payments are completed or for the next succeeding month, whichever is lower, but not more than $150 nor less than $110.

A variable-price option granted after September 30, 1958 will not qualify as a restricted stock option if its formula determines the purchase price by reference to the value of the stock prior to the exercise if that value exceeds the average value of the stock during the calendar month in which the option is exercised.

CERTAIN OPTIONS GRANTED AFTER DECEMBER 31, 1963. Under a transition rule, a restricted stock option may be granted after 1963 if it is issued pursuant to a binding written contract entered into before January 1, 1964. Such a stock option may also be issued pursuant to a pre-1964 plan if it is similar to an employee stock purchase plan.

Definitions and Special Rules on Stock Options

(a) CORPORATE REORGANIZATIONS, LIQUIDATIONS, ETC.
General rule
Corporate changes
Valuation
Employee rights
Other

(b) ACQUISITION OF NEW STOCK

(c) DISPOSITION

(d) ATTRIBUTION OF OWNERSHIP

(e) PARENT CORPORATION

(f) SUBSIDIARY CORPORATION

(g) SPECIAL RULE

(h) MODIFICATION, EXTENSION, OR RENEWAL OF OPTION
General rule
Definitions

(i) STOCKHOLDER APPROVAL

(j) CROSS REFERENCE

(a) CORPORATE REORGANIZATIONS, LIQUIDATIONS, ETC.

In the present era of business combinations, attention must be paid to the effect of corporate changes upon stock options which are outstanding. In many instances the stock option plan recites the procedures to be followed in the event of a corporate change. In other instances, the stock option plan is either completely silent or silent as to the type of corporate change which takes place. Section 425(a) sets forth the rules applicable to the tax-sanctioned substitution or assumption of a statutory stock option in prescribed corporate change transactions.

GENERAL RULE. In a situation where a new option is substituted for an old option or an option is assumed by a new corporation as a result of a corporate change, the rights and privileges of the optionee are preserved provided the following conditions are met [Regs. 1.425-1(a)]:

1. The aggregate spread between the option price and value of the stock after the substitution or assumption is not greater than the spread before the substitution or assumption.
2. The new option or assumption does not give the optionee additional benefits. For example, an extension of the time within which the option may be exercised is an additional benefit.
3. The corporate change otherwise affects the rights of the optionee.

Example: Haight holds statutory stock options to purchase 120 shares of West Corp. at $24 per share. On June 1, 1968 when West shares are worth $64 per share, West is merged into Gen Corp. whose shares are selling for $48. Gen issues statutory options at $18 per share to Haight for 160 shares of its stock in substitution for his old West options.

On a share-by-share comparison the ratio of option price to fair market value after the substitution (18/48) is no more favorable than the ratio before the substitution (24/64), Haight does not receive an additional benefit. In the aggregate the spread between the option price and the fair market value after the substitution (160 × $48 less 160 × $18 = $4,800) is not more than the spread before the substitution (120 × $64 less 120 × $24 = $4,800). Section 425(a) applies to the transaction.

CORPORATE CHANGES. For the purpose of this subsection, a corporate change must result in a substantial number of employees being transferred to a new employer or being discharged, or must result in the creation or severance of a parent-subsidiary relationship. The corporate changes contemplated by the subsection include a corporate merger, consolidation, purchase or acquisition of stock or property, separation, reorganization, or liquidation. The change may be a taxable transaction such as a purchase of stock or property for cash. It may be a reorganization regardless of whether covered by Section 368. It may be a liquidation regardless of Section 332 coverage. [Regs. 1.425-1(a)(1)(ii).]

Revenue Ruling 60-168 discusses the application of the substitution rules in the case of nontaxable "spin-offs."

VALUATION. In determining whether the excess of the spread between the aggregate fair market value of the stock subject to the option immediately after the assumption over the aggregate option price is not more than the excess of the aggregate fair market value of the stock subject to the option immediately before such assumption over the aggregate option price, any reasonable method may be used to determine the fair market value of the stock both before and after the assumption. In the case of a reorganization which is arrived at by arm's-length negotiations, the fair market value of the stock subject to the option before and after the assumption may be based upon the values assigned to the stock for purposes of the reorganization. In the case of a merger, if the parties treat each share of the merged company as being equal in value to a share of the surviving company, it will be reasonable to assume that the stocks are of equal value, so that the substituted option may permit the employee to purchase at the same price one share of the surviving company for each share he could have purchased from the merged company. [Regs. 1.425-1 (a)(7).]

Where a reorganization requires the issuance of stock to shareholders under a formula based upon future earnings, a substitution of options geared to the same formula may meet the requirements of Section 425(a). [Rev. Rul. 66-366.]

EMPLOYEE RIGHTS. The employee must lose his rights under the old options. He cannot receive new options in substitution while retaining his rights under the old options. He may, however, receive a partial substitution. [Regs. 1.425-1(a)(6).]

Example: Dugan has qualified stock options to purchase 100 shares of ABC Company at $50 per share. On June 1, 1968, when the stock is worth $100, ABC Company forms XYZ Company and distributes XYZ stock to the ABC shareholders. The ABC stock and the XYZ stock are worth $50 per share. Dugan works for both companies. XYZ gives Dugan a qualified stock option to purchase 100 shares of XYZ at $25 in substitution for his option to purchase 50 shares of ABC. This is a partial substitution. The unsubstituted stock options remain outstanding for purposes of Section 422 (c) (2). (See page 183.)

OTHER. The rule of this subsection applies to instances where a new employer makes the substitution or assumption or where it is made by a new parent or subsidiary. A qualified substitution or assumption does not constitute a modification. [Regs. 1.425-1(a)(2).]

An assumption or substitution may occur before or after the capital change. [Regs. 1.425-1(a)(5).] The corporation need not be under an obligation to assume or substitute an option. In fact, an assumption or substitution can occur even though the terms of the original option provide for termination in event of a capital change. [Regs. 1.425-1(a)(3).]

(b) ACQUISITION OF NEW STOCK

An optionee who receives new stock in respect of old stock under certain tax-free provisions of the Code—see definition of "disposition" in subsection (c)—is not considered to have disposed of his old stock if all other requirements of Sections 421 through 424 are met. The holding period of the new stock dates back to the exercise of the option. This rule applies also to a series of distributions. [Regs. 1.425-1(b).]

(c) DISPOSITION

The term "disposition" includes a sale, an exchange, a gift, or a transfer of legal title. It does not include a transfer from a decedent to his estate or a transfer by bequest or inheritance.

Example: On June 30, 1970 Hadden gives to his son 100 shares of XYZ stock which has a value of $145 per share. He received the stock under an option at $100 per share granted to him on January 1, 1966, which was exercised on January 1, 1967. The gift represents a disposition. Hadden realizes no income on the exercise or disposition. The son's basis is $100 per share plus the gift tax paid (if any). The gift tax value is $145 per share. A disposition by gift which is premature by reference to the required holding period can create compensatory income to the donor. (Compare the example on page 180, which also involved compensatory income.)

The term "disposition" excludes an exchange to which any of the following sections is applicable: Section 354 (exchanges of stock and securities in certain reorganizations), Section 355 (distribution of stock and securities of a controlled corporation), Section 356 (receipt of additional consideration), or Section 1036 (exchange of stock for stock of the same corporation).

The optionee may pledge or hypothecate the stock, but if the stock is disposed of pursuant to the pledge or hypothecation a disposition occurs. [Regs. 1.425-1(c)(1).]

Example: On January 1, 1968 Harvey receives 100 shares of XYZ Corporation pursuant to the exercise of a restricted stock option. On February 1, 1968 he pledges the stock to secure a short-term loan. The pledge is not a disposition. On June 1, 1968 Harvey defaults on the loan and forfeits the security. The forfeiture is a disposition. The disposition is within six months of the date the stock was received and so the restricted stock option is disqualified.

A disposition does not occur if a "put" is purchased on the same date that stock is acquired under a restricted stock option plan. [Rev. Rul. 59-242.]

A disposition does not occur if the optionee acquires stock in his name and that of another person jointly with right of survivorship, if it is later transferred to such joint ownership or transferred from such joint ownership to the name of the optionee. A disposition takes place if the stock is transferred from joint ownership to a third person or if it is transferred from joint ownership to the joint owner (other than the optionee). A disposition also occurs if, upon exercise of the option, the stock is transferred by the corporation to a person other than the optionee or to the optionee as trustee for another person. [Regs. 1.425-1(c)(2).]

(d) ATTRIBUTION OF OWNERSHIP

In determining the percentage of stock owned by an individual for purposes of qualifying a statutory stock option, attribution rules apply. Stock owned directly or indirectly by or for brothers and sisters (whole- or half-blood), spouse, ancestors, and lineal descendants is attributed to him. Stock owned directly or indirectly by or for a domestic or foreign corporation, partnership, estate, or trust is attributed to the stockholders, partners, and/or beneficiaries

[Regs. 1.425-1(d).] Double family attribution is not intended in Section 425(d). [Rev. Rul. 67-262.]

(e) PARENT CORPORATION

(f) SUBSIDIARY CORPORATION

(g) SPECIAL RULE

The option must be granted by the employer corporation, its parent, or its subsidiary. The terms "parent" and "subsidiary" include any member (other than the employer) of a chain of corporations connected with the employer by ownership of 50% or more of the combined voting power of all shares of stock of the next corporation in the chain. The required relationship must exist at the time the option is granted. It need not exist at the time the option is exercised.

Example:
Corporation A owns 60% of B
Corporation B owns 58% of C
Corporation C owns 55% of D
Corporation D owns 75% of E
Corporation E owns 48% of F
Corporation F owns 99% of G

If Corporation C is the employer, A and B qualify as parents and D and E qualify as subsidiaries. Corporations F and G are not subsidiaries because the chain is broken at Corporation E.

(h) MODIFICATION, EXTENSION, OR RENEWAL OF OPTION

GENERAL RULE. A modification, extension, or renewal of an option is considered to be a grant of a new option. The time of the modification, extension, or renewal is determined under the rules for determining the date of grant of an option. [Regs. 1.425-1 (e).]

If a modification, extension, or renewal takes place, the test of a statutory stock option must be met again on the date of the modification, etc. One test to be met is that the option price must qualify on the modification date. In the case of a stock purchase plan option or a restricted stock option, the fair market value to be taken into consideration is the highest of:

1. The value on the original grant date; *or*
2. The value on the date of modification, extension, or renewal; *or*
3. The value on the date of any interveninig modification, extension, or renewal.

Example: On January 1, 1967 Green receives an option to purchase one share of XYZ Corporation at $95; the value is then $100. On January 1, 1968 the option is modified to permit Green to purchase the share at $84; the value is then $88. This option does not qualify. The option price ($84) is not at least 85% of the higher of the value on the original grant date ($100) or the modification date ($88).

The above rule does not apply if the average value of the stock for the 12 months preceding the month of modification, extension, or renewal is less than 80% of the higher of its value at original grant date or its value at the date of any intervening modification, extension, or renewal, and the modification, etc. took place before 1964. [Regs. 1.425-1(e)(4).]

Example: Brown is granted an option in 1961 to purchase a share of ABC Corporation at $85; the value is then $100. On January 1, 1963, the value is $60, and the average value for 1962 is $79. On that date, Brown's option price can be reduced to $51 (85% of $60) without disqualifying the option.

DEFINITIONS. The term "modification" means any change in the terms of an option which gives the employee additional benefits.

Regulations 1.425-1(e)(5) consider the following changes:

1. Modifications:
   a. More favorable payment terms.
   b. Any change in terms for the purpose of qualifying an option.
2. Not modifications:
   a. A shortening of the period in which the option is exercisable.
   b. An acceleration of the time when the option is first exercisable.
   c. A change in the number or price of shares to reflect a stock dividend or stock split.

d. An increase in the number of shares subject to option. Such a change represents a new option insofar as the new shares are concerned.

e. A change in the number or price of shares under a qualified substitution or assumption.

f. A change to prevent transfer of the option except by will or by the laws of descent and distribution. A special rule exists for certain restricted stock options.

Recent Revenue Rulings have considered the definition of modification:

1. *Rev. Rul. 67-41.* A change in the terms of an option to permit exercise while in the employ of a subsidiary was a modification. The change was not handled as a substitution or assumption.

2. *Rev. Rul. 67-102.* A modification took place when the optionee was released from certain investment representations.

3. *Rev. Rul. 67-434.* This ruling discusses the tax effects of a reduction in price of stock subject to restricted stock options and a refund to optionees following a corporate change.

The term "extension" means a grant of additional time within which to exercise the option.

The term "renewal" means a regrant of the same rights and privileges under the same terms and conditions as an original option.

(i) STOCKHOLDER APPROVAL

If an option is granted subject to approval by stockholders, the date of the grant of the option is determined as if the option had not been subject to that approval.

(j) CROSS REFERENCE

This subsection is a cross reference to the reporting requirements under Section 6039 (see page 155).

Nonstatutory Stock Options

GENERAL STATEMENT

If a stock option does not qualify under Section 421 as a statutory stock option, it is considered to be a nonstatutory stock option. Nonstatutory stock options are created in several ways. The terms of the option when granted may prevent qualification as a statutory stock option. A statutory stock option may be modified in such a manner that it can no longer qualify as a statutory stock option. There may be a disqualifying disposition of stock acquired under a statutory stock option.

It has been established that an employee realizes taxable income when he acquires stock in a bargain purchase through the medium of a nonstatutory stock option. [*Com. v. LoBue,* 351 U.S. 243 (1956).] The taxation of the compensatory element in bargain purchases is provided for under Section 61 and Regs. 1.61-15. Regulations 1.421-6 sets forth the rules for taxing nonstatutory stock options to employees and independent contractors.

The regulations apply to employee options granted by an employer or its parent or subsidiary, by a stockholder, or by any other person. An option may be granted for any reason connected with employment to the employee, a member of his family, or any other person. [Regs. 1.421-6(a).] The terms "employee," "employer," and "employment" are limited to the employer-employee relationship covered by Section 3401(c).

The regulations do not apply to stock acquired prior to September 25, 1959 if the stock is subject to a significant restriction. They are not applicable if the option was granted before September 25, 1959 and exercised subsequent thereto if the grant provided for a restriction. If an option was granted before September 25, 1959 and sold before exercise, the new rules apply. In no event do the regulations apply to options granted before February 26, 1945. [Regs. 1.421-6(a).]

VALUE OF OPTION

The key to taxing nonstatutory stock options under the regulations is contained in the term "readily ascertainable fair market value." The term "readily ascertainable fair market value" is a new concept in tax law and first appeared in the *LoBue* case, in which the Supreme Court indicated that the receipt of an option might be a taxable event.

The regulations state that while an option may have a value when it is granted, it ordinarily does not have a readily ascertainable fair market value unless it is actively traded on an established market. [Regs. 1.421-6(c)(2).] This position would appear to eliminate virtually all employee options. The regulations do not entirely close the door, however, for if the option is not actively traded on an established market, the taxpayer may be able to establish a readily ascertainable fair market value if he can demonstrate that all of the following conditions are met [Regs. 1.421-6(c)(3)]:

1. The option is freely transferable by the optionee;
2. It is freely exercisable in full by the optionee;
3. Neither the option nor the stock underlying the option is subject to a restriction significantly affecting the fair market value of the option or the stock; *and*
4. The fair market value of the option privilege is readily ascertainable.

The first three conditions are conditions of fact: Either they exist or they do not. Employees' option agreements can be arranged to provide for or ignore them. The fourth condition is one of judgment and, consequently, will be the area of controversy.

The option privilege is the opportunity to benefit from any appreciation in value of the underlying stock during the option period without risk of capital. This privilege is separate from the value an option may contain to make an immediate bargain purchase.

Example: On January 1, 1968 Jones receives an option to purchase one share of XYZ Corporation stock at $60. The fair market value of the stock at the grant date is $100. The option is exercisable at any time during a ten-year period beginning with the grant date. The bargain-purchase aspect of the option can be measured on January 1, 1968 by the difference between the fair market value of the stock and the option price, or $40. It can be measured at any other date during the option period in the same manner. The option privilege aspect of the option, however, at January 1, 1968 is of a nebulous character; it is a measure of the value to Jones of the right to forgo the immediate bargain purchase in the hope that he can make a better bargain purchase on some day before January 1, 1978.

The value of the option privilege must be determined with reasonable accuracy. In determining the value, the regulations provide that the taxpayer shall consider the following factors:

1. Whether the value of the underlying stock can be ascertained; *and*
2. The probability of any ascertainable value of the stock increasing or decreasing; *and*

3. The length of time during which the option can be exercised.

Of primary importance to the timing of income is the point in time when the employee acquires an unconditional right to receive the stock—a right, that is, which is not subject to any conditions, other than conditions which may be performed by the optionee at any time.

Example: Under XYZ Corporation's nonstatutory stock option plan, the option price is payable either in a lump-sum amount or through payroll deductions. In the latter case, the employee can pay the remaining balance at any time. The shares are not transferred to the employee and the employee is not entitled to dividends until the full option price is paid.

If an employee exercises his options and authorizes payroll deductions, he realizes compensatory income at that time even though entitled to neither the stock certificates nor dividends on the stock. His right to receive the stock is conditioned only upon payment of the full option price—and he can do that at any time. [Rev. Rul. 66-346.]

OPTIONS WITH READILY ASCERTAINABLE FAIR MARKET VALUE

If an option has a readily ascertainable fair market value on the grant date, compensatory income is realized at the grant date in an amount equal to the excess of such fair market value over the cost of the option. [Regs. 1.421-6(c).]

OPTIONS WITHOUT READILY ASCERTAINABLE FAIR MARKET VALUE

TIME OF INCOME. If the option has no readily ascertainable fair market value, the time of realization of compensatory income depends upon the nature of the option. [Regs. 1.421-6(d).] The general rule is that the income is realized when the employee acquires an unconditional right to receive the stock—i.e., when his right is unencumbered by any conditions other than those which he can perform. Such a time may be the exercise date or a later date when his right becomes unconditional. If the stock is subject to a restriction which significantly affects its value (for example, a commitment to resell to the employer at book value if employment is terminated within two years of exercise of the option), the regulations [Regs. 1.421-6(d)(2)] take the position that the employee realizes income when the restriction lapses, or when the stock is sold or exchanged, whichever is earlier. If the option is sold or exchanged, income is realized when the option is transferred. If the employee dies while holding an option, the value of the option is included in the employee's estate and income is realized when the option is exercised or sold by the estate or beneficiary.

In the event the option or stock is disposed of in a non-arm's-length transaction, special rules apply. Income may be realized both at the time of the transfer and at the time of the removal of restriction, or the exercise, or the disposition in an arm's-length transaction by the transferee. [Regs. 1.421-6(d)(2),(4).] Special rules also are provided for computing the amount of compensatory income in nonarm's-length transactions.

Example: Jones receives an option on January 1, 1968 to purchase one share of XYZ Corporation at $50. The stock has a fair market value of $100 on the grant date. The option has no readily ascertainable fair market value. On August 1, 1968 Jones transfers the option to his wife for $20. Jones realizes compensatory income in 1968 of $20. On March 1, 1969, Mrs. Jones exercises the option. The stock has a fair market value of $140. In 1969 Jones realizes compensatory income of $70, computed as follows:

Value on exercise date	$140
Cost of stock	50
Total income	90
Income previously reported	20
Income in 1969	$ 70

A special rule applies to a disqualifying disposition of stock acquired under a qualified stock option plan. [Regs. 1.422-1(b)(2).] The rule is discussed on page 171.

AMOUNT OF INCOME. The amount of compensatory income received also depends upon the nature of the option. [Regs. 1.421-6(d).] If compensation is realized when the optionee acquires an unconditional right to receive the stock, the amount of the income is the excess of its fair market value on the date the right is received over cost. If the compensation is realized when a restriction lapses or when the stock is sold before a restriction lapses, the amount of income is the lesser of the following:

1. The difference between the cost of the stock and its fair market value at the date of acquisition, determined without regard to the restriction.
2. The difference between the cost of the stock and either its fair market value at the date of the restriction lapse or the amount received if earlier sold or exchanged.

Example:

Option price	$ 3	$ 3
Value of stock at acquisition date without regard to restriction	10	10
Value at date of restriction lapse	16	9
Compensatory income	7	6

OTHER CONSIDERATIONS

In the *LoBue* case the Supreme Court indicated that the receipt of an option might be a taxable event. The regulations make provision for this. [Regs. 1.421-6(c).] In *Robert Lehman,* 17 T.C. 652 (1951), *nonacq.,* the court held that termination of restrictions on stock having no market value when previously received for services was not a taxable event. The regulations are contra to that case. In *Harold H. Kuchman,* 18 T.C. 154 (1952), *acq.,* it was determined that if restrictions preclude a market for the stock, no taxable event occurs upon its issuance. This theory has been adopted by the regulations.

BASIS. The basis to an employee of the stock acquired pursuant to the exercise of an option is the amount paid for the stock plus any compensatory income includable in his gross income. If an option is transferred in a transaction which is not at arm's-length, the basis of the stock to the transferee includes the employee's compensatory income, but not if transferred in an arm's-length transaction. [Regs. 1.421-6(e).]

The basis of an option with a readily ascertainable fair market value when granted is increased by any includable compensatory income.

EMPLOYER DEDUCTION. The employer receives a deduction under Section 162 at the same time and in the same amount as the employee realizes compensatory income. The deduction, however, is subject to the tests of reasonableness. [Regs. 1.421-6(f).]

COMPENSATORY INCOME VS. CAPITAL GAIN. The ultimate benefit to the employee of the nonstatutory stock option is measured by the excess of the proceeds from the sale of the stock over the cost of the stock. In most instances, the employee desires the benefit to be taxed as capital gain, while the Commissioner wants the benefit to be taxed as compensatory income. The division of the benefit between capital gain income and compensatory income and the timing of the tax is determined by reference to the nature of the option, as discussed above and illustrated below.

Example 1: On January 2, 1967, Green receives an option to purchase one share of ABC Corporation at $70. The stock has a fair market value of $100 on that date. The option has no restrictions. It is determined that the option has a fair market value of $40. Green sells the stock on December 31, 1971 for $300. Green's benefit from the option is taxed as follows:

1967 compensatory income	$ 40
1971 capital gain	190
	$230

Example 2: Assume that the option has no readily ascertainable fair market value and that Green exercises the option on January 2, 1968, when the value of the stock is $160. Green's benefit from the option is taxed as follows:

1968 compensatory income	$ 90
1971 capital gain	140
	$230

Example 3: Assume the same facts as in Example 2 above, except that the option contract has a restriction which expires on January 2, 1970 when the stock has a value of $260 (value at date of exercise was $160). Green's benefit from the option is taxed as follows:

1970 compensatory income	$ 90
1971 capital gain	140
	$230

RESTRICTED STOCK PLAN

The nonstatutory stock option rules of Regs. 1.421-6 are used to create a deferred-compensation plan for high-tax-bracket executives who seek a substitute for current cash bonus or a bargain position in the corporation's equity. The plan avoids the restrictive provisions of the statutory stock option. Although it follows the rules of Regs. 1.421-6, the option feature of the nonstatutory stock option is omitted.

THE MECHANICS. The corporation gives to the executive certain shares of stock as a substitute for a cash bonus otherwise payable in cash. Alternatively, the corporation sells stock to the employee at a price below its fair market value.

The stock is burdened by a restriction which significantly affects its value. For example, the executive cannot offer the stock for sale to a third party during the restriction period unless it is first offered to the employer corporation at a predetermined price. The price may be book value, par value, or a stated figure. A provision for the company to repurchase the stock at fair market value at the offering date is not a restriction which significantly affects its value. The restriction period may terminate with retirement or other severance of employment or at a specified time — e.g., at the end of five years. The length of the restriction period determines the length of the tax deferral period. [Rev. Rul. 68-86.]

THE EMPLOYEE'S POSITION. The employee realizes taxable income in the year the restriction lapses or the stock is sold, whichever occurs earlier. [Regs. 1.421-6(d)(2).]

The amount of compensatory income is the lesser of the following:

1. The difference between the cost of the stock and its fair market value at the date of acquisition, determined without regard to the restriction.
2. The difference between the cost of the stock and either its fair market value at the date of the restriction lapse or the amount received if earlier sold or exchanged.

Any gain in excess of compensatory income is taxed as a capital gain when the stock is sold.

Example: XYZ Company sells 1,000 shares of its stock to Harper for $30 per share at a time when the fair market value of the stock is $50. The stock is restricted in that Harper must offer the stock to XYZ Company for repurchase at $30 if he wishes to dispose of it within five years. At the end of the five-year restriction period the stock is worth $70. Harper later sells the stock for $85 per share. Harper computes his tax in the following manner:

A. Cost of stock $30,000
B. Value of stock at acquisition date without regard to restriction 50,000
C. Value of stock at date of restriction lapse ... 70,000
D. Sales price 85,000

E. Ordinary income (B—A) 20,000
F. Capital gain (D—B) 35,000
G. Total income (D—A) $55,000

Factors affecting the employee are set forth below:

1. The employee's compensatory income is deferred until the restriction lapses. In order to minimize the impact of ordinary income, the restriction may be continued in full until retirement and thereafter removed in stages. For example, 20% of the stock may be freed from the restriction in each of five succeeding years.
2. The employee owns the stock during the restriction period. He is able to vote the stock, receive its dividends, and, unless prohibited by the restriction, collateralize the stock.
3. The holding period for long-term capital gain treatment begins when he receives the stock, not when the restriction is removed. Consequently, a capital gain can be realized as soon as the restriction lapses.
4. The stock may have to be valued for tax purposes at both the date received by the employee and the date the restriction lapses. This requirement may impose a hardship on the employee if he holds stock of a closely-held corporation.

THE EMPLOYER'S POSITION. Some of the benefits which accrue to the employer are as follows:

1. When the restriction lapses, the employer receives a tax deduction for compensation paid in the same amount as the employee's compensatory income.

2. Discrimination need not be considered. The plan may be offered to only one key employee.
3. If the restricted stock plan is used as a substitute for cash compensation by an employer who does not have a ready market for its stock, cash is conserved.
4. The plan is flexible. Restricted bonds or convertible notes may be substituted for stock, in which case, a tax deduction will be available for interest payments.

CROSS REFERENCE. See also other deferred compensation plans involving the use of stock in "Executive Compensation Plans," beginning on page 285.

WITHHOLDING OF TAX

In general, compensatory income is subject to withholding of income taxes. No withholding is required, however, with respect to payments made on account of retirement under a Section 403(a) annuity plan or a Section 405(a) bond purchase plan, or by an exempt employees' trust. (Sec. 3401.)

Compensatory income includable in gross income under Regs. 1.421-6 is characterized as supplemental wage payments. Supplemental wage payments are subject to withholding of income tax under Section 3402(a) because such compensatory income relates to services previously rendered by the employee to the employer.

The compensatory income may be in the form of property other than cash. For example, under a restricted stock plan, the restrictions lapse in a year prior to the year in which the stock is sold. The lapse of restrictions creates noncash compensatory income. The employer is required to withhold income taxes on account of noncash income. [Rev. Rul. 67-257.]

The collection of the withholding tax by the employer may be difficult where the compensatory income arises after termination of employment. Accordingly, it appears desirable that a procedure for collection of the withholding tax from the employee be incorporated in the original plan. In the case of the restricted stock plan, for example, the method of providing for the payment of any such withholding tax liability could assume any of several forms, depending on the particular characteristics of the plan employed. For instance, if the stock received by the employee is restricted in such a fashion that disposition of his securities can be made only to the employer, the proceeds representing the sales price can be tendered the employee net of any withholding tax. In other situations, since the original stock certificates issued an employee will be restricted visibly as to transferability on the face of the security, the employer can require that a payment of any withholding tax liability be tendered by the employee before transferable certificates will be issued.

A less important question (because of the $7,800 salary base) is whether the employer is required to withhold FICA taxes in regard to the compensatory income arising under Regs. 1.421-6. In general, supplemental wage payments are subject to withholding for FICA taxes [Rev. Rul. 57-92]. On the other hand, payments received under a plan which provide for retirement benefits are not subject to withholding for FICA. Consequently, the nature of the deferred-compensation arrangement which is taxed under Regs. 1.421-6 may determine the necessity for FICA withholding.

Any capital gain income arising from a nonstatutory stock option plan is not subject to withholding.

PROPOSED REGULATIONS—OCTOBER 26, 1968

As this book was going to press, the Treasury Department issued "proposed" regulations pertaining to options or other property subject to restrictions. [Prop. Regs. 1.61-2(d)(5) and Prop. Regs. 1.421-6(d)(1), (2), (3), (4) and (5).]

The proposed rules are aimed primarily at restricted stock options. (See pages 198 and 300.)

Under the proposed rules the compensatory income will be measured by the difference between the amount paid for the stock and the fair market value of the stock at the time the restrictions lapse. Consequently, in the example on page 199, ordinary income would be $40,000 and capital gain would be $15,000.

The proposed regulations apply to options or other property transferred after June 30, 1969. [TIR No. 1006.]

Exemption from Tax on Corporations, Certain Trusts, etc.

(a) EXEMPTION FROM TAXATION
(b) TAX ON UNRELATED BUSINESS INCOME

(a) EXEMPTION FROM TAXATION

Employees' trusts which are described in and qualify under Section 401 are exempt from taxation unless the exemption is denied because the trust engages in a prohibited transaction described in Section 503.

An employees' trust is required to file an annual return of information which specifically states its gross income, receipts and disbursements, assets and liabilities, and certain other information. [Sec. 6033.] The trust files Form 990-P. The information required by Regulations 1.401-1(b)(5)(ii), relating to prohibited transactions under Section 503, must be filed by the trustee. He must also file the information required by Regulations 1.404(a)-2 (page 92) unless he has received notification from the employer that such information will be submitted with the employer's annual tax return. If the employer has filed or will file the information required by Section 1.404(a)-2 or the statement required under Section 1.404(a)-2(d), the trust is not required to file such information with Form 990-P. In such a case the notification is to be retained as a part of the trust's records. [Regs. 1.6033-1(a)(3).] Form 990-P is filed on the basis of the regular annual accounting period of the trust and is due on or before the 15th day of the fifth month following its year-end.

An employees' exempt trust having an established annual accounting period can change to another annual accounting period by an administrative procedure. The trust files an application on Form 1128, Application for Change in Accounting Period, with the District Director of Internal Revenue for the district in which the trust files its return on or before the last day of the month following the close of the short period for which a return is required to effect the change of accounting period. Unless a letter is received by the trust from the District Director denying approval because the Form 1128 is not timely-filed, it may be assumed that the change has been approved. The trust then attaches a copy of the application to the return filed for the short period. [Rev. Rul. 56-374; Rev. Rul. 66-158; Rev. Proc. 66-13.]

The trust must also file Forms 1099 and 1096 for distributions to beneficiaries of more than $600 of taxable income in one year. [Regs. 1.6041-2(b).]

If the trust invests wholly or partly in insurance contracts, a special procedure is followed for supplying the information required by Section 6033. [Rev. Proc. 57-15.]

(b) TAX ON UNRELATED BUSINESS INCOME

The exemption from taxation does not extend to the unrelated business taxable income of the exempt trust. (See discussion beginning on page 219. The fact that the trust has such nonexempt income, however, does not affect the status of the trust as an exempt organization.

An employees' trust which is subject to tax on its unrelated business taxable income is required to file a return on Form 990-T in addition to Form 990-P. [Regs. 1.6033-1(i).] The filing of Form 990-P by an employees' trust does not, in and of itself, cause the statute of limitations to start running on assessment of tax on unrelated business taxable income if Form 990-T is not also filed. [Rev. Rul. 62-10.]

Requirements for Exemption Under Section 501

OVERALL CONSIDERATIONS

A loan of funds of an exempt employee trust to the employer or related and controlled interests must be adequately secured and bear a reasonable rate of interest, or the loan will be a prohibited transaction and result in the trust losing its qualified status and income tax exemption. A prohibited transaction can have the following important consequences and nullify the purpose for which the plan was established:

1. The income of the trust becomes subject to income tax.
2. The employer contribution to the trust is nondeductible, except to the extent that the contribution funds benefits which are nonforfeitable at the time the contribution is made. (See page 95.)
3. To the extent benefits are nonforfeitable at the time of the contribution, the contribution must be included in the employee's income in the year it is made. If the employee's rights are forfeitable at the time the contribution is made, the employee is not taxed at that time but instead at the time it is received or made available to him.

(a) DENIAL OF EXEMPTION TO ORGANIZATIONS ENGAGING IN PROHIBITED TRANSACTIONS

An employees' trust which is exempt under Section 501 may lose its exemption if it engages in a prohibited transaction. While this provision operates independently from the qualification provisions of Section 401, it may have an effect on them. For example, if a trust engages in a prohibited transaction and consequently loses its exemption for a limited period, such an event may cast a shadow on its qualifications under Section 401. The internal Revenue Service may contend that the trust is not operated for the exclusive benefit of the employees or their beneficiaries and therefore is not exempt under Section 501. [Regs. 1.503(a)-1.]

If a trust is denied an exemption, the denial is effective for any taxable year subsequent to the taxable year during which the Commissioner formally notifies the trust that it has engaged in a prohibited transaction.

Example: In 1965 a trust engages in a prohibited transaction. In 1966 the Commissioner informs it that the transaction was prohibited. The trust loses its exemption for 1967 and subsequent years.

The notification requirement does not apply if the purpose of the transaction was to divert trust income or corpus from its exempt purpose and if a substantial part of the total income or corpus of the trust was involved in the transaction. In such a case, the exemption can be denied for all taxable years. [Regs. 1.503-(a)-1(b).]

Example: In 1965 a trust, which was created in 1963, engages in a prohibited transaction which involves substantially all of its corpus. In 1966 the Commissioner denies the exemption for 1963 and all subsequent years.

If it is concluded that a prohibited transaction was entered into for the purposes of diverting corpus or income from the trust's exempt purpose, and if the transaction involved a substantial part of the corpus or income of the trust, its exemption is revoked, effective as of the beginning of the taxable year during which the prohibited transaction was commenced. No notification to the trust of the loss of its exemption is required under these circumstances. In all other prohibited-transaction cases, however, its exemption is revoked, effective as of the beginning of the first taxable year after the date of the revocation letter. Under these circumstances, a revocation letter is sent by registered or certified mail to the last known address of the trust. [Rev. Proc. 67-4, Sec. 806.]

(b) ORGANIZATIONS TO WHICH THE SECTION APPLIES

This subsection states that Section 503 applies to qualified employees' trusts.

(c) PROHIBITED TRANSACTIONS

The Code sets forth six types of transactions which are considered to be prohibited if they are engaged in by the trust with "tainted" persons. Whether or not the transaction is, in reality, prohibited is a question which must be determined from the facts in the particular situation. Either before or after the issuance of the notice, the trust may request a conference to protest the denial of the exemption. [Rev. Proc. 67-4.] The purpose of the section, insofar as employees' trusts are concerned, is to prevent a transaction in which the creator of the trust receives a private advantage or benefit to the detriment of the employees or their beneficiaries for whose benefit the trust was created.

A "tainted" person is defined as one who falls within one of the following categories:

1. The creator of the trust. The creator of an exempt employees' trust is the employer.
2. A person who has made a substantial contribution to the trust. In the case of an employees' trust, the contributor and the creator are the same party; therefore, this category is a duplication of the one above. The word "person" is construed to mean an individual, a trust, estate, partnership, association, company, or corporation. [Sec. 7701(a)(1).]
3. A member of the family of an individual who is the creator or substantial contributor. The employer, in this situation, must be an individual. The family of an individual includes only his brothers and sisters (whether whole- or half-blood), spouse, ancestors, and lineal descendants. [Sec. 267(c)(4).]
4. A corporation which is controlled by the creator or substantial contributor. "Control" is defined as ownership, directly or indirectly, of 50% or more of the total combined voting power of all classes of stock entitled to vote or 50% or more of the total value of shares of all classes of stock. "Indirectly" is not defined. No reference is made to the attribution of ownership rules. Ownership refers only to legal ownership. If a trust engages in a prohibited transaction with the parent of the corporation by whom it was created, it will not lose its exemption because the parent is neither the creator nor controlled by the creator. [Rev. Rul. 58-526.]

Example: Corporation P owns 100% of Corporation S. Corporation S has a pension trust which loans money without security to Corporation P. Section 503 does not apply.

The deposit of funds in a checking account is not a prohibited transaction, even if the bank is the employer. [Rev. Rul. 59-29.]

The deposit of funds by an exempt employees' trust in a savings account with the employer-grantor bank is a deposit, and as such is not a loan. Therefore an exempt trust making such a deposit is not engaging in a prohibited transaction. This conclusion is also applicable to national banks, state banks, savings and loan associations, and building and loan associations, properly chartered and subject to the usual Federal or state regulatory requirements, whose deposits are covered by insurance issued by the Federal Deposit Insurance Corporation, the Federal Savings & Loan Insurance Corporation, or their state equivalent. [Rev. Rul. 62-183.]

The deposit must be made, however, primarily for the benefit of the depositor — i.e., for safekeeping of the funds and the return of interest thereon. The deposit may or may not also be for the bank's benefit, depending on whether the deposited funds could, at the time, be placed in loans or suitable investments yielding a sufficient return to the bank. Even if the bank could so place the funds and be benefited thereby, the basic motive of the depositor is the overriding factor in denominating the transaction as a deposit rather than a loan. The primary purpose of benefiting employees or their beneficiaries must be maintained with respect to the investment of trust funds as well as in other activities of the trust.

There are six categories of prohibited transactions mentioned in the Code. Two of the prohibitions have little, if any, application to employees' trusts: i.e., the prohibitions relating to paying unreasonable compensation and to making services available on a preferential basis. The remaining four prohibitions are applicable to employees' trusts and relate to:

1. Lending money without adequate security and a reasonable rate of interest.
2. Purchasing securities or other property for more than adequate consideration.
3. Selling securities or other property for less than adequate consideration.
4. Engaging in any other transaction which results in a substantial diversion of income or corpus.

(d) FUTURE STATUS OF ORGANIZATIONS DENIED EXEMPTION

If an exempt trust is denied an exemption for a taxable year following the year in which the denial notice is received, the trust may reclaim its exemption by following prescribed procedures. [Regs. 1.503(d)-1.] In any year following the year the notice of denial was issued, the trust may submit to the District Director the information described in Regulations 1.404(a)-2 (information to be furnished by an employer claiming a deduction) together with a letter claiming an exemption and a written declaration, made under the penalties of perjury, that the trust will not knowingly engage in a prohibited transaction in the future. If the Commissioner is satisfied by the declaration, the exempt status will be returned to the trust for the succeeding year. [Rev. Rul. 67-9.] The timing of the steps is important in that it assures the Commissioner that the trust will be taxable for at least one year.

Example:
1965—Engaged in prohibited transaction.
1966—Received notice of denial of exemption.
1967—Denial effective.
   —Filed claim for exemption.
   —Exemption granted.
1968—Exemption effective.

If, upon examination of the return or returns of the trust, or from other sources, a District Director is of the opinion that a trust has entered into a prohibited transaction, the trust will be advised in writing that it is proposed to revoke its exemption and the reasons for such proposed action. The District Office will also advise the trust of its rights to protest the proposed action by submitting a statement of the facts, law, and arguments in support of its continued exemption, and of its rights to a conference in the District Office.

If, after considering the information submitted by the trust, both in writing and in conference, the District Office is still of the opinion that the exemption should be revoked, and the trust does not agree, the findings of the District Office will be forwarded to the National Office for consideration prior to further action. Such reference to the National Office will be considered a request for Technical Advice, and the procedures of Revenue Procedure 67-2 will be followed.

The trust will usually be permitted to submit its brief and to be heard in conference before final action is taken. However, the District Director may, in his discretion, issue the revocation letter prior to the receipt of the brief or prior to granting a conference. If it is later determined that the revocation was in error, it will be rescinded as of the date it was issued. [Rev. Proc. 67-4.]

(e) DISALLOWANCE OF CERTAIN CHARITABLE, ETC. DEDUCTIONS

This subsection concerns contributions to Section 501(c)(3) organizations and does not affect exempt employees' trusts.

(f) DEFINITION

This subsection defines the term "gift or bequest" as used in subsection (e) above.

(g) SPECIAL RULES FOR LOANS

The first enumerated prohibited transaction is one in which adequate security is not given for a loan to the creator of or contributor to a trust. "Adequate security" is defined [Regs. 1.503(c)-1] as something in addition to and supporting a promise to pay. It must be pledged so that it can be disposed of in the event the loan is not repaid. When it is pledged, its value and liquidity must be recognized by the lender as such that it may reasonably be anticipated that loss of principal or interest will not result from the loan. Examples of adequate security are mortgages or liens on property, accommodation endorsements of persons who are capable of covering the loan, and corporate securities. Evidences of indebtedness of a borrowing corporation will not be considered adequate security. However, if any such evidence of indebtedness provides for security that may be sold, foreclosed upon, or otherwise disposed of in default of repayment of the loan, there may be adequate security for such loan. Stock of a borrowing corporation is not adequate security. The following are examples of transactions in which the adequacy of security can be established by reference to recognized sources [Rev. Proc. 67-4, Sec. 8.02; Regs. 1.503(c)-1(b)]:

1. A surety bond issued by a recognized surety company doing a surety bond business under applicable state law.
2. An assignment of an insurance contract having a cash

surrender value sufficient to cover the loan, interest, and possible costs of collecting.

3. A first mortgage on real property in an amount not in excess of 50% of its assessed value for local tax purposes.

4. Collateral represented by securities listed on a recognized exchange of an aggregate value equal to twice the amount of the loan.

The National Office is permitted to issue rulings as to whether a trust has entered into, or proposes to enter into, a prohibited transaction, but a ruling will not be issued where the determination is primarily one of fact — e.g., market value of property, reasonableness of compensation, etc. Also, no rulings or determination letters will be issued concerning such transactions as sales and leasebacks, gifts and leasebacks, or other rental transactions of real or personal property directly or indirectly with the creator or a related or controlled interest.

There is an exception where the adequacy of the security for a loan is involved and a ruling may be issued, but only if there is a clear indication of value which can be established by reference to recognized sources without requiring physical valuation or appraisal. Examples of transactions in which the adequacy of security can be established by reference to recognized sources have been described above.

Such rulings may be issued only on proposed transactions and on completed transactions where the return for the first year for which the transaction is effective has not been filed or the filing date has not passed. [Rev. Proc. 67-4, Sec. 8.01 and 8.02.]

Also falling within the prohibited-transaction area is the purchase by the trust of the debentures of the creator of the trust. Such a purchase will be considered a loan to the creator, even if the debentures are acquired in an arm's-length transaction from a third party. [Reg. 1.503(c)-1(b)(1).] This rule, however, is tempered by subsection (h) below.

The language in a Sixth Circuit Court decision implies that a transaction may be a prohibited one where a trust borrows money under a chattel mortgage from a third party and purchases equipment which is then leased to its creator. [*Cooper Tire & Rubber Co. Employees' Retirement Fund v. Com.*, 306 F.2d 20 (6th Cir. 1962).]

A loan by a profit-sharing trust to an employer for an unsecured one-year promissory note has been held to be a loan without adequate security, and therefore a prohibited transaction. The Tax Court has stated that a reasonable interpretation of the law is that Congress did not intend unsecured promissory notes to be adequate security [*Van Products, Inc.*, 40 T.C. 1018 (1963).]

In another decision, the employer had directly contributed a five-year unsecured note to the trust. The Commissioner did not raise the question whether the mere contribution of the note was a prohibited transaction, but this is presumably only because he took the position that an unsecured note is not payment at the time of contribution. In this case, the Tenth Circuit Court reversed the Tax Court and considered the note deductible as a contribution in the year it was given.

Since the economic result of contributing an unsecured note and contributing cash and then borrowing back on an unsecured note is the same, the Internal Revenue Service may argue that a contribution of an unsecured note is tantamount to the making of an unsecured loan and therefore is a prohibited transaction. [*Wasatch Chemical Co. v. Com.*, 313 F.2d 843 (10th Cir. 1963).]

A loan made by an exempt employees' pension trust to the employer-creator is a prohibited transaction under Section 503(c) where the purported security for such loan is the excess of prior payments to the trust over the deductible limits under Section 404. Since an excess contribution becomes part of trust corpus, it cannot be used as security for a loan to an employer. [Rev. Rul. 67-266.]

A loan bearing a reasonable rate of interest, secured by a recorded chattel mortgage on specifically identifiable inventory having a fair market value equal to the loan, satisfies the adequate-security tests and is not a prohibited transaction. However, where a chattel mortgage on personal property which was intended to secure a loan made by a qualified employees' trust to its grantor was not recorded as soon as practicable, and where the property was not specifically identified, the loan was not adequately secured and constituted a prohibited transaction. [Rev. Rul. 66-324.]

Special consideration is given to loans which were made prior to March 1, 1954 by an exempt trust and which did not qualify under the adequate-security rule and/or the reasonable-interest rule. [Regs. 1.503(c)-1(b)(2)(v).] A loan made prior to March 1, 1954, repayable by its terms after December 31, 1955 may be held until maturity.

The adequate-security rule, as it relates to employees' trusts, has effective dates as follows:

1. March 15, 1956 — for loans other than debentures made after that date.
2. January 31, 1957 — for loans other than debentures made prior to March 16, 1956, if continued after January 31, 1957.
3. November 8, 1956 — for debentures purchased after that date.
4. December 1, 1958 — for inadequately secured debentures purchased prior to November 9, 1956 and held after December 1, 1958.
5. September 3, 1958 — for Section 503(i) loans.

(h) SPECIAL RULES RELATING TO LENDING BY SECTION 401 TRUSTS TO CERTAIN PARTIES

The Technical Amendments Act of 1958 contained a relief provision for trusts which purchase obligations of an employer in an arm's-length transaction. The purchase will not be considered a loan without adequate security if it meets the statutory requirements as to the purchase conditions and if it does not cause violation of certain percentage-of-ownership limitations. [Regs. 1.503 (h)-2.]

The obligation will be considered to have been acquired in an arm's-length transaction if acquired at the prevailing trading price, or if it is not traded, then at a price which is established by current independent bid and asked prices. It will also qualify if it is bought from an underwriter at the public offering price at which a major portion of the issue was acquired by independent persons. It may also be acquired directly from the employer at the same price as that paid by independent purchasers. There is no prohibition against the trust's acquiring the obligations at a price lower than that paid by outsiders. (See Rev. Rul. 46.)

If, as a result of the purchase, the trust owns more than 25% of the issue outstanding at the time of the acquisition, and if at least 50% of the entire outstanding issue is not owned by independent persons, the relief provision will be inapplicable.

The third condition which must be met is that immediately after the acquisition not more than 25% of the total assets of the trust may be invested in the obligations of the employer.

(i) LOANS WITH RESPECT TO WHICH EMPLOYERS ARE PROHIBITED FROM PLEDGING CERTAIN ASSETS

A second relief provision in the Technical Amendments Act of 1958 relates to employers who are prohibited, by law or regulation, at the time of making the loan or renewing the loan, from pledging their assets when borrowing from an exempt trust. Such loan will not be prohibited if it carries a reasonable rate of interest and if all of the following requirements are met:

1. The employer is prohibited from pledging a particular class or particular classes of its assets. The value of such assets must represent more than one half of the value of its total assets. This requirement must be met at the time that the loan is made or renewed. If, through a change in law or regulations, the employer is subsequently permitted to pledge the previously unpledgeable assets, such change will not alter the nature of the initial transaction.

2. A majority of the trustees who are independent of the employer must approve the loan as one which is in keeping with the primary purpose of the exempt trust. A majority of the independent trustees cannot have previously disapproved the loan.

3. The total of inadequately secured loans, including the loans made under subsection (h), must not constitute more than 25% of the value of the total trust assets. This test is also made at the time of the loan under subsection (i).

(j) TRUSTS BENEFITING CERTAIN OWNER-EMPLOYEES

This subsection contains special rules applicable to prohibited transactions and loans between trusts and certain owner-employees. See page 115 for a discussion of the Self-Employed Individuals Tax Retirement Act of 1962.

Imposition of Tax on Unrelated Business Income of Charitable, etc. Organizations

---

(a) CHARITABLE, ETC. ORGANIZATIONS TAXABLE AT
    CORPORATE RATES

(b) TAX ON CHARITABLE, ETC. TRUSTS

(c) EFFECTIVE DATE

(a) CHARITABLE, ETC. ORGANIZATIONS TAXABLE AT CORPORATION RATES

If an exempt organization is a corporation, this subsection subjects its "unrelated business taxable income" (defined in Section 512) to corporation tax rates. While the subsection expressly extends the tax to Section 401 organizations, such organizations are usually trusts. Consequently subsection (b) applies rather than subsection (a).

(b) TAX ON CHARITABLE, ETC. TRUSTS

An exempt employees' trust is taxed on its unrelated business taxable income as though it were a trust subject to the provisions of Subchapter J, except that the deduction for personal exemption provided by Section 642(b) is not allowed in computing the income subject to tax.

(c) EFFECTIVE DATE

The tax on unrelated business taxable income applies to exempt employees' trusts only for taxable years beginning after June 30, 1954.

Exempt organizations with gross unrelated business income for the taxable year not exceeding $5,000 will not be required to complete the entire Form 990-T for taxable years beginning after December 12, 1967. Instead they need only complete a specially designated small portion of the form setting forth aggregate gross income from unrelated trade or business, the aggregate deductions therefrom, and the tax payable, if any. A detailed breakdown of income and deductions is not required on Form 990-T where the new procedure applies. [TIR No. 974.]

Unrelated Business Taxable Income

(a) DEFINITION
(b) EXCEPTIONS, ADDITIONS, AND LIMITATIONS
(c) SPECIAL RULES APPLICABLE TO PARTNERSHIPS

(a) DEFINITION

Unrelated business taxable income is defined as the gross income less related deductions which is derived from the unrelated trade or business, which term is defined in Section 513. The general definition, however, is subject to certain exceptions, additions, and limitations (see (b) below). Aside from the exceptions, etc., taxable income is computed according to the rules set forth in Chapter 1 of the Code. Accordingly, if the exempt trust engages in several unrelated businesses, the gross income and deductions are aggregated in the computation of unrelated business taxable income. [Regs. 1.512(a)-1.]

(b) EXCEPTIONS, ADDITIONS, AND LIMITATIONS

While there are 14 exceptions, etc. which are applicable to the computation of unrelated business taxable income, the six set forth below are commonly encountered by employees' trusts:

1. Dividends, interest, and annuities are excluded together with directly related deductions.

2. Royalties and related deductions are excluded. This exclusion includes overriding royalties and mineral royalties measured by production or by reference to the gross or taxable income from the mineral property. For purposes of this subsection, in-oil payments are treated as royalties. Royalties do not include income received from a working interest in a mineral property which is burdened by development costs.

3. Rents and related deductions from real property and from personal property which is leased with real property are excluded. The rent exclusion does not extend to rents from public lodging places where services are also rendered [Regs. 1.512(b)-1(c)(2)] or to income from business leases as defined in Section 514.

4. Gains and losses arising from the sale or exchange of property are excluded except for those from the disposition of property constituting inventory and property held primarily for sale to customers, and timber as to which an election has been made under Section 631(a). The exclusion applies to gains and losses from involuntary conversions and casualties.

5. Net operating loss deductions are allowed if arising out of carryovers and carrybacks from a year in which the organization was subject to Section 511. The net operating loss is computed under the provisions of Section 172 except that items of income and deductions which are disregarded in the computation of unrelated business taxable income under Section 512(b) are not considered in the computation of the operating loss.

Example:

Unrelated business gross income $12,000
Dividend income (less directly related deductions)   3,000
                                                        _____
                                                        $15,000
Unrelated business expenses 17,000
                                                        _____
Net book loss .... $(2,000)
                                                        ========

The operating loss available for carryback or carryover is $5,000. The dividend income of $3,000 does not reduce the operating loss for this purpose because it is excluded from unrelated business taxable income under Section 512.

A net operating loss carryback or carryover can arise only from a year in which the trust was subject to the provisions of Section 511 or its counterpart, Supplement U, under the 1939 Code.

The net operating loss can be carried back three years and forward five years. If it is carried to a year not subject to the provisions of Section 511, it is not reduced by the income of that year. Nevertheless, such a year reduces the span of years to which the net operating loss can be carried.

Example: An exempt trust was subject to Section 511 for the years 1964 and 1966-1969 but not for the years 1961-1963 and 1965. It had income or loss as follows:

1961	$ 2,000
1962	4,000
1963	(1,000)
1964	(38,000)
1965	5,000
1966	7,000
1967	6,000
1968	3,000
1969	4,000

The 1963 loss is not a carryback or carryover because it arose in a year which was not subject to Section 511. The 1964 loss cannot be carried back to 1961 and 1962 because these were not Section 511 years. The 1964 loss must be carried first to 1965 which, being a non-Section 511 year, does not reduce the amount of the carryover available for 1966, but does reduce the span of carryover years. The 1964 loss is then carried to 1966, 1967, 1968, and 1969. The unused portion is lost.

6. A specific deduction of $1,000 is allowed in the computation of unrelated business taxable income. [Sec. 512(b) (12).] However, it is not allowed to increase a net operating loss under Section 172. [Rev. Rul. 68-59.]

Amounts distributed by a real estate investment trust, within the meaning of Section 856, to an exempt employees' pension trust do not constitute unrelated business taxable income where the distributions were made out of the earnings and profits of the real estate investment trust and hence were dividends. [Rev. Rul. 66-106.]

An exempt organization held title to a pipeline system consisting of right-of-way interests in land, pipelines buried in the ground, pumping stations, equipment, and other appurtenant property. It leased the system to an operating company and collected rents therefrom. Since the basic component of the pipeline system is an easement giving right-of-way interests in land constituting real property [See 3 Powell, Real Property, Paragraph 405 (1966)], the income derived from the lease is rent from real property within the meaning of Section 512(b)(3) and therefore is not unrelated business taxable income. [Rev. Rul. 67-218.]

However, Rev. Rul. 67-218 should be read in conjunction with the requirements of business leases in Section 514.

The investment credit is allowed if the Section 38 property is used predominantly in the unrelated business. [Sec. 48(a)(4).]

(c) SPECIAL RULES APPLICABLE TO PARTNERSHIPS

If the trust is a member of a partnership and the partnership carries on a business which, if it were carried on by the trust, would be an unrelated business, then the trust must include in its unrelated business taxable income its share of the partnership's gross income and deductions. In effect, the partnership computes its unrelated business taxable income under the rules in this section and passes to the trust its share of that income.

Example: An exempt trust is a 50% partner in a manufacturing business. During 1968 the business had taxable income as follows:

```
Gross income from manufacturing ............$100,000
Dividend income (less directly related deductions)    4,000
Interest income (less directly related deductions)    7,000
                                                  $111,000
Manufacturing and selling costs .............  (23,000)
Taxable income .........................$  88,000
```

The unrelated business taxable income of the partnership is $77,000, dividend and interest income being excluded under Section 512(b). The trust includes in its unrelated business taxable income 50% of $77,000, or $38,500.

If the year end of the trust and the partnership do not coincide, the unrelated business taxable income of the partnership for the year which ends during the year of the trust is used.

Unrelated Trade or Business

(a) GENERAL RULE
(b) SPECIAL RULE FOR TRUSTS
(c) SPECIAL RULE FOR CERTAIN PUBLISHING BUSINESSES

(a) GENERAL RULE

This subsection contains rules for determining whether a trade or business is unrelated to the functions of the exempt organization. Exempt employees' trusts are subject to the special rule set forth in subsection (b) and consequently this subsection does not apply to them.

(b) SPECIAL RULE FOR TRUSTS

This subsection provides that any trade or business regularly carried on by an exempt employees' trust is an unrelated trade or business. In this context, the term "any trade or business" is *per se* considered unrelated. The special rule also applies to partnerships of which the trust is a member.

The term "trade or business" has the same meaning in this section of the Code as it has in Section 162 under both sets of regulations, one effective for taxable years beginning after December 12, 1967, and the other effective for years beginning before December 13, 1967. [Regs. 1.513-1(b); 1.513-2(a)(3).]

A trade or business is regularly carried on when the activity is conducted with sufficient consistency to indicate a continuing purpose of the trust to derive some of its income from such activity. An activity may be regularly carried on even though its performance is infrequent or seasonal. [Regs. 1.513-2(a)(3).]

For example, the trustee of an employees' trust purchased railroad tank cars in the name of the trust. These cars were leased to an industrial company for a period of years with options for renewal. The full activity with respect to this venture is to receive the periodic rental income, the lessee having the responsibility for operation and maintenance of the cars. It has been held under these circumstances that the trust is subject to tax on the rental income from the personal property as unrelated business taxable income. [Rev. Rul. 60-206.] In a recent case, the Sixth Circuit Court of Appeals, affirming the Tax Court opinion, makes it clear that the leasing of personalty by an exempt trust is an unrelated business activity. [*Cooper Tire & Rubber Co. Employees' Retirement Fund v. Com.*, 306 F.2d 20 (6th Cir. 1962).]

A loan to the employer adequately secured and bearing a reasonable rate of interest or the purchase of employer stock are ways in which the *Cooper Tire* result can be evaded.

Rent from real property, however, including personal property leased with the real property, is specifically excluded from taxable business income. [Sec. 512(b)(3).] The latter should be read in connection with Section 514, referring to business leases and business lease indebtedness.

Under regulations effective for taxable years beginning before December 13, 1967, a trade or business is substantially related to the activities for which an organization is granted an exemption if the principial purpose of such trade or business is to further the purpose for which the organization is granted exemption. In the usual case, the nature and size of the trade or business must be compared with the nature and extent of the activities for which the organization is granted exemption in order to determine whether the principal purpose of such trade or business is to further the purpose for which the organization is granted exemption.

Regulations effective for taxable years beginning after December 12, 1967 introduce another test relative to the frequency and continuity with which the activities productive of the income are conducted and the manner in which they are pursued. This test is applied consistent with the purpose of the unrelated business income tax to place exempt-organization business activities upon the same tax basis as the nonexempt business endeavors with which they compete.

For example, specific business activities of an exempt organization will ordinarily be deemed to be "regularly carried on" if they manifest a frequency and continuity, and are pursued in a manner, generally similar to comparable commercial activities of nonexempt organizations. Business regularly carried on, intermittent activities, substantially related, size and extent of activities, income from performance of exempt functions, disposition of products, dual use of facilities, and the exploitation of exempt functions are terms and circumstances described in detail in new regulations adopted on December 11, 1967. [Regs. 1.513-1(c) and (d).]

(c) SPECIAL RULE FOR CERTAIN PUBLISHING BUSINESSES

The Code contains a relief provision for certain publishing businesses. It has no significance insofar as exempt employees' trusts are concerned.

Business Leases

HISTORY

Section 514 of the Code deals with business leases and extends the provisions of Section 423 of the 1939 Code to employees' trusts qualified under Section 401(a) and exempt under Section 501(a). The purpose of old Section 423 was to curtail the use of the sale and leaseback arrangement in which an exempt organization incurred indebtedness to buy business real estate and immediately leased the property back to the seller, who then took a deduction for rent paid.

(a) BUSINESS LEASE RENTS AND DEDUCTIONS

Although ordinary rents are excluded, if the trust holds a "business lease" the gross income and deductions attributable to such a lease must be considered in the computation of unrelated business taxable income. Note that if an employees' trust purchases business real estate without borrowing any funds or which is not subject to a lien (mortgage, etc.) and then leases the property, none of the rent it receives is taxable.

The percentage of rental income which is included in unrelated business taxable income is determined by a formula the numerator of which is the "business lease indebtedness" and the denominator of which is the adjusted basis of the property covered by the business lease. The percentage cannot be greater than 100%. The business lease indebtedness and the adjusted basis are computed as of the end of the year. The adjusted basis of the property is determined under Section 1011. Consequently, depreciation is accumulated from the date the property was acquired regardless of whether the trust was subject to Section 511 during the intervening years and regardless of whether all or a part of the premises is covered by a business lease.

If only a portion of the property is under a business lease, an allocable portion of the business lease indebtedness and adjusted property basis is used in the determination of the percentage.

Example: A trust owns a building which it acquired in 1958 at a cost of $100,000, $75,000 of which was borrowed. It has a useful life of 50 years. It leased one-half of the building for 20 years under a business lease, the annual rental from which is $3,000. The other one-half produces $2,000 rent annually from nonbusiness leases. At the end of 1968 it had an adjusted basis of $80,000 and the debt was reduced to $60,000. The includable rent was $2,250, computed as follows:

$$\frac{\text{Business indebtedness: } \$30,000}{\text{Adjusted basis of premises: } \$40,000} \times \text{Rent: } \$3,000$$

The percentage which is used in computing the business lease rent is also used in determining the business lease deductions. The deductions which can be taken are (1) taxes and other expenses, including depreciation, applicable to the property under the business lease and (2) interest on the business lease indebtedness. As in the case of rents, if only a portion of the property is subject to a business lease an allocable share of the deductions is allowed. If the deductions exceed the rent, the resulting loss is taken into account in the computation of unrelated business taxable income. [Regs. 1.514(a)-2(b).]

Example: In 1968 the trust mentioned in the above example paid interest on the business indebtedness of $3,000. It paid taxes of $500, paid other expenses of $1,500, and incurred depreciation of $2,000. Its total deductions were $7,000. One-half of the deductions, or $3,500, was applicable to the business lease property. Of the $3,500, three-fourths

($30,000/$40,000), or $2,625, was allowable. In determining unrelated business taxable income, the loss of $375 ($2,250 less $2,625) is taken into account and offset against other unrelated business income.

Using accelerated methods of depreciation can create a cash flow from depreciation which can be used to reduce mortgage indebtedness in appropriate amounts, so that over a period of time the combination of accelerated depreciation and reduction of debt will result in very little, if any, tax imposed on net business lease rental income. This makes for an attractive investment of pension funds in combination with a mortgage and a lease of the property to the employer.

Example: A pension trust builds a structure costing $1,300,000 using a 5½%, 15-year mortgage for $1,000,000. The trust receives $153,000 annual rental, pays $20,000 in real estate taxes, and uses double-declining-balance depreciation over 20 years. In this situation the cash flow will reduce debt at a rate sufficient to virtually eliminate net business lease rental income.

(b) DEFINITIONS OF "BUSINESS LEASES"

The first requirement for taxability of rents as unrelated business income is that a "business lease" exist.

A business lease is a lease by the trust, or by a partnership of which it is a member, of real property for a period of more than five years provided a business lease indebtedness exists on the property at the end of the taxable year. In this instance, personal property is considered to be real property if leased in connection with the real property. [Regs. 1.514(b)-1(a).]

In determining whether the lease has a term of more than five years, a renewal option must be taken into account. Thus, if a lease has a term of four years with an option to renew for an additional three years, the "Section 514 term" is considered to be seven years. If the lease is renewed, the "Section 514 term" includes the period of the prior lease.

Example: A one-year lease is executed for 1968 with an option to renew for 1969. At the end of 1969, the parties execute a lease for 1970 with an option to renew for 1971. The same arrangements are made for 1972 and 1973. Under the rules above, in 1972 a "Section 514 term" exists. Under the first rule 1973 is added to 1974, and under the second rule the period 1966-1971 is added, for a total of six years.

Where the property is acquired subject to a lease, the term of the lease for purposes of Section 514 begins on the date the property was acquired.

A "Section 514 term" cannot be avoided by executing successive one-year leases. If the lessee occupies the same premises for more than five years a "Section 514 term" exists after the fifth year regardless of the method of leasing (but see below for an exception). The term will not commence prior to the acquisition date of the property by the trust. The term "lessee" in this case includes the parties set forth in Section 267(a), concerning disallowed losses.

The lease is not a business lease if it is executed primarily for reasons substantially related to the exempt purposes of the trust (aside from the need for income), or if the premises are in a building designed for and used by the trust. This relief provision is seldom, if ever, of help to an exempt employees' trust.

Neither is the lease a business lease if some of the leases of the property have terms in excess of five years and some have terms of five years or less, provided none of the following conditions exists:

1. Rents from the leases with terms of more than five years equal 50% or more of the total rents obtained from the property.
2. The area occupied under leases with terms of more than five years is, at any time during the year, 50% or more of the total area rented at such a time.
3. Rents from a tenant under a lease with a term of more than five years equal more than 10% of the total rents from the premises during the year.
4. The area occupied by a tenant under a lease with a term of more than five years equals, at any time during the year, more than 10% of the total area rented at such a time.

For purposes of conditions 1 and 2, the "Section 514 term" does not include the "tacking on" of successive one-year leases under Section 514(b)(2)(B); the "tacking on" does apply, however, for conditions 3 and 4. For purposes of conditions 1 and 2, if during the last half of the term of a lease of five years or less a new lease is made which is to become effective at the end of the old lease, the unexpired term of the old lease is not added to the term of the new lease to determine whether the new lease has a term of more than five years. This relief provision does not apply if the new lease is made pursuant to an option contained in the old lease.

(c) BUSINESS LEASE INDEBTEDNESS

The second requirement for taxability of rents as unrelated business income is that "business lease indebtedness" exist. This term means an unpaid indebtedness incurred by the lessor under any of the three following circumstances:

1. Incurred in acquiring or improving the property which is the subject of a business lease.
2. Incurred before the acquisition or improvement of the property if the indebtedness would not have been incurred had the trust not acquired or improved the property.

   Example: An exempt trust borrowed funds from a bank in 1967 by pledging certain of its securities. In 1968 it used the funds to purchase an office building. The office building is leased under ten-year leases. The indebtedness is business lease indebtedness.

3. Incurred after the acquisition or improvement of the property if the indebtedness would not have been incurred had the trust not acquired or improved the property and if, at the time the property was acquired or improved, the incurrence of the indebtedness was foreseeable.

   Example: An exempt trust purchased an office building in 1967 for cash. In 1968, in order to replenish its cash so that it could continue to pay out pension benefits, it borrowed funds from a bank by pledging certain of its securities. At the time of the acquisition, the trust knew that it would be necessary to replenish its cash in the next year by borrowing. The indebtedness is business lease indebtedness.

If the property is acquired by the trust subject to a lien (mortgage, etc.), the indebtedness secured by the lien is business lease indebtedness. This rule applies even though the trust does not assume or agree to pay the indebtedness. It applies regardless of how the property was acquired; purchase, gift, bequest, devise, or contribution by an employer. Insofar as a Section 401(a) trust is concerned, it does not apply to indebtedness incurred prior to March 1, 1954 in respect of property which was leased prior to that date. Neither does it apply to indebtedness which was incurred on or after March 1, 1954 and which was necessary to carry out the terms of a lease which was in effect before that date. These two exceptions also apply to a title holding company. [Sec. 501(c)(2)] which was wholly owned by the trust prior to March 1, 1954.

Example: In 1953 an exempt trust purchased an office building subject to a $100,000 mortgage. The building was leased for the period 1945-1964 to an insurance company. Under the terms of the lease, the lessor was required to install an additional elevator not later than 1958. In 1957 the trust borrowed $20,000 and installed the elevator. Neither the $100,000 mortgage nor the $20,000 is considered to be business lease indebtedness.

An employer may have two or more Section 401(a) trusts. If a trust lends money to a brother trust, the loan will not be considered indebtedness of the borrowing trust except to the extent that the lending trust borrowed money to make the loan. The same rules apply to the lending trust, with regard to borrowing before or after the loan to the brother, as apply under Section 514(c)(1). If the loan is indebtedness of the borrowing trust, it is business lease indebtedness if used for the acquisition or improvement of property subject to a business lease. [Regs. 1.514(c)-1(h).]

Example: Trust A, created under an hourly pension plan, and Trust B, created under a salaried pension plan, are brother trusts related to one employer. Trust A borrowed $100,000 from a bank by pledging certain of its securities. Trust A loaned $150,000 to Trust B, which amount consisted of the $100,000 borrowed plus $50,000 of its own funds. Trust B purchased an office building subject to a business lease, using $150,000 which it borrowed from Trust A plus $125,000 of its own cash. The business lease indebtedness of Trust B is $100,000.

The above rules also apply to supplemental unemployment benefit trusts exempt under Section 501(e)(17) for taxable years beginning after December 31, 1959.

(d) PERSONAL PROPERTY LEASED WITH REAL PROPERTY

When used in Section 514, the terms "real property" and "premises" include personal property if leased in connection with the lease of real property.

Funding Media

GENERAL STATEMENT

In pension planning, the first major step is to decide the extent of retirement benefits to be made available to employees. The next step is to determine how the funds will be provided to pay the pension benefits. This chapter considers some of the more common media of funding pension benefits.

UNFUNDED PLANS

The unfunded plan is one under which the benefits are paid from current income as they accrue ("pay-as-you-go method") or from accounting provisions previously made to meet the liability for the benefits. The preferential tax treatment of Sections 401 through 404 does not apply to an unfunded plan. The employer is entitled to a deduction only when the benefits are paid to the beneficiary.

TERMINAL FUNDING

Terminal funding represents a compromise between an unfunded plan and a funded plan. In general, the benefits credited to active employees are entirely unfunded, while the benefits payable to retired employees are entirely funded. The employer funds the benefits upon retirement of an employee by the purchase of an annuity or by the transfer to a trust of an amount actuarially determined to be sufficient to provide the benefit payout. The compromise may be further compromised, as, for example, in the seven-year plan under which the plan is unfunded as to a participant until he reaches an age which is seven years from his retirement date. He is then fully funded over the seven-year period. The employer is entitled to a tax deduction, within the limitations of Section 404(a), when funds are transferred to the insurance company or the trust. [P.S. No. 67.] Terminal funding is sometimes used in union-negotiated plans.

FUNDED PLANS

TRUSTEED PLAN. A pension plan may be funded through the medium of a trust. The employer pays contributions to the trust, which may invest in stocks, bonds, other intangible assets or tangible assets (an invested trust) or insurance contracts (an insured trust), in accordance with the trust agreement. If no insurance is involved, the benefits are paid directly to the retired employees from the general assets of the trust and the plan is operated under the supervision of an actuary. If insurance is involved, the trustee usually purchases individual annuity contracts (which may or may not contain life insurance) for the individual for the amount of benefit provided by the plan. The policies are held by the trustee until retirement. The plan may be self-administered (run by an administrative committee appointed by the company) with a bank, a trust company, or even an individual or individuals as trustee; or it may be jointly administered by the company and union representatives, or may even be union-administered with the same choice as to the trustee or trustees being a bank, trust company, etc.

POOLED INVESTMENT TRUST. A trusteed plan usually offers more flexibility than an insured plan. (See, for example, the discussion of trust investments beginning on page 239.) The small employer, however, may find that the trust which he creates is uneconomical to administer and too limited to permit proper diversification of investments. Pooled pension trust fund arrangements are maintained by some banks and others to overcome the limitations of the small trust.

Under the pooling arrangement, the contributions are transferred from the employees' trust to the pooled trust fund maintained by the bank or other party. The commingled funds of all small employers under the arrangement are invested as one fund. The small employer through the pooling mechanics obtains the advantages which accrue to the large employer in terms of diversification, yield, growth, liquidity, and investment management.

Periodically, a separate accounting is made to each participating trust as to its share in the total assets, the income, etc. of the pool.

While the pooled investment trust overcomes the handicaps carried by the small employer in the areas of administration and investment, the pooled concept does not solve the problem of unfavorable mortality. Mortality experience is not pooled under this plan. The insured plan may offer protection in this area, although many modern insurance contracts provide fiduciary services only, thus taking on the total appearance of a trusteed plan. These types of insurance contracts are normally made available to only the very large plans.

NONTRUSTEED PLAN. The following types of nontrusteed plans involve insurance contracts:

1. *Deposit administration plan.* A group plan whereby employer contributions are paid to and held as a fund by the insurance company and not initially allocated to the accounts of the employees. When an employee retires, his

annuity is purchased from the fund in accordance with the provisions of the plan. The insurance company guarantees the interest rate and premium rate for a specific period — usually five years. The employer assumes the risk of pre-retirement mortality. Contributions are determined by an actuary. This type of plan has some of the flexibility of a trusteed plan. Dividends, if any, are unilaterally determined by the insurer. A variation of the deposit administration plan is the "IPG plan." In this plan the insurance company pays the benefits from the fund instead of purchasing the annuity. The employer assumes all mortality risks. The insurance company does not guarantee a rate of return on the fund, but does credit to it an earnings credit based on the earnings rate of its total portfolio. The insurance company would normally buy annuities for retired employees if the plan is terminated or if another insurance company is selected to administer the plan.

2. *Group annuity plan.* An old-type plan, not extensively installed currently, under which contributions in the form of premiums are paid to an insurance company and which is similar to the deposit administration plan except that paid-up units are purchased each year for each employee covered by the plan. The units mature at the retirement date and the retirement income is the total of all units purchased while the employee was covered. A contract exists between the company and the insurance company under which the plan is underwritten and administered. The purpose of the plan is to cover a large number of employees and so an employee minimum is required (in some cases, as few as ten). Premium rates are usually guaranteed for five years.

3. *Group permanent plan.* A plan which combines group life insurance with group annuities into one contract with a level basis premium. The group life accumulates a cash value (unlike regular group term life insurance) which can be converted to an annuity upon retirement of the employee. During working years the employee is protected by life insurance. During retirement years the annuity is operative. The insurance protection feature must adhere to the "100 to 1" rule (see page 19).

The principles of group underwriting and administration are used. The trustee is replaced by the insurer.

4. *Individual annuity plan.* An employer may purchase a nontransferable individual annuity contract in the name of each participant. This plan operates independently of the principles of group underwriting and consequently may be more costly than a group annuity. On the other hand, it is available to the small employer who does not have enough employees to qualify for group underwriting.

While the individual annuity contract may be used in the nontrusteed plan, generally it is used in the trusteed plan or the custodial account plan. In the latter case, the contract need not be nontransferable because it is controlled by the third party. If an individual retirement income contract is purchased, a trust must be employed. [Rev. Rul. 56-673.]

COMBINATION PLANS. The various types of insured plans and the features of the insured plan and the trusteed plan are used in many combinations to provide the employer with the mixture of flexibility and security which he seeks. Combination plans commonly seen are as follows:

1. "Split funding" means that a portion of the assets is invested in annuity or life insurance contracts and the remainder is invested through a bank, a mutual fund, or other type of investment institution.
2. Group annuities are mixed with individual annuities. The former may provide for current service and the latter for past service. Alternatively, the group annuities may cover lower-paid employees (to reduce turnover administration) while individual annuities cover the higher-paid employees.
3. A self-administered trust may invest solely in annuity contracts. This is not quite an anomaly. The trust transfers the total risk to the insurance company but retains the functions of premium payment, record keeping, etc. The trust acts as an administrative buffer between the employer and the insurer.

SPECIAL FUNDING METHODS. Under the Self-Employed Individuals Tax Retirement Act of 1962, any qualified retirement plan may depart from traditional methods and fund the plan through the following types of investments:

1. Shares in an "open end" regulated investment company through a custodial account in a bank.
2. Annuity, endowment, or life insurance contracts through a custodial account in a bank.
3. Face-amount certificates, regardless of whether a trust is created.
4. Specially designed U.S. bonds, purchased either by the trust under the plan or directly by the employer.

These funding methods are encumbered by certain restrictions and should be carefully examined before being employed. (See the chapter on qualified bond purchase plans on page 99, and also the chapter on retirement plans for the self-employed beginning on page 115.)

Investment of Trust Funds

GENERAL STATEMENT

There is almost an infinite number of ways of investing employee benefit funds held by an exempt trust. The investment patterns vary somewhat depending upon whether the exempt trust is part of a plan for pensions or for profit sharing. Generally speaking, pension trust funds place greater emphasis upon safety and liquidity because specific beneefits must be paid out of the trust fund upon the retirement of participants under the plan. On the other hand, there are no specific payout requirements under a profit-sharing plan; consequently, conservation is replaced to some degree by the desire for fund growth.

As economic conditions and retirement philosophies evolve, the trends of trust investment change. It was once thought that pension and profit-sharing funds should be invested in government bonds and the fixed obligations of financially solid public corporations with yields of 2½% to 3%. The primary considerations in this philosophy of investing were safety of principal, assurance of yield, and liquidity. This philosophy de-emphasizes capital appreciation through speculation. As retirement trusts moved away from this investment pattern, trust funds were invested in preferred stocks and then in common stocks. A further movement shifted the investments from "blue chip" corporations to those corporations which offered greater growth possibilities. The investment program of the fund, however, maintained a balance between conservatism and the new-found liberalism.

Of late years, surveys show that trust funds are being placed in such investments as mortgages, mutual funds, savings and loan associations, real estate, leasebacks, personal property, real estate investment trusts, and mineral production royalties.

This chapter concerns itself with the restrictions placed upon the investment program of exempt trusts, transactions between the employer and the trust, and some of the more sophisticated investment patterns found in the present pension society.

TRUSTEE RESTRICTIONS

Pension trusts are subject to the same local laws as are other trusts. Local law must be examined for restrictions on the investment policies of trusts. While some states may limit trustees to investing in government securities and a select list of corporate securities, many states have varieties of the "prudent man" rule which permit trustees to invest trusteed funds as though they were dealing with their own funds and seeking a reasonable income coupled with conservation of capital.

The trust instrument may override local law. If a specific investment policy is laid down in the instrument, the trustee may follow that policy regardless of the fact that it runs contrary to local law, provided the policy does not do violence to the public good. For example, the trustee, even though expressly authorized by a liberal trust instrument, may not invest, without reproach, in a marijuana plantation. And the instrument must be specific as to each instance in which local law is suppressed. Authorization to override local law in one area does not permit similar action in another area. If the instrument is silent as to a specific action, the trustee will be governed by local law.

Conversely, the trust instrument may prohibit investments which are allowed under local law. Consequently, both local law and the trust instrument must be examined.

If local law or the provisions of the trust instrument are violated, the trust itself may be held not to be a part of a qualified plan. [P.S. No. 49; Rev. Rul. 65-178 Part 2(k)(1); Rev. Proc. 67-4, Sec. 3.03.] As a consequence, the employer's deduction will be threatened, the trust income will be taxed, and the employees may be required to pay tax on the employer's contribution to the extent of any nonforfeitable interests.

TAX RESTRICTIONS

The Internal Revenue Code does not specifically place any limitations upon the investments which may be made by an employees' trust. [Regs. 1.401-1(b)(5).] The Code, does, however, contain a number of provisions which work indirectly to limit the investment policy of an employees' trust, and the Commissioner's regulations and rulings have added further limitations.

The statutory provisions which have a limiting effect can be classified as follows:

1. *The "benefit" test.* The first condition to be met under Section 401 for qualification of a plan is that the plan must be for the exclusive benefit of the employees or their beneficiaries.
2. *The "prohibited transaction" test.* The pension receives its tax-exempt status through Section 501 of the Code.

Section 503 denies an exemption to pension trusts which engaged in certain enumerated transactions, directly or indirectly, between the creator of a trust and the trust. (See page 205.)

3. *The "unrelated business taxable income" test.* Section 511 imposes a tax on the income of a pension trust which qualifies as unrelated business taxable income. (See page 217.)

BENEFIT TEST. The benefit provision does not place, in itself, any limitation upon the investment policy of the pension trust but it does provide the general language from which the Commissioner has devised limitations in his regulations and rulings. The provision merely states that any investment made by the trustee must be made for the exclusive benefit of the participants under the pension plan. It does not provide that a third party cannot benefit from the investment. Its spirit is, however, that the transaction be at arm's-length, that it provide for a fair purchase price and a fair rate of return, and that it not endanger the proper liquidity of the trust. Generally, if the appropriate state law governing the action of trustees is complied with, the trustee will be above criticism for his investments. If the transaction violates the benefit test, the plan may cease to be a qualified plan under Section 401 and thereby forfeit the tax advantages of the qualified plan to the employer and employee.

PROHIBITED TRANSACTION TEST. While the prohibited transaction limitation applies to a number of tax-exempt organizations, only the following four of the six categories of transactions outlined in Section 503 have application to the pension trust:

1. Lending money without adequate security and/or a reasonable rate of interest.
2. Purchasing securities or other property for more than adequate consideration.
3. Selling securities or other property for less than adequate consideration.
4. Entering into any other transaction which results in a substantial diversion of trust income or corpus.

Any of the above transactions are considered prohibited by Section 503 only if they are entered into with what is called a "tainted person." In general terms, a "tainted person" is one who is related, directly or indirectly, to the trust. Section 503 sets forth explicit definitions of "tainted persons" and reference should be made to those definitions if the transaction is between any related person other than the creator of the trust. The creator of an employee trust is generally the employer. The creator is always a "tainted person." (See page 207.)

If the person is not a "tainted person," one of the above transactions may be consummated without danger of being labeled a prohibited transaction. It must be remembered, however, that the four transactions outlined above are not usually considered arm's-length transactions. A trustee who is bold enough to enter into such a transaction, even though safe from the prohibited transaction limitation, flouts danger in two other areas: He may violate the fiduciary duties entrusted to him by local law or he may fail the benefit test mentioned earlier.

The loss of exemption to the trust need not be a permanent loss. Procedures are available by which the exemption may be recaptured, but the procedures are so designed that the exemption will be lost for at least one taxable year of the trust. Obviously, Section 503 is an effective limitation on the investment policies of a pension trust.

UNRELATED BUSINESS TAXABLE INCOME TEST. Section 513 provides that any trade or business carried on by a pension trust is an unrelated trade or business. It is immaterial that the trade or business may provide income which, in turn, serves to provide greater retirement benefits to the participants under the pension plan. For the purposes of this limitation, the term "trade or business" has the same meaning as it has under Section 162 of the Code. Excluded from the definition of unrelated business taxable income is income of a type which is usually thought of as an investment income — dividends, interest, annuities, royalties, capital gains and losses, and certain rents. The purpose of this provision is to prevent the profits of a trade or business from escaping taxation merely because the trade or business is operated by a tax-exempt trust. (See page 223.)

If a pension trust has unrelated business taxable income (defined as gross income less related deductions), such income is taxed at the rates applicable to individuals, but no deduction for personal exemption is allowed. However, the first $1,000 of unrelated business income is exempt from tax.

Ordinary rents from real property are not included within the definition of unrelated business taxable income. However, net income from so-called "business leases" is included within the definition. Section 514 defines "business leases" and prescribes the rather complex rules under which the taxable income is computed. (See page 227.) Defined broadly, a business lease is one which leases, for a period of more than five years, real property which is subject to indebtedness at the end of the taxable year. The business lease provisions do not apply to personal property unless it is leased in connection with real property. Again with a broad brush: The portion of net rental income which is included in unrelated business taxable income is determined by applying to the total the ratio of business lease indebtedness to adjusted basis of the property at year-end.

INVESTMENT IN EMPLOYER STOCK

It is not uncommon for an employees' trust to invest in the stock of the employer. Instances can be pointed out in which the trust acquired all or substantially all of the employer's stock. An investment in company stock can be made if the benefit and prohibited-transaction tests are met. The unrelated business taxable income test does not apply because income from such an investment (i.e., dividends) is excluded from the definition of unrelated business taxable income.

The trust must pass the first test by showing that the investment is for the exclusive benefit of the employees covered by the plan. This requirement, however, does not prevent others from also deriving some benefit from a transaction with the trust. For example, a sale of securities at a profit benefits the seller, which may be an employer, but if the purchase price is not in excess of the fair market value of the securities at the time of sale and the applicable investment requisites have been met, the investment is consistent with the exclusive-benefit-of-employees requirement. These requisites are: (1) the cost must not exceed fair market value at the time of purchase, (2) a fair return commensurate with the prevailing rate must be provided, (3) sufficient liquidity must be maintained to permit distributions in accordance with the terms of the plan, and (4) the safeguards and diversities that a prudent investor would adhere to must be present. Upon compliance with these requisites, if the trust instrument and local law permit investments in the stock or securities of the employer, such investments are not deemed to be inconsistent with the purpose of Section 401(a). [Rev. Rul. 65-178, Parts 2(k)(1).]

The second test may require the trust to prove to the Commissioner that the transaction was arm's-length in that the purchase price was right, the rate of return was properly considered, and the quality of the investment was taken into consideration. Under either test the trust may borrow funds to make the purchase. The District Director, however, is to be notified if trust funds are invested in stock or securities of, or loaned to, the employer or a related or controlled interest, so that a determination may be made whether the trust serves any purpose other than constituting part of a plan for the exclusive benefit of the employees. Such notification is to be made as a part of the annual Information Return, Form 990-P, unless an advance determination letter is requested and, if so, at the time of making a request to the appropriate District Director of Internal Revenue for such letter. [Rev. Rul. 65-178, Part 2(k)(1).]

These two tests, while stated separately in the law (one applies only to pension trusts and the other applies also to certain other tax-exempt organizations), have a single purpose: to assure the beneficiaries of the plan the best use of the dollars of the trust which are put out for investment. Given $1 of funds for investment, these sections require that the trust put that $1 to work in the most advantageous manner and reap the most benefit for the employees. If the best place to invest the money is in company stock, these sections will permit such an investment. However, the plan may lose its qualification or the trust its exemption, or both, if the Commissioner finds that the transaction serves some interest other than that of the employees. Consequently, an extremely dangerous situation exists if the transaction has a purpose such as buying out a troublesome stockholder, providing liquidity for the estate of a deceased shareholder, shifting control between shareholders, bolstering a market, or providing a new market for the shares. While such transactions are not fatal *per se*, they at least are symptoms of a fatal purpose.

No-DIVIDEND STOCK. Investment in closely-held corporate employer stock which has no history of dividend payments and, perhaps, little prospect of dividend payments in the foreseeable future requires careful consideration. The Revenue Service may be reluctant to approve such an investment without a clear showing that growth income is inherent in the stock. Investment yield can be in the form of dividend income or capital gains or both. The trustee must convince the Revenue Service that the best interests of the participants are served by the particular form of investment.

The exclusive-benefit test presumably is met if the no-dividend stock is purchased by a trustee upon direction given by each participant involved. Accordingly, only the electing participants would benefit from an increase in the stock's value or bear a loss for a decrease. Provision for such earmarked investments should be made a part of the plan and trust agreement. [Rev. Rul. 65-178, Part 5(r).]

INFORMATION. The investment must be reported to the Commissioner so that a determination can be made whether the best interests of the employees were served by the purchase. The information which must be reported [Rev. Proc. 67-4] is as follows:

1. Balance sheets of the employer for the last two taxable years, comparative income statement for the last five years, and an analysis of the surplus account for the last five years, specifically setting forth the amount and rate of dividends paid.
2. A statement which accounts for all material changes in the financial statements from the end of the last taxable year to the date of filing the information.
3. A statement of the trust assets.
4. A statement concerning the investment—covering amount, type, present rate of return, security if a loan is involved, and the reason for the investment.

The required information must be filed by the trust with its annual Form 990-P if the transaction has been consummated, or with a request for determination if one is sought before consummation. It is considered prudent to obtain a determination from the Commissioner prior to the time the transaction is consummated.

LOANS TO EMPLOYER COMPANY

Section 503 provides that lending money without adequate security and/or without reasonable interest is a prohibited transaction. This type of transaction usually occurs only if the loan is made to the employer or a person related to the employer. The determination of a reasonable rate of interest may not be as difficult as the determination of what is adequate security. The Commissioner's regulations define the term "adequate security" as something in addition to and supporting a promise to pay. It is something which can be disposed of in the event of loan default, and its value and liquidity can be recognized. It takes such forms as mortgages, liens, corporate securities, and accommodation endorsements.

At one end is the loan secured in an unquestionably adequate way. At the other end is the unsecured demand note. The former clearly is not a prohibited transaction. The latter clearly is. Between these two ends appear the many types of employer obligations which require careful study before being categorized as prohibited or not. The purchase of an employer debenture may be a prohibited transaction even though the purchase is made from an outsider in an arm's-length transaction; however, the harshness of this rule is alleviated by the following qualification. The purchase of the debenture will not be considered a loan without adequate consideration if acquired in an arm's-length transaction and if, after the purchase, the trust owns not more than 25% of the issue outstanding when purchased, at least 50% of the issue outstanding is owned by independent third parties, and not more than 25% of the trust's assets are invested in the obligations of a "tainted person." The term "arm's-length transaction" is defined in Section 503(h). (See page 205.)

As in the case of investment in company stock, loans to an employer are limitied by the prohibited transaction test and the benefit test. If it is apparent that loans are to be made because the employer is unable to borrow elsewhere, danger is inherent in the transaction.

PURCHASE AND LEASE OF REAL PROPERTY

The purchase of real property and the subsequent lease of the property to the employer is a common occurrence. The transaction may take the form of a purchase and leaseback. As with all investments of the trust, the benefit test must be passed. In addition, the rentals must be neither too low nor too high. If the former, the investment is not in the best interests of the employees; if the latter, the excessive rent might be considered an additional contribution to the trust by the employer subject to the statutory limitations for contributions set forth in Section 404.

Another danger exists if the transaction with the employer takes the form of a purchase and leaseback. Particular care must be given to providing an arm's-length purchase price. If the purchase results in a gain to the employer, the gain will be recognized. A loss, however, will not be recognized because Section 267(b) prevents the recognition of loss in a transaction between an employer and an employees' trust.

This danger may be avoided if the employer transfers the property to the trust as a contribution under Section 404 for the purpose of funding the benefits under the plan. The amount of the contribution is the fair market value of the asset at the time of the transfer and, while the contribution might be in excess of the amount deductible under Section 404 in the year of the contribution, it probably can be absorbed in subsequent years through the contribution carryover provisions contained in Section 404(a)(1)(D). If this plan is adopted, it is preferable that newly acquired property be transferred because its fair market value is established. No gain or loss can then result to the employer, since the tax basis to the employer and the value upon transfer are presumably equal.

The two methods, purchase with leaseback and contribution with leaseback, may give the employer identical financing benefits. Under the former, he increases working capital by converting a fixed asset into cash. Under the latter, he retains cash he would otherwise expend for funding contributions.

Still a third danger lies in the unrelated business income test. While rents are ordinarily excluded from the definition of unrelated business income, net rents received under business leases are included. If the trust borrows money to acquire or improve the property, if it acquires property subject to a mortgage, and if it borrows money before or after the acquisition or improvement of the property and such indebtedness would not have been necessary if the acquisition or improvement had not transpired, the trust probably will lose its tax-exempt status as to all or a portion of the net rents from the real property. While the purchase and lease of real property represents the easiest and commonest method by which the employer can make use of the trust funds, care must be used in shaping the transaction because all three of the tests have application.

PURCHASE AND LEASE OF PERSONAL PROPERTY

Can a pension trust purchase personal property, either from an outsider or from the employer, and lease it to the employer? As in the case of purchase and lease of real property, the benefit test and the prohibited-transaction test can probably be passed if the transaction is truly at arm's length. The third test, however, presents the hurdle. Does the leasing of personal property constitute engaging in a business? The Revenue Service believes that it does. The question does not arise where real property is leased because Section 512 excludes from unrelated business taxable income rents from real property except as they might come from "business leases." Section 512 is silent as to rents from personal property leased separately from real estate. The point is important because pension trusts are increasingly viewing this type of investment with interest. If the profits from such leasing are taxed to the trust, the investment may lose its savor. On the other hand, a taxable transaction, properly structured with accelerated depreciation, investment credit, etc., may present a favorable investment.

INTANGIBLE ASSETS

The trust may purchase trademarks, trade names, patents, and intangible assets of similar nature. Royalty income received is generally classified as passive investment income and not unrelated business taxable income. Transaction between the trust and the employer may be handled successfuly within the limits of the benefit test and the prohibited transaction test.

MINERAL ROYALTIES

Employee retirement trusts invest in producing oil and gas royalties and other mineral royalties. The term "royalty" as used in the oil and gas business denotes the ownership of a definite share in the oil or gas and the revenue derived from its production from a specific piece of land. Generally, the royalty interest is a one-eighth interest although it may be a different fraction. The owner of the royalty interest bears no part of the exploration or drilling costs on the lease. He receives a percentage of the gross revenue free of all drilling and operating expenses. His interest runs in perpetuity. The working interest is retained by the lessee of the oil or gas lease and he has the responsibility for producing the mineral.

The producing oil and gas royalty interest is of interest to some pension funds for the following reasons:

1. A typical royalty interest has an average life in excess of 20 years. The cash flow from the royalty is realized monthly, spread over its productive life. Consequently, the oil or gas royalty interest is a partial solution to the constant reinvestment problem of the trustee.

2. The yield from a royalty interest is normally higher than the yield average from alternative investments. The royalty yield is generally expressed in what is called a "discount rate of return" which is that interest rate which will reduce the total income over the life of the property to equal the initial cash outlay.

   Example: If a royalty that cost $1,000,000 had a producing life of 25 years and yielded $2,750,000 over its productive life, the rate of return would be that interest rate which discounted $2,750,000 to its present-day value of $1,000,000 — in this case, approximately 11% p.a.

3. Income from a producing oil and gas royalty interest is passive investment income to the retirement trust (see page 220). Because of this tax-free status, the retirement trust is able to pay more for a royalty interest than a party

who must take into account his tax liability in computing his expected yield. In making the comparison, it must be noted that the retirement trust is not allowed a deduction for percentage depletion, while the taxable party may claim percentage depletion.

4. The royalty interest is a relatively liquid asset. In general, the demand for royalty interests is high and the retirement trust can dispose of the interest without great difficulty.

REAL ESTATE VENTURES

As fund managers seek higher yields and broader investment diversification, the acquisition of real estate and mortgages as investments for pension trusts becomes more substantial. The form which the investment may take ranges from acquisition of raw land to the construction and ownership of entire towns. The record made by major U.S. corporations in this area indicates the extent to which pension trusts may be employed. Some of the units which have been brought into existence through employee trust funds are imaginative new towns, urban redevelopment, single-structure office buildings, shopping centers, and motels. The size of the fund dictates the practical participation that a particular fund might undertake. The larger fund may be capable of carrying the entire project. The smaller fund might be able to handle only a small portion of the total project. For example, in the construction of a shopping center, one fund may acquire the land. Another fund may carry the structures. If the participating funds are very small, a joint venture between several funds may be required to finance the land or the structures. Alternatively, one fund may finance the construction within the shopping center of the theatre, a second fund may finance the bowling alleys and other funds may finance the retail store buildings.

Some of the activities of the retirement trust in this area may bring it into contact with the unrelated business taxable income provisions of Section 512. Many pension trusts have been proceeded regardless of this fact because it has been found that, even with the penalty of Section 512, investment in real estate ventures can be beneficial to the employee participants under the plan. A sophisticated approach to the structuring of the transaction is a responsibility of the trustee of the plan.

BOOTSTRAP ACQUISITIONS

A bootstrap acquisition is one in which the cash flow from the acquired asset is sufficient to provide the amortization of a debt financed purchase price. In a taxable situation the cash flow is impeded by income taxes.

The use of a tax exempt organization such as the employees' trust accelerates the cash flow by removing the income tax feature. Such a bootstrap acquisition is revealed in *Commissioner v. Brown*, 380 U.S. 563 (1965). The situation in that case (somewhat modified for purposes of illustration) may be summarized as follows:

Clay Brown owned the stock of Clay Brown and Company, with sawmills and lumber interests. He sold his stock to a charity, California Institute for Cancer Research, which was exempt under Section 501(c) for $1,300,000, payable $5,000 down and the balance within ten years from the earnings of the company's assets.

Simultaneously with the acquisition of the stock, the Institute liquidated the company and leased the assets to a new corporation, Fortuna Sawmills, Inc., which was formed and wholly owned by the attorneys for Clay Brown. While Clay Brown was neither a stockholder nor a director in Fortuna, he had a management contract with Fortuna at an annual salary and the right to name any successor manager if he resigned.

Fortuna paid to the Institute 80% of its operating profit without allowance for depreciation, and 90% of such payments were paid by the Institute to Clay Brown to apply on the note. The note was non-interest-bearing and the Institute had no obligation to pay on the note other than from the rental income which it received from Fortuna.

The issue before the Supreme Court was whether the receipt of payments by Clay Brown was capital gain or ordinary income. The Commissioner contended that such payments constituted ordinary income. The Court held that the payments were taxable as capital gain.

Looking beyond the issue before the Court, the framework of the bootstrap acquisition can be seen:

1. The Institute was exempt from taxation under Section 501(c) except for any unrelated business taxable income under Section 512.
2. The Institute immediately liquidated the corporation and leased the assets to Fortuna, a corporation which was un-

related to the Institute, the former corporation, or Clay Brown. This action structured an arm's-length relationship for future steps in the transaction.

3. The lease of the assets to Fortuna for a five-year term was the first step in accelerating the cash flow. The Institute could have held the stock in Clay Brown and Company and received its income in the form of dividends. The dividends would not have been taxable to the Institute. The corporation, however, would have been taxed on its profits, thus cutting in half the amount available for dividend payments. The Institute leased the assets. The rental income from the lease was not taxed to the Institute—it was income from a lease of real and personal property and thus was not unrelated business taxable income. There was no business indebtedness as contemplated by Section 514 because the term of the lease was only five years. The Institute had put itself in a position to receive tax-free income from the lease. The next step was to make that income as much as possible.

4. Fortuna's rental payment formula eliminated any erosion from income taxes. When it paid over 80% of its operating profit before depreciation, it was entitled to a deduction for rent expense. The remaining 20% of operating profit was subsequently eliminated by its depreciation deduction. No income taxes were paid.

5. The Institute received in the form of rental income 80% of Fortuna's pretax earnings. Fortuna retained 20% to replace its depreciable property. The Institute paid over 90% of the 80% to Clay Brown to be taxed to him as a capital gain.

6. The flow of pretax earnings of the lumber business was this:

   a. 20% retained in the depreciation reserve of Fortuna.
   b. 7.2% retained by the Institute for its role in arranging the transaction.
   c. 72.8% to Clay Brown to be taxed as capital gain.

7. After the obligation to Clay Brown was discharged, the Institute was entitled to the full 80% of Fortuna's operating profit.

The Clay Brown type of transaction can be adapted to the exempt employees' trust as an investment device. It must be noted however, that the Internal Revenue Service is seeking ways and means to prevent the spread of the use of the transaction. Legislation has been introduced which, if adopted, will change the unrelated business taxable income provisions of Section 512 and the business lease provisions of Section 514 in such manner as to remove the attractive tax benefits from the transaction. (H.R. 12663.)

EARMARKED FUNDS

The investment of employee retirement funds does not have to be an activity far beyond the understanding and influence of the employee. Some retirement plans provide means for the employee to play a role in providing for his own retirement by letting him choose the investment media for his share, or a portion of his share, of the employer contribution. An example of this sharing of the trustee duties is the plan which provides for three funds:

1. *Fund A.* This fund is used to provide for a basic retirement program for the employee. The Fund A monies are prudently invested by the trustee and the employee does not direct or authorize any investments within this fund. In a pension plan, the largest portion of the employer's contribution will flow to this fund.

2. *Fund B.* The smaller portion of the employer contribution flows to Fund B or Fund C. If the employee elects Fund B, he is furnished with a list of investments and is advised periodically of the progress of his portion of the fund. The list of investments might include blue-chip and less seasoned equities, mortgages, and investment of moderate speculation.

3. *Fund C.* The election of this fund introduces the employee to speculative investments. It is in the nature of a special-situation fund. It might include leasebacks, land speculation, new industries, joint ventures with the employer, etc.

Earmark funding has many variations, depending upon the type of retirement plan (it is more suited to profit-sharing plans than pension plans because of the fixed payout of the latter), the size of the plan (it is easier to manage in a smaller plan), and the degree of interest of the employer in involving his employees in the investment aspect of the fund. For example, in a profit-sharing plan the employee may have an election under which all of his share of the employer contribution goes into Fund C and the trustee is given an absolute direction to invest in the employer's stock. Under appropriate circumstances such an action will be beneficial to the employee (he becomes a proprietor) and the employer (as a source of financing). [See Technical Advice Memo., January 17, 1968, *Prentice-Hall Pension and Profit-Sharing Service*, 11,983.] Another variation would be to divide Fund B into investment areas and permit the employee a choice between equities, mortgages, etc. Alternatively, the employee may have complete freedom to direct the trustee in all investments as to his share.

Investments made through earmarked funds require segregated accounting within the trust so that the participant benefits or loses from his own actions. [Rev. Rul. 65-178, Part 5(r).]

Integration Rules

IN GENERAL

Adjusting a plan so that, when supplemented by social security, it is not discriminatory in favor of officers, stockholders, supervisory employees, or highly compensated employees is known as "integrating" the plan with social security. Various formulas for such integration have been approved by the Treasury Department. [Mim. 5539; Mim. 6641; T.D. 6447; Rev. Rul. 60-337; Rev. Rul. 61-75; Rev. Rul. 62-152; Rev. Rul. 65-178, Part 4(j).] If a plan covers an owner-employee (see page 115), the integration rules are different, in that it is the social security contributions which enter into the computations rather than the benefits. The following comments relate to plans which do not cover any self-employed persons.

Plans properly integrated at $3,000, $3,600, or $4,200 are not required to make any change.

Where the plan excludes employees earning not more than $4,800 per year, or where the first $4,800 of employees' compensation is treated differently from the compensation in excess of such amount, the test of discrimination is whether the relative or proportionate differences in benefits are offset by the Social Security Act retirement benefits which are not attributable to the employees' contributions.

INTERIM GUIDES, 1965 AND 1967 SOCIAL SECURITY AMENDMENTS

1967 amendments increased the social security wage base to $7,800. The Revenue Service has issued proposed regulations and a draft of a proposed revenue ruling describing and explaining new integration rules to reflect this increase and the new integration percentage of 30%. [Prop. Regs. 1.401-3, 1.401-11, and 1.401-12; Treas. Dept. Release F-1297.] (But see page 262.)

1965 amendments had increased the wage base to $6,600. The Revenue Service, however, will accept plans which integrate under existing rules pending the issuance of new regulations. Thus, new plans integrated at $4,800 are allowed to provide a retirement benefit of up to 37.5% of average earnings, and plans integrated at $6,600 are allowed to provide benefits of up to 27.27%. [Rev. Rul. 67-10.] See example on page 261.

The integration percentage for a profit-sharing plan at the $6,600 level is reduced from 9⅜% to 6.8% as follows: 9⅜% x $4,800 ÷ $6,600 = 6.8%. See example on page 260.

TRANSITIONAL RULES

To enable existing plans to adapt gradually to the proposed standards and the new integration percentage, the proposed regulations contain transitional rules for these plans. The Treasury noted that transitional rules of this nature were not included in the 1966 announcement but have been added as a result of the comments which have been received. Specifically, these transitional rules will permit the following:

— No change will be required in existing plans before January 1, 1971. This will give employers a period of time within which they and their advisors can determine what action, if any, needs to be taken.

— Only benefits accrued for service after December 31, 1970, need conform to the new integration percentage.

— For benefits for service after December 31, 1970, a plan may retain its present integration wage level (i.e., the wage level at which the private plan replaces social security), although this may not technically meet the new standards. For example, if a pension plan presently provides a 37½% pension on wages in excess of $4,800 and no pension on wages below that level, it may, under the proposed rules, continue to integrate at the $4,800 wage level with respect to future benefits (even though social security benefits are now being earned on the first $7,800 of wages rather than $4,800, as was the case prior to 1966). To retain a nondiscriminatory character, it must, however, on or before January 1, 1971, either add a 7½% pension on wages below that level or reduce the rate of benefits on wages above that level, so that the difference is no more than 30% with respect to wages below that level. [Treas. Dept. Release F-1297.]

INTEGRATING A PENSION PLAN

Integration is a process of building a private pension plan upon the foundation of the social security program so that the relative or proportionate differences in benefits for various classes of employees are offset by the social security benefits provided by the employer's contributions. Rules for integrating a pension plan, and examples of computations, are illustrated on pages 260 and 261.

The rules laid down by the Internal Revenue Service are premised on at least two assumptions: (1) that the total amount of social security benefits is equivalent to 150% of the primary benefit, and (2) that the employee contribution pays for 22% of the total monthly benefit. [Regs. 1.401-3(e)(3).] The Revenue Service is presently reconsidering these assumptions.

INTEGRATING A PENSION PLAN

Formula: For a plan which excludes employees making $4,800 or less—

Benefits under plan	Cannot	Social security benefits
Wages over $4,800	exceed	Wages under $4,800

Types of plans to be integrated:

1. Excess plans — Employees earning less than a stated amount are excluded from the plan.
2. Offset plans — All eligible employees are covered but plan benefits are reduced by a percentage of the employees' social security benefits.
3. Step-up plans — All leligible employees are covered but a larger percentage is contributed for over-$4,800 employees than for $4,800-and-under employees.

Integrating the flat benefit $4,800 excess plan:

A. Rules for the plan which excludes employees earning less than $4,800:

1. Normal annual retirement benefit cannot exceed 37½% of average annual compensation in excess of $4,800 for any employee.
2. No death benefit before retirement.
3. Straight life annuity normal form used.
4. Normal retirement benefits for employees who reach normal retirement with less than 15 years' service cannot exceed 2½% of average annual compensation in excess of $4,800 for each year of service.
5. Normal retirement age must be 65 (male) and 60 (female).
6. Actuarial equivalents must be used for early retirement.

B. Computation of 37½%:

Social security benefits —

Maximum monthly compensation
($4,800 ÷ 12) $400
58.85% on first .... 110 = $ 65
21.4% on remainder .... $290 =   62
Primary benefit $127

All benefits considered to be 150% of primary
150% of $127 = $190.50 (total benefit)
$190.50 ÷ $400 = 47.625% of monthly compensation
Portion attributable to employee contribution: 22%
47.625% less 10.48% (22% of 47.625%) = 37½%
(rounded)

Result: A worker covered by social security is assumed to receive a straight life annuity at age 65 of 37½% of his maximum average monthly wage of $400.

C. Illustration:

Abel Corporation has a pension plan which excludes employees earning less than $4,801. Jones retires at age 65 after 20 years' service. His average annual compensation for his highest five consecutive years was $28,000. The maximum annual benefit he can receive under an integrated excess plan is $8,700, computed as follows:

Average earnings	$28,000
Base	4,800
Excess earnings	$23,200
Benefit at 37½%	$ 8,700

D. If the plan contains provisions more favorable than those above numbered A.2 through A.5, the basic limitation of 37½% must be adjusted. Examples:
  1. 33⅓% if a death benefit exists.
  2. 33¾% for an annuity for ten years certain and then life.
  3. 30% for retirement with 12 years' service.

Integrating the offset plan:

A. The limitation is expressed as a percentage (117%) of the primary social security benefit:

Total benefit	$190.50
Less portion due to employee's contribution (22%)	41.91
	$148.59
Limitation ($148 ÷ $127)	117%

B. The plan is integrated by deducting from the plan's benefits an amount not in excess of 117% of the primary social security benefit.

C. The 117% offset plan also requires observance of the excess plan rules A.2 through A.5. More favorable provisions require adjustment of the 117% limitation.

Integrating the step-up plan:

A higher rate is provided for compensation in excess of $4,800, and therefore such amount is integrated under the rules applicable to the excess plan. As to the amount contributed with respect to the first $4,800, this is uniform for all employees and therefore poses no problem.

INTEGRATING A PROFIT-SHARING PLAN

A profit-sharing plan cannot logically be integrated. On the one hand, the social security program provides definitely determinable benefits; on the other, the profit-sharing plan is prohibited from providing definitely determinable benefits.

Notwithstanding the lack of logic, the Internal Revenue Service will approve the integration of a profit-sharing plan provided the following conditions are met:

1. The plan must provide benefits only upon retirement or separation from service.
2. The employer must have no other integrated plan based on the same compensation.
3. All contributions must be allocated on a nondiscriminatory basis with no weighting for service or other factors.
4. The amount of employer contributions plus forfeitures allocated to any participant in any year must not exceed 9⅜% of his actual compensation for the year in excess of $4,800, except that a minimum allocation not exceeding $60 may be provided for each participant in any year that allocations are made. [Rev. Rul. 61-75.] However, a profit-sharing plan may provide death benefits, or benefits upon retirement for disability, subject to the general requirements of Section 401(a). [Rev. Rul. 67-426.]

Illustration:

A Company pays $600,000 compensation to its 84 employees, none of whom receives less than $4,800. The contribution which would yield the maximum advantage to the highly paid is as follows:

Total compensation	$600,000
Exclusion, $4,800 × 84	403,200
Total excess	$196,800
Contribution, 9⅜% of total excess	$ 18,450

Jones, receiving a salary of $25,000, would have a credit of $1,894 ($20,200/$196,800 × $18,450).

Under a nonintegrated plan, a company contribution of $45,452 would have been required to give him a credit of $1,894 ($25,000/$600,000 × $45,452).

If the company had contributed only $18,450 to a nonintegrated plan, Jones's credit would have been $769 ($25,000/$60,000 × $18,450).

If the company had contributed $90,000, the 15% statutory limitation, the excess of $71,550 would be allocated without reference to the social security exclusion.

Jones received 4.167% of the total compensation. He would be credited with $2,981 (4.167% of $71,550). This credit added to his credit from the $18,450 would make his total credit $4,875 or $1,125 more than under a nonintegrated plan.

Under a nonintegrated plan, Jones would have received a credit of $3,750 ($25,000/$600,000 × $90,000).

REGULATIONS ADOPTED NOVEMBER 12, 1968

As this book was going to press, regulations relating to integration were adopted. (See pages 34 and 258.)

The integration rate is lowered from 37½% to 30%. The effective date of the change for existing plans is January 1, 1972. Final regulations permit an employer to keep present funding arrangements intact during the transaction to the new integration percentage.

Business Combinations

GENERAL STATEMENT

As used in this chapter, "business combination" is a generic term which includes such tax-free acquisition patterns as a merger or consolidation [Section 368(a)(1)(A)], an exchange of stock for stock [Section 368(a)(1(B)], and an exchange of stock for assets [Section 368(a)(1)(C)]. It also includes the taxable acquisition of assets or stock for cash or other property.

The term "qualified plan" refers to the employee pension, profit-sharing, and stock bonus plans which are given special tax treatment under Sections 401 to 404 of the Internal Revenue Code as to qualification, taxability, and contributions.

Business combinations affect the tax treatment of qualified plans. The plans of the participating parties may be modified, terminated, or combined. New plans may be activated. Each such step may have an effect upon the tax posture of the participating parties and their employees. Tax planning before the business combination may insure a favorable tax posture after the transaction.

MERGERMAKER'S OVERVIEW

The role of the mergermaker is to take the various elements of the present and rework them into something which, hopefully, will be more acceptable to the future. A further responsibility exists to do as little damage as possible to present bystanders in the conversion processes.

So it is particularly with employee retirement plans. In the beginning there are two groups of employees. (It is assumed that the business combination involves two corporations.) Each group was acquired, employee by employee, at a competitive price set in the marketplace and fashioned into a talent pool which operates under a compensatory package which is absolutely unique. No two compensation programs are alike. Presumably each group is considered to be an asset of the present business that must be preserved through the business combination transition into the business of the future. As the mergermaker looks at the business with which he must work, he might be fairly dazzled by the splendor of the varie-gated forms and methods of qualified plans in existence: Pension and profit-sharing plans. Annuity and stock bonus plans. Industry and salaried-only plans. Contributory and noncontributory. Over-funding and underfunding. Trusteed and insured. Investments at cost and at fair market value. Vested and nonvested. The list goes on. Each plan, each method, each feature, an integral part of a whole. Each part, each whole to be investigated and understood before the formation of the business combination design.

CONVERSION CHANGES. A careful reading and detailed analysis of the retirement programs of all parties to the business combination prior to the execution of any acquisition agreement is imperative in order to make intelligent decisions on how to convert the present raw material into a suitable retirement program for the future. The steps to the future are these:

1. Understand the present retirement benefits.
2. Determine the future retirement benefits goal.
3. Examine the ways and means of converting the present into the future.

At the outset basic choices might be looked at, such as these:

1. Should all plans be discarded and a new plan adopted?
2. Should the acquiring corporation's plan be extended to the transferor's employees or should the reverse action be adopted?
3. Should all plans be continued in the same or amended form?

A choice made, whether one above or some other, generally requires the application of conversion changes which cause or affect:

1. Terminations
2. Coverage
3. Benefits
4. Discrimination
5. Vesting
6. Funding
7. Deductions

While the list is incomplete, the important point is that when changes in a qualified plan are made, the tax life of the plan responds. Pre-acquisition investigation and planning must be within the overview of the mergermaker.

ACQUISITION PRICE. The employee retirement responsibilities involved in a business combination may influence the acquisition price. Questions which arise in this area are as follows:

1. What is the amount of the unfunded past service costs?
2. Will a new retirement program increase the transferor's unfunded liabilities?
3. Are the assets in the transferor's retirement fund undervalued or overvalued? Is there overfunding in the plan?
4. Does the transferor have unused contribution carryovers? (See discussion under "Employer Deductions.")

The last item tends to increase the purchase price if the carryovers can be deducted by the acquiring corporation.

It may be found that the assets in the transferor's retirement fund are overvalued, thus increasing the unfunded past service costs assumed by the purchaser. The assets may be undervalued to an extent that unfunded past service costs are reduced or eliminated entirely. The condition may be so extreme that the plan is overfunded and future normal costs are reduced.

If the answer to the second question is in the affirmative, should the purchase price be adjusted or is this a cost chargeable against future operations?

The amount of the unfunded past service cost should also be considered. If substantial in amount, and if assumed by the acquiring corporation, a reduction in purchase price is indicated. The situation is to be handled gingerly, however, because Section 381(c)(16) provides, with respect to certain tax-free reorganizations, that if the acquiring corporation assumes an obligation of the transferor corporation which gives rise to a liability, and such liability, if paid by the transferor, would have been deductible, the acquiring corporation shall deduct such item when paid as though it were the transferor, but no deduction will be allowed if the purchase price is reduced because of the obligation. The effect of Section 381(c)(16) is not clear. This section must be read in connection with Section 381(c)(4) and Section 381(c)(11). While Section 381(c)(16), when read alone, appears to deny a deduction, the authors believe that if it is read in conjunction with the other two sections, the deduction is available to the tax-payer.

EMPLOYEE TAXATION

The termination of a qualified plan usually requires a distribution of benefits to the employee beneficiaries. (See Rev. Rul. 67-213, where the interests in a transferor's terminated pension plan are transferred to the transferee's stock bonus plan without taxation to the employees.) Depending upon the terms of the plan, the distribution may take the form of a lump-sum distribution or some type of annuity payment. Generally speaking, an annuity payment is taxed as ordinary income and a lump-sum distribution is taxed as a capital gain.

The business combination may result in a termination of a qualified plan of one or more of the participating parties. The termination may be by design or it may be by misdesign. The termination may occur as an integral part of the business combination or as a subsequent, and perhaps unforeseen, event.

The problem is the lump-sum distribution arising from the termination of a plan which is caused, directly or indirectly, by a business combination. The specific question is: Will the lump-sum distribution be taxed to the employee as capital gain or as ordinary income?

Capital gain taxation. Section 402(a)(2) provides that an employee shall treat a lump-sum distribution from an exempt employees' trust as a long-term capital gain provided certain conditions are met.

1. The distribution must be a total disbursement of all funds standing to the credit of the employee's account. Much consideration has been given to what constitutes a total distribution. [Regs. 1.402(a)-1(a)(6)(ii).] Definitions on this point have developed to an extent that it presents no problem in the case of well-cared-for plans.

2. The distribution must be paid within one taxable year of the recipient. The distribution does not have to be in

the same year in which the employee severs his employment.

3. The distribution must be paid on account of the employee's death or other separation from the service of the employer.

Section 403(a)(2), relating to the taxation of the employee annuities, contains a similar capital gain provision.

A business combination may result in a terminated qualified plan. A terminated plan may cause a total distribution to be paid to an employee. The final link in this chain of events is the taxation of the distribution to the employee. The final link is forged by reference to the phrase "separation from the service of the employer." If separation occurs, the distribution is taxed as a capital gain. If there is no separation, the distribution is taxed as ordinary income under Section 72.

The framers of the business combination must understand the relationship between separation and taxation if they have a desire to control the tax fortunes of the employee.

SEPARATION FROM THE SERVICE. Unfortunately, tax consequences flow from a tax phrase which is defined neither in the Code nor in the regulations. Any definition of the key phrase must come from court cases and Revenue Service rulings. Despite the bramblebush nature of such source definitions, certain benchmarks are visible.

1. Look to the severance of the employer-employee relationship. Generally, the employment tax regulations are a guide to when a severance occurs.

2. Do not look to the termination of the plan. The termination may cause the distribution of benefits, but it does not determine its taxability.

3. Do not look to a mere change in stock ownership; it does not produce a seed from which capital gain will sprout.

Separation may occur in two ways in a business combination. First an employee may be completely severed from his employer. He quits or is discharged or he retires. He is out and away. The separation from service definition is not an issue insofar as a lump-sum distribution is concerned.

The second type of separation is the troublesome one. For

example, an employee stands behind the counter nonchalantly selling fish hooks to the same old customers while around him, unnoticed, swirl the machinations of acquisition, merger, reorganization, liquidation, etc. In the midst of demonstrating a No. 3 snelled hook, the business changes hands. He continues his demonstration. Has the employee changed employers?

ILLUSTRATIONS — CASES. *U.S. v. Johnson*, 331 F.2d 943 (5th Cir., 1964). Lee purchased the stock of Waterman. Waterman terminated its qualified plan and made a distribution. Subsequently, Lee merged downstream into Waterman, which continued in business. Capital gain income was denied to Waterman's employees. The distribution was on account of the termination of the plan, and such termination did not sever the employment relationship between Waterman and its employees. Neither the change in stock ownership nor the subsequent merger severed the relationship. Waterman employees still worked for Waterman.

Jack E. Schlegel, 46 T.C. 706 (1966). Worthington purchased the stock of Annin. At a later date, Annin was liquidated into Worthington. Worthington took over Annin's employees, one of whom was Schlegel. Worthington also took over Annin's profit-sharing plan, but soon terminated it. Schlegel was denied capital gain treatment because the lump-sum distribution was made to him on account of the termination of the plan. At the time of termination it was Worthington's plan. Schlegel was Worthington's employee before and after the termination.

Robert E. Beaulieu, TCM 1965-303. P purchased the stock of S. S terminated its qualified plan and made a lump-sum distribution. S was later liquidated into P. The distributions were taxed as ordinary income to the recipients because they remained in the employ of S after the termination of the plan. There was no separation from the service.

These three cases are set forth to illustrate the benchmarks. The cases are by no means unusual. These benchmarks appear time and again as cases, favorable and unfavorable to the taxpayer, are reported. See among others: *E. N. Funkhouser*, 44 T.C. 178 (1965), aff'd (4th Cir. 1967); *U.S. v. Peebles*, 331 F.2d 955 (5th Cir. 1964); *Edward J. Glinske, Jr.*, 17 T.C. 562 (1951); *Clarence F. Buckley*, 29 T.C. 455 (1957); *Estate of Edward I. Rieben*, 32 T.C. 1205 (1959); *Lester B. Martin*, 26 T.C. 100 (1956); *Mary Miller*, 22 T.C.

293 (1955), aff'd (6th Cir. 1955); *Estate of Frank B. Fry,* 19 **T.C.** 461 (1952), aff'd (3rd Cir. 1953); *McGowan v. U.S.,* 277 F.2d 613 (7th Cir. 1960).

ILLUSTRATIONS — RULINGS. The Revenue Service has attempted to clarify the separation-from-service issue through a series of revenue rulings. The rulings relate largely to business transfers — i.e., business combinations, as that term is used in this chapter, and transfers of businesses by liquidation. It will be noted that these rulings further illustrate the benchmarks set forth above.

1. *Sale of a division.* The assets of a division are sold for cash. The qualified plan covering the seller's employees is continued by the seller, but a total distribution is made to the employees who are taken over by the purchaser. There is a separation from service. After the sale the divisional employees work for a different employer. *Benchmark:* Look to the severance of the employer-employee relationship. [Rev. Rul. 58-97.]

2. *Sale of a subsidiary.* One qualified plan serves the employees of both a parent company and a subsidiary. The subsidiary's stock is sold to other interests. The qualified plan is discontinued as to the subsidiary's employees. A total distribution is made to the employees of the subsidiary. There is no separation from service. *Benchmark:* Do not look to a mere change in stock ownership. [Rev. Rul. 58-99.] In this situation, the employment relationship does not change. The employees work for the same employer before and after the change in ownership. The distribution was caused by the partial termination of the plan (as to the subsidiary's employees) which was caused by the change in ownership.

3. *Sale of assets.* In preparation for liquidation, a corporation sells all of its assets for cash. The qualified plan is terminated and all employees receive a total distribution. There is a separation from service even as to those employees who incident to the sale of assets go over to the purchaser. *Benchmark:* Look to the severance of the employer-employee relationship. [Rev. Rul. 58-96.]

4. *Tax-free acquisition of assets.* The P corporation exchanges its voting stock for all of the assets of the M corporation,

which assets are then transferred to the S corporation, a subsidiary of the P corporation. The reorganization is tax-free under Section 368(a)(1)(C). The qualified plan of the M corporation is terminated as a part of the reorganization. The employees of the M corporation become employees of the S corporation. A separation from service occurs. *Benchmark:* Look to the severance of the employer-employee relationship. [Rev. Rul. 58-94.] (But see page 274.)

5. *Merger of businesses.* In this ruling, two corporations enact two tax-free transactions under one plan of reorganization. First, there is an exchange of stock so that S becomes a subsidiary of P. Second, the subsidiary is merged into the parent. The qualified plan of the subsidiary is terminated as part of the second transaction — the merger. A total distribution is made at this point. A separation from service takes place and the subsidiary's employees are in position to claim capital gain treatment. *Benchmark:* Look to the severance of the employer-employee relationship. [Rev. Rul. 58-383.]

This transaction is in reality an exchange of stock for assets. One step, not two. [See Rev. Rul. 67-274.] If two steps had been involved — i.e., two separate reorganizations — the consequences might have been different. The first would have been a Section 368(a)(1)(B) transfer of ownership (no separation), and the second would have been a Section 332 liquidation (separation possible, but read immediately below).

CERTAIN TECHNICAL SEPARATIONS. A lump-sum distribution plus a separation from service should result in a capital gain. There are circumstances, however, under which a separation occurs in a technical sense but nothing of real substance takes place insofar as the employee is concerned. An example of this might be the liquidation of a mature subsidiary under the tax-free provisions of Section 332 and the continued operation of the business of the subsidiary as a division of the parent. A technical separation has occurred. The employee has left one employer and joined another — although he may not have been fully aware of it.

The legislative history of Section 402(a)(2) indicates that a reorganization of liquidation must bring about a "substantial change" in the make-up of the employees if capital gain status is desired for the distribution. [Rev. Rul. 58-94.] The term "substantial change" will be defined with difficulty in many instances, but ordinarily a distribution incident to the tax-free liquidation of a controlled subsidiary will be taxed as ordinary income even though a separation from service takes place.

The liquidation of a controlled subsidiary may be more than a mere technical separation.

Example. The P Corporation wishes to acquire the operating assets of S corporation and continue the business of S as a division of P. P purchases the stock of S for cash. P liquidates S. Incident to the plan of liquidation, the qualified plan of S is terminated and a total distribution is made. A separation from service exists. [Rev. Rul. 58-95.]

The form of this two-step transaction would appear to preclude a real separation from service. The first step, the acquisition of stock for cash, was a mere change in stock ownership. [Rev. Rul. 58-99.] The second step, the liquidation of a wholly-owned subsidiary, generally does not result in the necessary substantial change in the make-up of employees. [Rev. Rul. 58-94.]

In substance, however, this transaction was a one-step acquisition by P of the assets of S. [Section 334(b)(2).] In reality, and regardless of the form of the transaction, a separation from service occurs. [Rev. Rul. 58-96.]

At the present time, considerable uncertainty exists in the capital gains area. In *Victor S. Gittens,* 49 T.C. No. 44, January 25, 1968, the court held that no separation from the service existed in a "C"-type reorganization (see page 273) because there was no substantial change in the make-up of the employees. Not only is the validity of Rev. Rul. 58-94 placed in jeopardy by *Gittens,* but also the severance-from-employment benchmark.

In a majority of business combinations, there is no substantial change in the make-up of employees as understood in *Gittens.* An extension of the *Gittens* holding may eliminate capital gain possibilities from substantially all business combinations. Alternatively, separation from service may have to be decided on a case-by-case basis, with no benchmarks to guide the taxpayer.

TAX PLANNING. In retrospect, it would appear that pre-acquisition investigation and planning, coupled with an understanding of the three benchmarks, could have produced capital gain situations in *Johnson, Schlegel,* and *Beaulieu.*

In *Johnson,* Lee bought Waterman, Waterman terminated its plan, Lee merged downstream into Waterman. If Waterman had merged upstream into Lee, and if the Waterman plan had been terminated as a part of the merger, Johnson would have been in a capital gain position. His severance of employment with Waterman would have related to receipt of the distribution. The termination of the plan would have been related only as a part of the mechanics. The change in stock ownership would have been an unrelated factor.

In *Schlegel,* the subsidiary was liquidated and the parent took over its qualified plan, only to terminate it at a later date. In *Beaulieu,* the subsidiary's plan was terminated and then the subsidiary was liquidated into the parent. In each instance the employee was forced to the sands of termination from which to claim the capital gain advantage. In each instance, if the plan had been terminated as part of the liquidation transaction, the employee could have stood on the solid grounds of separation from the service of his employer.

Rearranging the events in *Johnson, Schlegel,* and *Beaulieu* by the application of hindsight in order to reach a satisfactory tax result is done only to further validate the benchmarks. Hindsight here ignores the reality that tax considerations must at times give way to conflicting nontax considerations in business combinations. When this happens, other ways must be examined to avoid or soften the sharp edges of ordinary income taxation. The following might be considered:

1. The lump-sum distribution is postponed until the day of real separation from service (retirement, death, resignation, etc.)

    To accomplish this end the plan will be "frozen." The plan will be adopted by the successor company so that the employee will receive the payout as a result of separation from the employment of the successor company. The exempt trust will remain in existence to hold the assets of the plan. No further contributions will be made under the plan. This approach may lend itself to planning for a combination of capital gain and ordinary income for retirement:

    a. The terminated plan of the earlier business will pay out in a lump-sum distribution, taxable at capital gains, to provide immediately available funds for travel, purchase of a retirement home, investment, etc.

    b. The operating plan of the successor employer will pay out in installments to provide low-tax-bracket income during the retirement years.

2. The trust assets are converted into annuities which will begin to pay out only upon the occurrence of a future event such as retirement. The annuities can be distributed to the employee without incurring a tax. This method will permit the termination of the exempt trust. It does not produce capital gain taxation but it does permit low-bracket taxation in the retirement years, an alternative which may be more advantageous.

3. The distribution of benefits of the terminated plan is made in installments designed to level out taxable income. The provisions for "income averaging" may assist in this approach.

Essential to tax planning of the sort described above is a thorough analysis of the qualified plan itself. The plan must be flexible enough to contain the shape of the tax idea. If it is not, it must be properly amended. The need for change is developed in the pre-acquisition investigation.

PLANNING OUT THE CAPITAL GAIN. In some cases, a lump-sum distribution from a qualified retirement plan to an employee, even though taxed at capital gains rates, is less desirable than distributions taxed as ordinary income. The net-of-tax amount retained by the employee from the total benefit paid is the important thing. The amount retained depends upon the tax bracket at which the benefit will be taxed. The mergermaker must remember that in this decision area he is dealing with high-bracket and low-bracket taxpayers as well as the many who fill the in-between brackets.

Ideally the qualified plan will be structured so that all recipients may be served to their best interests — some as capital gains, some as an annuity, and some to their advantage under the "income averaging" provisions of Sections 1301 to 1305. It requires a sophisticated plan, a patient planner, and a careful technician.

GUIDELINES. The qualified retirement plan must be created and maintained with the best interests of the employees in mind. The designer of the business combination will see that the spirit of this requirement extends beyond the formalized procedures which protect the interests of the employees during the operating life of the plan. He will realize that he has a responsibility to guard the interests of the employees as to their tax posture in the event a distribution is necessitated by a business combination. With such a responsibility, he will no more thrust upon the employees an avoidable tax burden than he would permit shareholders to be damaged through his actions.

It is competent mergermanship to:

1. Understand the tax impact of a total distribution and a separation from service.
2. Plan for a total distribution, or any distribution, if one is necessary so that the employees attain the best tax posture.
3. Assure the employee tax posture through expert opinions and, where possible, an advance ruling from the Internal Revenue Service.

EMPLOYER DEDUCTION

Qualified retirement plans are a creation of the tax statute. It should follow that the cost of providing the benefits of a qualified plan is a tax-deductible expense. And so it is — within limitations, some of which are carefully prescribed by law, some of which are administrative fiat. One series of limitations concerns itself with the timing of the tax deduction. In substance these limitations place a maximum upon the amount of tax deduction which may be claimed in any one taxable year, regardless of the amount of retirement cost actually funded during that year. [Sec. 404(a).] As a consequence of the limitations, certain "contribution carryovers" come into existence. If the retirement plan is funded in an amount which is greater than the maximum tax deduction for that year, the excess contribution becomes a contribution carryover to the future and may be deducted in a future tax year, provided it can be fitted within the limitations which apply to that future year. (See page 84.)

Contribution carryovers are an asset of the business. While they are not the type of assets which normally appear on the books of the business, nevertheless, they represent a deferred tax benefit which, if properly nurtured, may turn into cash through a reduction in Federal income tax liabilities.

The mergermaker should have a knowledge of how the contribution carryover arises and what pressures it is subjected to in the atmosphere of business combinations. If a contribution carryover exists, it should at least be recognized and, if possible, given a chance to convert into a real asset of the survivor of the business combination. While it may be exchanged in negotiation for other benefits, it should not be thrown away through neglect.

SOURCE OF THE CARRYOVER. In the case of a qualified pension plan, the tax deduction for contributions for any taxable year is initially limited to an amount not in excess of 5% of the compensation otherwise paid or accrued to all employees who are participants under the plan. [Sec. 404(a)(1)(A).] The 5% figure may be reduced by the Internal Revenue Service if it is found to be more than is required to fund the benefits under the plan. It may be found also that the 5% limitation is insufficient to fund the cost of past and current service credits when such credits are distributed as a level amount or level percentage of compensation over the remaining service of each employee under the plan. In such a case, the required amount in excess of 5% of compensation is also deductible. [Sec. 404(a)(1)(B).] As a third choice, the employer may claim a deduction based upon the normal cost of the plan plus 10% of its past service cost. [Sec. 404(a)(1)(C).]

In the case of a profit-sharing or a stock bonus plan, the deduction for contributions is limited to an amount equal to 15% of the compensation otherwise paid or accrued during the taxable year to the employees covered by the plan. [Sec. 404(a)(3).] If an employer has at least one employee who is covered under a pension plan and is also covered under a profit-sharing or a stock bonus plan, there is a special limitation on contributions. [Sec. 404(a)(7).] In any taxable year the total allowable deduction for contributions under all plans cannot exceed 25% of the total compensation to all participants under all plans.

Regardless of the limitation adopted for the taxable year, if the employer makes a contribution which is in excess of the applicable limitation for such year, the excess of the amount paid over the limitation may be carried forward to a later year. (See page 84.)

Making use of the unused carryover is usually not a difficult task for the employer under normal operating conditions. It is treated as a contribution in the later year. The later year, of course, has its own limitations, but the employer reduces the actual contribution under the plan to an amount below the limitation so that the combined actual contribution and the phantom contribution from the past can be fitted within the limitation of the later year. If it does not fit, it moves forward to a succeeding year. In the case of a business combination in a later year, new rules are infused and some of the old rules become difficult for both the transferor and the transferee.

TRANSFEREE IN GENERAL. For purposes of demonstrating the problems of the acquiring corporation in a business combination, the assumption is made that the transferor corporation is possessed of an unused contribution carryover. The unused carryover is the "asset" that the acquiring corporation wants. Whether it will pass over to the acquiring corporation will depend upon the shape of the combination transaction and the decision of that corporation to continue or to terminate the transferor's qualified plan.

SANCTIONED TRANSACTIONS. Under Section 381 of the Internal Revenue Code, an acquiring corporation steps into the shoes of the transferor corporation insofar as the deductibility of a contribution carryover is concerned, provided the business combination is a "sanctioned transaction." This is the same section that covers the tax attributes (operating losses, accounting methods, earnings and profits, etc.) which pass from one corporation to another in tax-free corporate reorganizations. The contribution carryover applicable to qualified retirement plans is considered to be a tax attribute for purposes of this section. The types of transactions which are sanctioned are as follows:

1. The liquidation under Section 332 of a controlled subsidiary into its parent.

   No sanction, however, is bestowed upon a Section 332 liquidation where the basis of the assets is determined by Section 334(b)(2). The latter section of the statute is designed to cover a situation where, instead of purchasing assets for cash, a corporation purchases stock in a corporation and then liquidates the corporation. The substance of the transaction is a cash purchase of assets. When the corporation is liquidated, the cost of the stock is apportioned to the assets. A Section 334(b)(2) liquidation differs. It is treated as a taxable liquidation, rather than a tax-free Section 332 liquidation, for purposes of Section 381.

2. A tax-free merger or consolidation under Section 368(a)(1)(A).
3. A tax-free exchange of stock for assets under Section 368(a)(1)(C).
4. Certain other tax-free reorganizations which are not relevant to this chapter.

It will be noted that the Section 368(a)(1)(B) method of acquisition — i.e., the exchange of stock for stock — is not a sanctioned transaction. The reason for this is that the transaction merely creates a parent-subsidiary relationship. The corporate walls remain intact. The retirement plans within the walls are undisturbed. The reorganization does not create tax attributes. The "B"-type acquisition, however, is often followed by the liquidation of the subsidiary into its new-found parent. If that happens, the liquidation will qualify as a Section 332 liquidation, a sanctioned transaction. The tax attribute arises at the point of the Section 332 liquidation.

Another Section 368(a)(1)(B) bypass exists. If the exchange of stock for stock and the subsequent liquidation of the subsidiary into the parent are separate steps in one business combination plan, the two steps will be ignored and a single step substituted. The legal niceties of the stock for stock plus liquidation will be brushed aside. The whole affair will be considered as an exchange of stock for assets under Section 368(a)(1)(C), a sanctioned transaction. [Rev. Rul. 67-274.]

If the acquisition transaction is sanctioned by Section 381, excess contribution carryovers under a pension, profit-sharing, or stock bonus plan are eligible for passage into the acquiring corporation. The acquiring corporation is considered to be the transferor corporation for all purposes of deduction contributions under a qualified retirement plan. [Regs. 1.381(c)(11).]

DEDUCTION — CONTINUED PLAN. The tax attribute provisions may be generally stated as follows:

1. If the excess contribution of the transferor becomes available to the transferee, it may be deducted by the latter.

   If the transferor's plan is continued, the acquiring corporation may absorb the contribution carryover within the normal rules of limitation applicable to the plan. If, however, the plan is terminated, special limitations are applicable. These special rules are discussed below as a part of the problems of the transferor.

2. The continuation of the transferor's plan may be accomplished in one of three ways:

   a. It may be continued as a separate plan.
   b. It may be consolidated with another qualified plan.
   c. It may be replaced with a comparable plan.

3. A pension plan and an annuity plan are "comparable." Neither is comparable to a profit-sharing plan or a stock bonus plan, but a profit-sharing plan and a stock bonus plan are comparable.

4. Unused contribution credits may be carried over and used by the acquiring corporation.

   The term "unused contribution credit" has not been used heretofore. It is not a deduction as such, but it might be considered as a passport to a future deduction. It arises only in the case of a profit-sharing plan or a stock bonus plan when an employer contributes less than the 15%-of-compensation limitation in any taxable year. The excess of the limitation over the amount actually funded becomes a credit carryover to the future, thus permitting the employer in a later year to contribute more than the 15% limitation of the later year.

   The unused contribution credit is considered to be a "phantom" asset, but certainly not of the status of the unused contribution deduction. It may pass from the transferor to the transferee corporation under Section 381 if the latter corporation continues the former's plan as a separate plan, consolidates it with another qualified plan, or replaces it with a comparable plan; however, such plan must be qualified in the year the excess credit is used.

In summary, it would appear that the acquiring corporation may make use of the carryover benefits if the transferor's plan is properly handled and if the vehicle used to transport the benefit from the transferor to the acquiring corporation is sanctioned by Section 381.

NONSANCTIONED TRANSACTIONS. Not all acquisitions follow the sanctioned routes of Section 381. The purchase of assets for cash in a taxable transaction, for example, does not qualify under Section 381 and yet this is a well-traveled acquisition trail. In the event the unused carryover benefit is not a tax attribute under Section 381, the surviving corporation cannot use it. If it is to be used at all, the transferor corporation must find a way to do it.

TRANSFEROR IN GENERAL. The transferor corporation has a myriad of problems of its own — similar and dissimilar to those of its partner in merger. Its problems must also be considered by the mergermaker for a satisfactory result for the business combination. The transferor with an unused contribution deduction must look for a way to convert the phantom asset into a real asset.

SANCTIONED TRANSACTIONS. The sanctioned transactions of Section 381 provide the avenue to the elimination of the unused contribution deduction (and the unused contribution credit) from the transferor's area of influence. The deferred tax benefit passes over to the acquiring corporation and out of control of the transferor.

CONTINUED CORPORATION. A business combination may be structured as an acquisition of the assets of a business for cash (a taxable transaction) with the transferor corporation remaining in existence. New business assets are purchased and a new business enterprise undertaken. Alternatively, the corporation converts the cash into investments of some sort and remains in existence for the benefit of its shareholders as an investment holding company. In any event, the employees of the former business, presumably, travel with the assets from the transferor to the acquiring corporation.

The acquiring corporation may have taken over the transferor's qualified retirement plan at the time it received its purchased employees. It may not have accepted the plan; the transferor corporation may have terminated it when its employees left to go with the acquiring corporation.

Regardless of the actual mechanics, the transferor corporation now has an unused contribution deduction, a terminated qualified plan, and a burning desire to deduct a prior year's unused contribution in a taxable year after the sale of its business assets.

One problem has been put to rest. The transferor may deduct the unused contribution carryover in a taxable year subsequent to the termination of the plan. [Regs. 1.404(a)-7(b).]

With the end of that question, which indeed haunted the past, a new one arises: *How* does the transferor deduct the unused contribution carryover in a year after the termination of the plan?

The pattern for deducting the pension plan's unused deduction is found in Regs. 1.404(a)-6 and 7. If the amount is deducted in a year in which the pension trust or annuity plan is not qualified, or which ends after the trust or plan has terminated, the 5%-of-compensation limitation and the "level amount" limitation do not appear to be applicable because there are no employee-participants upon which to base a computation. The excess contribution seems to be allowable only to the extent of the limitation based upon past service credits—i.e., 10% of past service or supplementary cost as of the date the past service or supplementary costs are provided under the plan.

The Revenue Service, however, has ruled, under a specific factual situation, that a current deduction is computed by the level-amount method. [Rev. Rul. 60-132.] The ruling lacks clarity, and it is difficult to judge its application beyond the factual situation to which it was addressed.

It would appear that the transferor merely has to retain its patience and work out the unused contribution deduction at the 10% rate. But anxiety may overhang the trail. The corporation may extinguish its existence before the full amount is recovered, in which case the unrecovered amount will be lost.

Under the pattern for a profit-sharing or stock bonus plan, the unused contribution deduction may be deducted in a year subsequent to the termination of the plan but only to the extent of 15% of the compensation otherwise paid or accrued to the employee-participants during the year the deduction is claimed. [Regs. 1.404 (a)-9(b)(2).] And where are the employee-participants? They are now being paid by the acquiring corporation. The transferor has funded the retirement plan in advance. The advance-funded benefits accrue to the participants who will be taxed upon them at some point in time. But the employer, he who provided the benefits, is deprived of a tax deduction because of a formula which comes out to zero. The answer may be right for the operating business which terminates its plan, but it offers no help to a transactor corporation.

It might be noted that the door to the courthouse may be ajar on this issue. The regulations say that the limitation is based upon compensation paid to the employees "by the employer" — i.e., the transferor corporation. The Code says it is based upon compensation paid to the employees. The phrase "by the employer" is not in the Code. Did the Code intend the limitation to be computed with reference to the compensation paid by the acquiring corporation?

These special rules of limitation are applicable also to the carryover deduction of a terminated plan in the hands of the acquiring corporation, but they are not as troublesome there. The acquiring corporation has the employees.

LIQUIDATED CORPORATION. It has been noted above that the unrecovered contribution deduction will be lost if the transferor corporation is liquidated. This point should not be lightly considered by the mergermaker, because it is likely to happen.

Section 337 of the Code contains a most important relief provision which is often availed of in a taxable acquisition that follows the cash-for-assets pattern. The transferor corporation and its shareholders avoid double taxation on their side of the transaction. In general it works like this: The corporation adopts a plan of liquidation and within twelve months thereafter completes its liquidation. During the twelve-month period, the corporation sells its assets. The gain on the sale of the assets is not taxed to the corporation. The shareholders, of course, are taxed in the usual manner on the gain arising from the liquidation. No tax on the corporate level; tax at the shareholder level. Without Section 337, tax falls at both levels. A liquidation carried out under Section 337 requires propitious timing if the unused contribution carryover is to be recovered. Total recovery must be accomplished within the twelve-month period—an unlikely event. Section 337 usually sounds the death knell for the carryover.

CONCLUSION

Qualified retirement plans live only by the grace of the tax law. Each plan is uniquely created and administered for a particular group of employees. The very process of molding a business combination exerts pressures on the plan which affect its tax life. The pressures must be understood. The effects must be controlled. Perhaps these are tasks for the technician. Certainly they are the responsibility of the mergermaker.

Executive Compensation Plans

GENERAL STATEMENT

The purpose of the executive deferred-compensation plan is to currently recognize the executive's contribution to the business organization without permitting high tax rates to erode the value of the instrument of recognition. The procedure is to shift current income from present high-tax-bracket years to future years when, presumably, it will be taxed at lower rates.

Of the many types of unqualified executive plans which are employed, five are discussed below. The deferred-salary arrangement is the fundamental plan. All other plans, to some degree, inherit the characteristics of the deferred-salary arrangement.

THE DEFERRED-SALARY ARRANGEMENT

THE MECHANICS. The typical arrangement is where an employer agrees to pay to an employee an annual amount after his retirement from active service for the remainder of his life or for a specific number of years. The arrangement may be contractual or noncontractual, funded or unfunded, forfeitable or nonforfeitable—the tax effect of the agreement varying accordingly. The agreement may call for special services to be rendered by the employee and may provide for payment to a beneficiary in the event of the death of the executive.

THE EMPLOYER'S DEDUCTION. Under normal circumstances the employer wants a tax deduction currently; that is, he wants to match his deduction against the income which he believes the executive or key employee is producing for him. He is educated by his experience with the qualified plan to believe that possible. He finds, however, that the rules applicable to the qualified plan do not extend to the nonqualified plan.

The regulations [Regs. 1.404(a)-12] provide that in the case of a nonqualified plan, the employer is allowed a deduction only in the year that the payment is made and then only if the right of the employee to the payment is nonforfeitable. This means that, in order to receive a deduction currently, the employer must pay cash directly to the employee, make a payment into a trust, or purchase an annuity contract for him.

If the payment is made into a trust or an annuity is purchased, the right of the employee must be nonforfeitable at the time of the payment. If the employee has a nonforfeitable right in these circumstances, the income will be taxed to him immediately and the primary purpose of the deferred-salary contract will be defeated. If the employee has a forfeitable right at the time the payment is made to the trust or the annuity purchased, he will not realize taxable income, but the employer will not receive a deduction in the year of the payment or in any other taxable year. [Regs. 1.404(a)-12.]

This reasoning can best be seen by reference to a payment to a trust: If the employer makes a payment to an irrevocable trust on behalf of an individual who has a forfeitable interest, he will receive no deduction even though he has irrevocably parted with his money. An irrevocable trust is not an agency of the employer. Therefore, the Commissioner argues, when the trust subsequently pays over the monies to the individual, it is not distributing monies which belong to the employer, for he lost control over the monies at an earlier date. The deduction, if any, belongs to the trust, and the employer has lost the deduction forever. The fact that the employee had a forfeitable interest at the time of the payment to the trust but, prior to the distribution, acquired a nonforfeitable interest does not change the result. The acquisition of a nonforfeitable right does not simultaneously secure a deduction for the employer. The Court of Claims, however, has held the regulations under the 1939 code to be invalid and allowed deductions in the year of payout by the trust. [*Russell Manufacturing Co. v. U.S.*, 175 F. Supp. 159 (Ct. Cl. 1959); *Mississippi River Fuel Corp. v. U.S.*, 314 F.2d 953 (Ct. Cl. 1963).] The Internal Revenue Service refuses to follow the Russell Manufacturing Co. case on the issue of deductibility of benefit payments. [Rev. Rul. 59-383.]

In two district court cases, deductions have been allowed for contributions to nonqualified profit-sharing plans. In one case, contributions were nonforfeitable as to a group of employees. In the other, the employer was allowed to deduct his contribution to a nonqualified deferred profit-sharing trust in the year in which the trust made nonforfeitable payments to the employees, even though employee rights were forfeitable when the contributions were made. [*Bank of Sheridan* (D.C. Mont., 1963); *U.S. v. Russell Manufacturing Co.* (D.C. Conn., 1964), aff'd (2nd Cir. 1965); see also *Buttrey Stores, Inc.*, 375 F.2d 799 (Ct. Cl. 1967).]

An exception to the above rule exists in the case where the employer makes the contribution to a revocable trust. Here the employer obtains a deduction under Section 162 in the year in which distribution or payment is made to the employee from the trust. [Rev. Rul. 55-525.] The rationale of this ruling lies in the fact that the revocable trust is merely an agency for the employer, and thus a transfer of funds to the agency has no tax significance—

the funds are merely shifted from one pocket of the employer to another.

Because of Section 404(a)(5) the employer cannot get a deduction before the employee receives taxable income. The desire of the employer for an immediate tax deduction must be sacrificed to the desire of the employee to postpone his taxable income.

The employer may wish to fund the contract for nontax reasons. He can do this, without accelerating the employee's tax, by purchasing an endowment life insurance policy on the life of the employee. The policy should be applied for and entirely owned by the company. It should be subject to the demands of creditors as are other assets. The proceeds should be payable to the company and not to the employee, nor to a trust created for him, nor to his beneficiary. The purchase of the policy should not be related to the deferred-salary contract. The premiums will not be deductible by the employer [Sec. 264(a)(1)] and the proceeds if paid because of death will not be taxed to him [Sec. 101(a)]. Under these circumstances, the Revenue Service will not contend that the contract is funded. [Rev. Rul. 59-184, announcing agreement of the Revenue Service with *Casale v. Com.*, 247 F.2d 440 (2nd Cir. 1957); see also Rev. Rul. 68-99.]

If an accrual-basis employer has an arrangement having the effect of a pension, profit-sharing, stock bonus, or similar plan deferring the receipt of compensation, no deduction is allowed until the year in which the compensation is paid. However, if an accrual basis employer has an incentive bonus plan, where bonuses based on profits are determined through a formula in effect before the end of the taxable year, and the employer before year-end has notified the employees, either individually or as a group, of their proportionate shares, deduction is allowed in the year of accrual. The fact that the bonuses are not actually paid until after the end of the year, as soon as the amounts can be determined, does not make the arrangement a deferred compensation plan. [Rev. Rul. 57-88; *Avco Mfg. Co.*, 25 T.C. 975 (1956), acq.]

Similarly, if an employer defers payment of compensation after the accrual year merely because of inability to pay such compensation in the year of accrual, liability accrues in the earlier year and the deduction is allowed, provided that Section 267, disallowing certain deductions between related taxpayers, is not applicable. [Regs. 1.404(b)-1.] (See also Revenue Ruling 61-127.)

THE EMPLOYEE'S INCOME. From the point of view of the employee, the primary object of the contract is to shift income from the present to the future. In addition the employee wants some assurance that he will receive the funds while he is in retirement years. At first blush he feels that the funds should be put aside for him through the medium of a trust fund, annuity, or other sequestration of funds for his protection in the event of the financial failure of his employer. He further wishes a vested right to the funds. Such an approach, while giving him the security he desires, would in all probability cause him to be taxed on the funds as they are set aside for him through either the theory of constructive receipt or the doctrine of economic benefit. As a result of this threat, the principal characteristic of the contract is that it is supported only by the employer's simple promise to pay the funds in the future.

For a great many years tax authorities have felt that the deferral of tax is not assured even though supported only by a simple promise to pay. There has been a fear that the Revenue Service might attack the arrangement with the weapon of the doctrine of economic benefit. Under this doctrine an employee receives taxable income when his employer grants to him certain benefits which are payable in the future if such benefits have a present ascertainable value. This fear should no longer exist in the light of Revenue Ruling 60-31, referred to below, which sets forth the present liberal position of the Revenue Service with respect to the taxation of unfunded deferred-salary arrangements. So far as a funded arrangement is concerned, the employee is taxable at the time of the funding if at that time he has nonforfeitable rights to the funds. (See *Sproull v. Com.*, 194 F.2d 541 (6th Cir. 1952), and also Revenue Ruling 60-31). However, if the employee's rights are forfeitable when contributions are made, no income is realized until payout. [Regs. 1.402(b)-1.]

Revenue Ruling 60-31 gives a series of five "cases" or situations in which deferral of tax is considered. These are described below.

Case 1 relates to an executive who is entitled to additional compensation in a stated annual sum, which compensation is credited to a bookkeeping reserve account and to be paid in five annual installments after the happening of certain contingencies. Even though there is a lack of conditions precedent to the executive's enjoyment of the benefits of the plan, the Service ruled that the additional compensation is taxable only when and as received.

Case 2 permits an executive to enter into an agreement with his employer whereby a stated share of profits is determined for the executive but not then paid to him. The employer takes this sum (diminished by the amount of tax which the corporation would have saved if it had paid the share of profits immediately) and invests it in stocks, etc.; any gain or income realized on these investments is added to the profit-sharing reserve being accumulated for the executive. Then, pursuant to the agreement, the fund is paid out at certain intervals in the future—after retirement, death, resignation, and the like. Since the corporation derives a tax deduction at the time of the payout, the tax saving then realized is added to the payout. The executive (or his beneficiaries) is required to pay a tax only at the time the benefits are received by him. The case is interesting because the sterility of the funds (with respect to the employee) which is so common in nonqualified executive compensation plans is avoided. The amounts set aside for the executive earn income. Also, the tax on any dividends received by the corporation on the investment of funds set aside is taxed at only 7.5% in 1964 and 7.2% in 1965 and years following (giving effect to the 85% dividends-received deduction).

Case 3 involves an author and a publisher who have executed an agreement under which the author granted to the publisher the exclusive right to print, publish, and sell a book he had written. The agreement provides that the publisher will pay the author specified royalties on the actual cash received from the sale of the published work, render semiannual statements of the sales, and at the time of rendering each statement make settlement for the amount due. On the same day, another agreement was signed by the same parties, mutually agreeing that, in consideration of, and notwithstanding any contrary provisions contained in the first contract, the publisher shall not pay the taxpayer more than a specified maximum amount in any one calendar year. Any excess accruing in any one calendar year is to be carried over by the publisher and paid in succeeding years.

Since the supplemental agreement was made before the royalties were earned, the Service ruled that the author is required to include the royalties in his gross income only in the taxable years in which they are actually received in cash or other property.

Case 4 concerns a football player who entered into a two-year standard player's contract with a football club in which he agreed to play football and engage in activitieis related to football during the two-year term only for the club. Although the football player could have demanded and received payment of a bonus at the time of signing the contract, it was at his suggestion that the standard contract form be altered to provide substantially as follows:

"The player shall receive the sum of 150 x dollars upon signing of this contract, contingent upon the payment of this 150 x dollars to an escrow agent designated by him. The escrow agreement shall be subject to approval by the legal representatives of the player, the Club, and the escrow agent."

The escrow agreement was executed and the escrow agent, a bank, agreed to pay this amount, plus interest, to the football player in installments over a period of five years. The escrow agreement also provided that an account be established by the escrow agent to bear the football player's name; that payments from such account be made only in accordance with the terms of the agreement; that the agreement be binding upon the parties thereto and their successors or assigns; and that in the event of the football player's death during the escrow period the balance due will become part of his estate.

The Service ruled that the bonus was includible in the gross income of the football player in the year in which the club unconditionally paid such amount to the escrow agent.

Case 5 in Revenue Ruling 60-31 concerns an agreement between a boxer and a boxing club which deferred payment of the boxer's share of the receipts from a match. No deferment was permitted. The boxer was considered a joint venturer in the match. He constructively received his share of the receipts.

In *Ray S. Robinson*, 44 T. C. 20 (1965), a factual situation quite similar, the Court brushed aside the joint venture argument. The contract made no mention of joint venture, sharing of profit or losses, or participation in management. No escrow, trust, or other security arrangement was created. The fight proceeds were commingled with other funds of the promoter. Robinson was an unsecured creditor of the promoter. Deferral was allowed.

The official examples and explanations of Revenue Ruling 60-31 indicate that the forfeiture provisions previously mentioned above do not appear to be necessary. The essential factor in a successful tax deferment is a substantial limitation or a restriction on the employee's right to receive the deferred compensation. The examples in the ruling indicate that an agreement to pay compensation in a future year or years itself is the necessary restriction or limitation, notwithstanding that there are no provisions for forfeiture in the agreement.

However, in a later ruling, the Revenue Service referred to substantial forfeiture provisions contained in a deferred-compensation contract as grounds for deferral. The contract permitted awards of supplemental compensation to key employees to be paid in equal cash installments in each of four years beginning with the year of the award.

Under the plan, an award installment was payable only if, during the entire period from the date of the award until December 31st of the year preceding that in which such installment is payable, the employee (1) continued in the employ of the employer or, if employment terminated for a reason other than death, (2) refrained from engaging in the business of manufacturing specified products in competition with the employer, or from entering the service of any organization engaged in competition with the employer, and (3) made himself available upon request at reasonable times and upon a reasonable basis to consult with, supply information to, and otherwise cooperate with the employer with respect to any matter that was handled by him or under his supervision while he was in the employ of the employer.

Each installment of an award in addition could be further deferred, at the employee's election, until after termination of employment, at which time payment could be arranged to be made in one or more installments of cash or the employer's common stock. The right to receive any payment was dependent on the same conditions aforementioned during the period from termination of employment until December 31st of the year preceding that in which such installment was due.

The initial four-year election of installment payments was required to be made not later than December 15th of the year preceding the year in which an installment would otherwise become payable. The subsequent election was required prior to termination of employment.

The Revenue Service ruled that, in view of the substantial forfeiture provisions, the compensation deferred will be taxable only in the year in which it is actually received unless otherwise made available to the employer at an earlier date. [Rev. Rul. 67-449.]

The above ruling does not refer to Revenue Ruling 60-31 and creates some uncertainty because of its reliance on "substantial forfeiture provisions" as the factor which is the substantial limitation or restriction required by the regulations.

The Revenue Service will now consider requests for advance rulings in regard to deferred-compensation arrangements. [Rev. Rul. 64-279.]

In order to insulate the deferred-compensation arrangements from the threat of the doctrine of economic benefit, it has been customary to incorporate within the contract a number of conditions which the employee must meet in the future. The theory is that so long as the employee is capable of violating the conditions some time in the future, and thus voiding the contract, the contract can have no possible present value to tax under the doctrine of economic benefit. Phrased another way, if the employee has a forfeitable interest in the contract until the moment that the cash reaches his pocket, he can have no taxable income until the cash travels.

Typical forfeiture clauses which have appeared in deferred-salary contracts are as follows:

1. *Service-age clause.* The executive must remain in the employ of the company for a stated number of years. The executive must reach a specified age before he becomes entitled to the payments. Either or both of these requirements can be used in a single contract.
2. *Noncompete clause.* The executive must not compete with the company either during his period of employment or during the period in which he receives the benefits.
3. *Consulting clause.* The executive must hold himself available for consulting services during the payout period.
4. *Income clause.* This may take several forms. It may restrict or eliminate payments if the company's profits fall below a stated level. It may also restrict or eliminate payments if the executive's income (other than the contract income) surpasses a stated level. It may also be correlated with the executive's cost of living and family circumstances.

It can be seen in most of the forfeiture clauses that the employee can commit some act or refrain from some act which will void the contract. These clauses, however, have certain weaknesses which are discussed below:

1. Insofar as an age-service clause is concerned, the condition is met at the end of the workout period, whether that be ten years or at age 65. If there are no other conditions to be met, the executive may acquire a nonforfeitable interest in the contract at that time. The Revenue Service may then be in a, position to apply the doctrine of economic benefit and assign a value to the contract. The present value might be taxed to the executive in the year the workout period ends — presumably a high tax rate year — and thus the objective of the deferred-salary contract might be destroyed. In reality the executive may be in a poorer position than if he had taken the additional income annually. Because of this danger, the age-service clause should be viewed only as a means of deferring the tax during the workout period. A separate clause should be employed to defer the tax into the retirement years. Note that in the stock option situation the expiration of a restriction is held to be a taxable event. [Regs. 1.421-6(d)(2)(i).]

2. The noncompete clause must be realistic and have meaningful limitations as to time and location if it is to be considered valid. The employer may terminate the business with which the employee has agreed not to compete. The restraint becomes valueless and, if there are no other conditions to be met, the employee may acquire a vested right capable of being valued under the economic-benefit doctrine. The employee may die before the end of the payout period with the result that the payments go to a beneficiary who is incapable of competing with the company. The restriction becomes meaningless.

3. The consulting clause may also lose its validity if the business of the employer is terminated or if the employee dies or becomes disabled. The executive may leave the employ of the company under such circumstances that it is obvious that he will never be called upon to render consulting services. Such an event might give him a vested right in the contract. In addition the

clause should be reasonably specific as to the type of consulting services which the employer has in mind.

The consulting clause, perhaps the most widely used of all the forfeiture clauses, may cause trouble in three other areas:

a. If the retired executive is required to render consulting services, such activities might make his post-retirement receipts "wages" or "earnings from self-employment" for social security tax purposes and subject to that tax. However, payments other than vacation or sick pay made to an employee after the month in which he attains the age of 65, if he did not work for the employer in the period for which such payment is made, are exempt from social security taxes. But it has been held that bonuses attributable to services performed as employees, but paid in installments to former employees after termination of the employment relationship are remuneration for services performed in "employment" and therefore constitute "wages" at the time of payment for both FICA and FUTA tax purposes. [Rev. Rul. 57-92.]

b. In addition, such wages or earnings may reduce or eliminate the retired executive's social security benefit until he reaches age 72.

c. To avail himself of the capital gain treatment as to a lump-sum distribution from a qualified pension, profit-sharing, or stock bonus plan, the retired executive must separate himself from his employer. [Sec. 402(a)(2).] It has been held that an employee was not "separated" from the service of his employer where he was required to perform consulting services after termination of regular employment. A lump-sum distribution from a qualified pension trust was therefore not taxable as capital gain under Section 402(a)(2). [*William S. Bolden*, 39 T.C. 829 (1963). See also Rev. Rul. 56-214.] See discussion of this point on page 49. However, also see Letter Ruling dated December 22, 1960 at ¶ 11,981 of *Prentice-Hall Pension and Profit-Sharing Service* contra.

4. The income clause, if tied to the income of the employer, is of particular value to the small employer in that it

protects against the payout of low-level earnings. The executive may be cool to such a clause because he wants no contingencies in the path of his eventual receipts except those which he can control. Generally the income clause has validity only if used by a small employer. There is some doubt that the clause has any value if it is related to the employee's income because this income is a factor somewhat within his control.

Forfeitures clauses are used in various combinations in deferred-salary contracts in an attempt to postpone taxable income until a future date. What happens if a contract contains none of these or similar clauses?

Example: A company agrees to pay Jones $20,000 per year for ten years after his retirement. There are no strings whatsoever attached to the agreement.

Can the Revenue Service place a present value on this simple enforceable contract? The courts have held that an employer's promise to pay amounts in the future to a cash-basis employee has no present value and therefore cannot be taxed until the payments are received [*Com v. Oates*, 207 F.2d 711 (7th Cir. 1953)] unless the promise is made by an insurance company (by an annuity). See also *Olmsted Incorporated Life Agency*, 35 T.C. 429 (1960), *nonacq.*, aff'd (8th Cir. 1962). This principle draws a distinction between a simple promise by a commercial company and a promise by an insurance company on the grounds that the latter is a promise by a third party. This is a dubious distinction at best. If a simple enforceable promise cannot be valued, the forfeiture clauses, which are often used as window dressing, can be eliminated unless their inclusion is desired for nontax purposes.

Of particular interest in connection with forfeiture clauses is a Tax Court decision, *Estate of Edward H. Wadewitz*, 39 T.C. 925 (1963), aff'd (7th Cir. 1964). The case involved the question of whether the benefits under a deferred-compensation contract were includable in the gross estate under Section 2039. In holding that they were so includable, the Court stated that the rights were really nonforfeitable, since compliance with the forfeiture provisions was within the decedent's exclusive control.

In Revenue Ruling 60-31, the Commissioner has removed the threats of constructive receipt and economic benefit insofar as simple promises and unfunded arrangements are concerned. He indicates that contingency clauses are unnecessary. He acquiesced in the *Oates* case, but he also reaffirmed his position in the *Sproull* case for nonforfeitable funded arrangements. But see Rev. Rul. 67-449.

A discussion of deferred compensation contracts is not complete without reference to two cases which were decided against the taxpayer in each case by the lower courts (the Tax Court in one case, the District Court in the other) but were subsequently reversed on appeal by the Sixth Circuit Court of Appeals in decisions which leave something to be desired from the standpoint of certainty and clarity.

In *Drysdale v. Com.*, 277 F.2d 413 (6th Cir. 1960), the Circuit Court, in reversing the Tax Court, held that there had been no constructive receipt and no economic benefit in the following set of facts: The taxpayer, employed by Briggs Manufacturing Co., had entered into a deferred compensation contract providing deferred payments over a ten-year period following termination of the taxpayer's full-time activities or upon his attaining the age of 65. By the terms of the contract, the taxpayer was obligated to serve Briggs in an advisory and consulting capacity while he received the deferred payments, and to refrain from employment with any interests adverse to the activities of Briggs. In the event of any breach, any amount of deferred compensation not yet received by the taxpayer was to be forfeited. The agreement contained a "spendthrift" provision prohibiting assignment of benefits, etc.

Prior to a sale of its business by Briggs to Chrysler Corporation, the agreement was amended to cut the total amount of deferred compensation in half, to be paid over a period of five years instead of ten. Such payments were to be made to a trustee commencing one month after the sale of Briggs's business to Chrysler and continuing until the principal amount had been paid to the trustee. The advisory and consulting services of the taxpayer were required for the duration of the payments to the trustee. The trustee in turn was to pay over to the taxpayer on an identical scale of monthly payments, beginning with the attainment of age 65 or retirement from regular employment requiring full-time effort, whichever event first occurred. There was a provision for payments over to the taxpayer's wife or estate in the event of his death. The spendthrift provision was apparently retained in the contract.

The Tax Court had held the taxpayer to be taxable upon

amounts paid to the trustee in years prior to the taxpayer's attaining age 65 or retiring. The Circuit Court had no trouble disposing of the constructive-receipt contention on the grounds that at no time was the taxpayer entitled to receive any money and that the amendment to the contract had been an arm's-length negotiation prior to his being entitled to receive anything. So far as the economic-benefit theory of the *Sproull* case went, the Circuit Court stated that a crucial distinction in the instant case was that the taxpayer was restricted by the terms of the contract from exercising any dominion over the funds in possession of the trustee. In the *Sproull* case the trust funds were not spendthrifted.

In *Doty v. U.S.*, 323 F.2d 649 (6th Cir. 1963), involving identical contracts but a different taxpayer, the District Court held in favor of the Government and the Circuit Court again reversed. The Government contended that there should be a different result in *Doty* from *Drysdale* because the Court's attention in *Drysdale* had not been called to Section 402(b) of the Code. The Circuit Court stated that, in its opinion, the forfeiture provisions of the contract were still in effect and that:

"... Violation by Doty of the provisions of the contract as amended would result in forfeiture of his interest in the contribution made by Briggs under the trust agreement. Since the contributions were forfeitable, Section 402 did not apply.

"In any event, *stare decisis* compels that we follow the rule in Drysdale."

The confusing part of the above statement is that, in the agreement as amended, it is not at all clear that there would be a forfeiture of amounts already paid to the trustee upon a subsequent violation of any of the conditions or agreements to be performed by the taxpayer.

If the foregoing cases serve no other purpose, they certainly tend to emphasize the importance of forfeiture provisions.

THE NONQUALIFIED STOCK BONUS PLAN

THE MECHANICS. The nonqualified stock bonus plan compensates the efforts of selected employees by giving them shares in the employer company. It is similar to the simple cash bonus plan with two exceptions: (1) the payment is made in shares of the company, thereby giving the employee a proprietary interest in the company; and (2) the plan has a deferred-compensation feature in that the shares are transferred to the employee subsequent to the time that they are allotted to him.

As is characteristic of all executive compensation plans, the form of the stock bonus plan varies in accordance with the specific needs of the employer. A typical plan might have the following elements:

1. The plan is administered by a company committee which determines who is eligible for bonus and the amount of bonus allocable to each eligible person.
2. An amount, determined by reference to a predetermined formula based upon the annual earnings of the company, is set aside in a reserve account.
3. After the total amount is credited to the reserve account, the committee determines the allocation of the annual bonus. The date on which the allocation is made is termed "the award date." As of the award date, the dollar amount of each employee's bonus is translated into terms of shares of stock. For example, an employee is awarded a bonus of $5,000. The company stock is selling for $50. Therefore, his award account represents 100 shares of the stock of the company. Any portion of the total annual bonus which is not awarded is carried over at its dollar amount and awarded in future years.
4. The company acquires sufficient shares of its stock to cover the number of shares represented in the reserve account. The acquisition may be by purchase on the market or by transfer of treasury shares. If unissued shares are used, their effect upon the value of outstanding shares must be recognized.
5. One-fifth of the shares which have been awarded are distributed to the employee in each of the five years subsequent to the year of the bonus. The distributions are earned through continued employment on a monthly basis. If an employee is discharged or resigns, he is entitled only to the portion of the annual distribution which he has earned. If an employee dies before full distribution, the unpaid portion is paid to his estate or beneficiary. If an employee retires before full distribution,

the annual distributions are continued to him so long as he does not violate a noncompete agreement.

Example: As of December 31, 1967, Jones is awarded a bonus of $5,000, representing 100 shares of XYZ Company stock. In January 1968 a distribution of 20 shares is made to him. In January 1969 he receives another 20 shares. On July 1, 1969 he resigns. He is entitled to an additional ten shares.

6. When the shares are paid to the employee, he also receives an amount equal to the dividends which he would have received had he been the owner of the distributed shares from the award date.

THE EMPLOYER'S DEDUCTION. No distributions are made until the employee's rights become nonforfeitable. Under Section 404(a)(5), the employer receives a deduction in the year in which the distributions are made. Revenue Ruling 62-217 states that the employer is entitled to a deduction for the full market value of the stock, notwithstanding that under Section 1032(a) no gain or loss on the distribution is recognized. Low-cost treasury stock may therefore be used to satisfy obligations under a nonqualified stock bonus plan without causing a reduction of the compensation deduction allowable.

THE EMPLOYEE'S INCOME. The workout provision and the noncompete provision represent forfeiture clauses which are sufficient to prevent taxation to the employee until he actually receives the distribution.

THE "STOCKLESS" STOCK BONUS PLAN

THE MECHANICS. The "stockless" stock bonus plan was popularized by Koppers Company, Inc., although two other Pittsburgh companies (H. J. Heinz and Consolidation Coal) had similar plans earlier. A district court has restrained Consolidation Coal Company from further utilization of its plan because the benefits bore no reasonable relation to the services of the employee. [*Berkowitz v. Humphrey*, 163 F. Supp. 78 (D.C. Ohio, 1958).] Under the Koppers-type plan, which has been upheld in court, a specific number of deferred-compensation units are created and are awarded from time to time to a select group of executives. Each unit corresponds in value to one share of common stock of the company. When an executive is awarded a number of units, his account under the plan is credited with the fair market value of a similar number of shares of common stock as of the day of the award. When dividends are paid on the common stock, the executive's account is credited with a like amount of "dividends." While the units do not represent any actual proprietary interest in the company, they have many of the attributes of actual shares. Thus, the units are affected by stock dividends, stock rights, mergers, etc., and the accounts of the executives are adjusted accordingly.

On the day the executive retires, his units are revalued at the then market value of the common stock. Upon retirement the individual is entitled to (1) the "dividends" which his units earned during the period when he held them plus (2) the increase in the market value of the units during his holding period, as measured by the value of the actual stock of the company. These benefits are paid to him in quarterly installments over a ten-year period.

The plan contains forfeiture clauses in that the executive must agree to the following conditions:

1. He will remain in the employ of the company for five years from the award date, or until retirement, if earlier.
2. He will not compete with the company during the payout period.
3. He will be available for consulting work during the payout period.

The plan also has these features: If a participant dies before retirement, his beneficiary succeeds to his benefits as of the date of death. If the employee terminates his employment after the five-year employment period (other than by death or retirement), he receives the "dividends" earned on his units, plus such portion (none, part, or all) of the increase in the value of his units as may be awarded to him by the administrative committee. If he terminates his employment during the initial five-year workout period, the committee may award him a distribution if it feels that the circumstances surrounding his termination are unusual. If, at the date of death or retirement, the market value of the common stock is depressed, an election may be made to value the units at a date during the three years which follow the termination or death, provided the optional value thus assigned does not exceed the highest value which existed during the entire workout period. This privilege of optional value may be extended to a termination by other than death or retirement upon action of the committee. The company reserves a block of authorized but unissued common stock which may be sold to finance the plan.

The plan may have other variations. For example, relating the value of the units to the book value of the stock rather than to its fair market value makes the plan adaptable to the small closely held corporation.

THE EMPLOYER'S DEDUCTION. The employees have no vested rights under the plan. No payments are made until after retirement. The employer, therefore, receives a tax deduction in the year that the benefits are paid to the employee. [Sec. 404(a)(5).]

THE EMPLOYEE'S INCOME. The forfeiture clauses prevent taxation of income to the employee until the cash is received. At any time prior to the receipt, the employee can commit certain acts which will deny him further benefits. In addition, this plan represents a promise to pay in the future made by a commercial company (see discussion at page 296). See, however, *Frank Cowden, Sr.*, 32 T.C. 853 (1959).

In the *Cowden* case (remanded by the 5th Circuit (289 F.2d 20, 1961) to determine the discounted value of certain contracts involved, and found by the Tax Court (20 TCM 1134) to be of at least as great a value as the Commissioner had placed on them), the taxpayer had sold oil interests for $511,192, payable $10,224 in 1951, $250,484 in 1952, and $250,484 in 1953. The obligation of the purchaser, Stanolind Oil Co., was represented by separate, non-interest-bearing instruments. The Courts held the obligations to be the equivalent of cash because they were of a solvent obligor, payable unconditionally, assignable (and in fact assigned), and of a kind which was becoming more frequently assigned to a banking institution at a discount not shown to be unreasonably high.

THE RESTRICTED STOCK PLAN

The advantages of restricted stock as a deferred compensation device was analyzed earlier, beginning on page 198. See also Revenue Ruling 68-86, which approves a plan under which an employee, by an early election, may choose between a cash bonus or a restricted stock bonus.

The restricted stock plan is based upon the rules applicable to bargain purchases with restrictions added to defer the imposition of tax. It would appear that property other than employer stock might be used in the plan without affecting the end result — e.g., securities in another corporation, employer bonds, land, etc.

JOINT VENTURES

EQUIPMENT LEASING. The leasing partnership is used as a vehicle for reducing the taxes of high-tax-bracket individuals through the effective employment of partnership tax law, accelerated depreciation, and the investment credit. As one of the most sophisticated of tax control devices, it requires careful handling in the areas of state partnership law, tax law, leasing, and financing. It may be adapted to a deferred-compensation situation, as illustrated below:

Example: Ten executives (together with a general partner) form XYZ, Ltd., a limited partnership. Each limited partner contributes $10,000. XYZ, Ltd. purchases $2,000,000 of industrial equipment which has a life of 20 years. The purchase is financed by a bank. The liability for the debt runs to the property. The equipment is leased for 20 years to a third party for a rental sufficient to amortize and service the debt. The executives are in the 70% bracket.

In this situation, each partner will reduce his taxes during the first year of partnership operations by $24,920 as follows:

Deductions and credits	Tax reduction
Investment credit	$14,000
First-year depreciation	2,800
Partnership loss	8,120
Total tax reduction	$24,920

During the earlier years, the partnership will have operating losses which will be available to the executive to reduce his taxable income. Each year the loss will be smaller than the previous year because of decreasing deductions within the partnership for interest

and accelerated depreciation. Eventually the partnership will operate at a profit, and the partner will increase his taxable income
by including the partnership profits. If structured as a deferred compensation device, however, the partnership profits will flow back
during retirement years — i.e., low-tax-bracket (say 30%) years.

The illustration highlights these features:

1. The $10,000 initial investment is exchanged for $14,000
   reduction in taxes due to the investment credit.
2. The operating loss-gain of the partnership removes income from a 70% year and places it in a 30% year.
3. The executive assumes the management of the cash flow
   from 1 and 2 above to provide income and cash flow
   required in the retirement years.
4. Operating the plan requires that close attention be paid
   to avoiding the limitations on partnership losses and taxation of the partnership as an association.

LAND PURCHASE. A limited partnership is formed with the
employer corporation the general partner (50%) and the ten executives as limited partners (50%). A land parcel is purchased for
$1,000,000, payable $200,000 down and $80,000 per year for 10 years
at 6%.

The corporation, as its capital contribution of $500,000, makes
the $200,000 down payment and pays the annual installments of
$80,000 until an additional $300,000 is paid. It carries the interest
on the $300,000.

The ten executives pay the interest on the second $500,000 —
about $3,000 each annually. They also pay local taxes. These ex-
penses are deductible, presumably in high-tax-bracket years.

At about the time the limited partners are required to make
capital contributions to amortize the debt, the land is sold and the
profits are divided. As a deferred-compensation device, the plan is
structured to flow the profits to the lower-tax-bracket retirement
years of the executives.

Reasonable Executive Compensation

GENERAL OBSERVATIONS

How much to pay corporate executives of a business enterprise is a question of some magnitude. In addition to attracting and retaining capable persons, there are matters of taxation, renegotiation, cost considerations, etc. These matters are further translated under Federal income tax laws and regulations into determinations of what is a "reasonable allowance" for services actually rendered. The phrase "a reasonable allowance" first appeared in the Revenue Act of 1918 and has remained unchanged in our income tax structure to this day.

What is "reasonable" under various circumstances is a question which has probably undergone more litigation and debate under our tax system than any other subject. Controversy, no doubt, could have been avoided in many cases if either the employer or the executive, or both, had been more aware of the principles and rules which have developed over the years for establishing and justifying executive compensation. Furthermore, the principle of "reasonableness" is essentially a determination based on all of the facts applicable in a given case. Generally, no case is conclusive as to the issue in another, and each case must be decided on its own facts. There are no rigid formulas which can be applied without modification and correlation to a set of specific circumstances. Decided cases can do no more than furnish guidelines to be used to determine the reasonableness of an executive's compensation.

GUIDELINES

The Revenue Service many years ago published a ruling describing the factors to be used in appraising a particular employee's compensation to determine reasonableness and deductibility. The standards to be used in any scrutiny are as follows [T.B.M. 44]:

1. Character and amount of responsibility.
2. Ease or difficulty of the work itself.
3. Time required.
4. Working conditions.
5. Future prospects.
6. Living conditions of the locality.
7. Individual ability.
8. Technical training.
9. Profitableness to the employer of the services rendered.
10. Number of available persons capable of performing the duties of the position.

Paralleling the Revenue Service's ruling is a set of guidelines promulgated by the Tax Court in the case of *R. P. Farnsworth &*

Co., Inc., 203 F.2d 490 (5th Cir. 1953) rev'g. T.C. Memo. The Tax Court referred to a number of guidelines it considered reliable as the minimum necessary to establish reasonableness in compensation cases. They are as follows:

1. Employee's qualifications, background, and skill.
2. Economic conditions.
3. Availability of others to compete for the job.
4. Time of year compensation is determined.
5. Comparison of compensation paid to employees of comparable businesses and positions.
6. Ratio of compensation to gross receipts, gross or net income.
7. Size and scope of the business.
8. Extent and nature of the employee's work and responsibilities.

See also *Mayson Manufacturing Company,* 178 F.2d 115 (6th Cir. 1949).

Unlike the Revenue Service's ruling, the *Farnsworth* and *Mayson* cases establish that the ratio of compensation to gross income, the time of determination of the amount of the executive's compensation, and the comparison to other companies in the industry are important criteria to be used for testing reasonableness.

Unreasonable-compensation cases usually involve circumstances of small, closely-held companies where the employer and the employee are not dealing at arm's length. Arm's-length situations generally do not create controversies. Relationships by blood, or by marriage, or by stockholdings generally neutralize the concept of arm's-length dealings. [*Harold's Club,* 340 F.2d 861 (9th Cir. 1965).]

An outstanding exception in connection with the payment of compensation in proportion to stockholdings is a case where 1,900 employees participated in a company plan. [*R. J. Reynolds Tobacco Co.,* 260 F.2d 9 (4th Cir. 1958).]

As a general rule, no single set of circumstances, nor any specific combination of several, can offer a formula for success in a particular case. The factors used are many and varied, and the emphasis is usually keyed to the particular facts of a specific case. However, the more factors present to justify reasonableness, the better the opportunity for allowance of the deduction to the payor.

COMPANY POLICY

A comparison of the company's general salary policy toward all employees is important. For example, the existence of employee salary increases over a period of years may indicate percentage increases in low-level employee brackets which are greater than the percentage increases granted the higher-level executives. Individual comparison of salaries paid to other employees in the same company by nature of duties is also helpful. For instance, where compensation paid to an employee salesman who was the husband of the chief stockholder was questioned, the amount paid was allowed after it was shown that the compensation paid to other, unrelated, salesmen in the same company was comparable. [*Eagle Office Equipment Co., Inc.*, TCM Dec. 46,264 (1946).]

An executive's salary history may on occasion establish reasonable compensation in a later year. [*Stern-Slegman-Prins Co. v. U. S.*, (D.C. Mo. 1938), Govt' appeal dism'd, 106 F.2d 1020.]

ABILITIES AND RESPONSIBILITIES

The ability of the executive and his assumption of responsibility, and the time required of him to perform his services, are significant elements in establishing reasonable compensation. His salary worth to a company is demonstrated ultimately by the executive's past attainments and the prospects of his future performance. Competent executives command rewards commensurate with better-than-average and/or outstanding service.

Executives who assume wide and varied duties also shoulder significant responsibilities and are usually rewarded generously. Where the success of a business can be traced directly to the efforts of an executive or executive group, better-than-average salary allowances are in order. Where the prosperity of a company is better than average, measured by growth in a particular industry or the normal inflationary trend of the economy, a substantial salary for the responsible executive or executive group is not uncommon. Normally, greater emphasis is to be given to the factors evidencing the value of the executive's services by reason of his qualifications, duties, and achievements rather than the time spent in performing such services.

In some cases a company's financial performance is directly related to the abilities and services of an executive who has assumed a combination of duties as president and chief executive officer, including responsibilities for sales, engineering, and general management. Where this is the case, the savings and benefits derived are normally directly attributable to the services of the executive and he should be compensated accordingly. Where the company has enjoyed an unusual return on investment and a rate of growth attributable to the efforts of an executive or an executive group, it is obvious that any stockholder group or board of directors would be pleased at such results and would have little difficulty in approving the amounts which are paid. [*Despatch Oven Company*, TCM Dec. 45,219 (1945); *Jewell Ridge Coal Sales Co., Inc.*, TCM 1957-30.]

A substantial salary and bonus paid to the president of an auto agency was allowed in the year 1941, although he had entered the United States Navy but was stationed nearby. He operated the agency at night. He spent long hours, and because of his direct efforts the agency was successful. His compensation was determined to be reasonable. [*Ernest Burwell, Inc. v. U.S.*, 113 F. Supp. 26 (D.C. S. Carolina 1953).]

An important element in many cases has been the extent of the responsibility assumed by an executive. [*Bringwald, Inc.*, 334 F.2d 639 (Ct. Cl. 1964).]

Performing the functions required of two positions for the same company does not necessarily mean that the executive is entitled to the combined compensation of both. However, it does entitle him to increased compensation for the greater amount of responsibilities assumed. [*Express Publishing Co.*, 143 F.2d 386 (5th Cir. 1944).]

DIVIDENDS, EARNINGS, GROWTH

There is a tendency in the closely-held corporation situation where stockholders are also executives to be liberal with executive compensation. Deductible compensation is preferable to nondeductible dividends. This inclination on the part of the closely-held corporation accounts in part for the frequency of nonpayment of dividends, and is a factor considered often in compensation cases, though it is not always controlling.

In and of itself the nonpayment of dividends does not justify a conclusion that compensation is unreasonable. Nonetheless, absent other favorable factors or in conjunction with unfavorable factors, it has been considered in a number of cases. [*Glenshaw Glass Co.*, 13 T.C. 296 (1949), *acq.*; *Bringwald, Inc.*, 334 F.2d 639 (Ct. Cl. 1964).]

Considered objectively, if sales, earnings, and growth are at high levels, higher compensation is justified even apart from contingent compensation arrangements discussed later. Where sales, earnings, and growth are the results of the activities of an executive or group of executives, they should command high levels of compensation. [*Ernest Burwell, Inc., v. U.S.* 113 F. Supp. 26 (D.C. S. Carolina 1953).]

Very often the assembly of statistical data for a period of, say, ten prior years as to net sales, net earnings, rate of return on net worth, and a comparison of executive compensation to net sales and net earnings can indirectly reveal the executive's worth to a company and show appropriately whether or not his salary is increasing at a comparable rate.

INDUSTRY COMPARISONS

The validity of the factor of comparable salaries in the same industry or in comparable industries depends on true comparability. Individual company characteristics can either weaken or strengthen comparability. Differences or equality in size and complexity can be used either to distinguish or to strengthen the validity of the comparison. It is by no means an all-inclusive factor in a reasonable-compensation case. However, it has been used with some success. [*Faucette Co., Inc.*, 17 T.C. 187 (1951), *acq.*; *Rust-Oleum Corp. v. Sauber*, (D.C. Ill. 1958).]

ECONOMIC CONDITIONS

The general price level of the economy and economic conditions are frequently used as supporting factors in some compensation cases. In the early years of World War II, this factor at least in part was considered to justify high compensation. [*Roth Office Equipment Co. v. Gallagher,* 172 F.2d 452 (6th Cir. 1949).]

In appropriate situations, consumer price indices and similar criteria might justify increases for executive salaries which have not kept pace with such price indices.

PAST SERVICES

It is well established that the reasonableness of compensation can be measured in all instances against past as well as present services. Current compensation can often be justified by establishing that the executive was paid inadequate compensation in a prior year or years.

In the leading case, *Lucas v. Ox Fibre Brush Co.,* 281 U.S. 115 (1930), the Supreme Court concluded that both past and present services can be used to justify compensation as reasonable for a current year. In the case, the company's corporate directors in 1920 voted a substantial bonus to two corporate officers, partly because they had been underpaid in prior lean years. Admittedly, the bonuses were unreasonable in relation to the services rendered in 1920, the year in which the payments were made. The resolution of the board referred specifically to the underpayment of compensation in prior years. The Supreme Court determined that the amounts paid in the current year were reasonable when viewed in relation to inadequate compensation paid in past years.

Justification based on past services should be used cautiously. After past services have been adequately compensated, compensation of future years may be affected, since reliance then must be placed on current-year circumstances.

BONUSES AND CONTINGENT COMPENSATION

The test of reasonableness is applied to the total compensation paid to an executive, and the total includes any and all bonuses.

If in the aggregate his total compensation, including the bonus, is reasonable, then the bonus is reasonable and deductible. Regulations require that bonus payments to be deductible should be made in good faith and as additional compensation for services actually rendered. [Regs. 1.162-9.]

The question in bonus cases involving stockholder-executives is whether the additional compensation is a distribution of earnings, a disguised dividend. Dividend consequences are increased when the payments are in proportion to stock holdings and either result in absorbing as a practical matter all of a corporation's earnings or are determined at a time near year-end when corporate earnings are known. [*Bridges-Smith Co., v. Glenn,* 116 F.2d 934 (6th Cir. 1940).]

Bonuses paid in the same ratio as stock holdings are probably more subject to scrutiny than direct payments of compensation. Despite the fact that year-end bonuses were admittedly paid to stockholder-officers in proportion to their stock ownership, the total compensation paid including the bonuses were determined to be reasonable. [*Safety Engineering & Supply Co., Inc. v. U. S.,* 374 F.2d 885 (5th Cir. 1967).]

The form or method of fixing executive compensation is not decisive as to deductibility. While any form of contingent compensation invites scrutiny as a possible distribution of earnings of the enterprise, it does not follow that payments on a contingent basis are to be treated fundamentally on any basis different from that applying to compensation at a flat rate. Contingent compensation contracts based on profits, sales, etc. are approved by the regulations if:

1. It is paid under a free bargain between the employer and the executive; *and*
2. The agreement is made before the services are rendered; *and*
3. The arrangement is not influenced by any consideration on the part of the employer other than that of securing on fair and advantageous terms the services of the executive. Compensation agreed to and paid thereunder "should be allowed as a deduction even though in the actual working out of the contract it may prove to be greater than the amount which would ordinarily be paid." [Regs. 1.162-7(b)(2).]

The regulations consider that the circumstances to be taken into consideration in the determination of reasonableness are those existing at the date when the contract for services was made, not those existing at the date when the deduction is questioned. The statement of the regulations is of great importance, since it can be argued that compensation is deductible in a year even though unreasonable in amount for that year, provided it is paid in accordance with a bona fide contingent compensation agreement entered into at a time when the circumstances taken into consideration made the terms of the agreement a reasonable one.

A contingent bonus based on profits can be upheld as reasonable if the arrangement is made well in advance before large earnings are apparent or realized.

A district court has allowed a deduction for contingent compensation paid to a husband and wife under a contract with a corporation entered into shortly after they had acquired the stock. The corporation had been experiencing serious financial difficulties. It allowed the corporation a deduction for the entire amounts paid to the husband and wife for the years in question as reasonable compensation. Both worked long hours and performed many duties involved in operating a manufacturing business, such as buying, inventory control, hiring and firing, accounting services, etc. The Court found that the corporation's success was due primarily to the wife's designing of new products and the husband's creation of new machines to produce the items. [*W. R. Vermillion Co., Inc. v. U.S.*, (D.C. Mo. 1968).]

However, changed circumstances may have an effect on later payments of compensation. The regulations state that, "In any event, the allowance for the compensation paid may not exceed what is reasonable under all the circumstances." [Regs. 1.162-7(b)(3).]

In *Hoffman Radio Corporation*, compensation disallowed as unreasonable was paid as a part of a contingent compensation arrangement. When the contract was executed in 1941, the company was in poor financial condition. In 1943, due to the circumstances of World War II and not to any increased services or demands on the executive, the company became successful. Because of the changed circumstances brought about by the War and lack of comparability to compensation paid to other employers, the Court said:

"It is not thought that the Regulations, considered in their entirety, establish the hard and fast rule that a contingent contract, fair and equitable when made, becomes permanently immune from scrutiny regardless of how radically conditions may alter; ..."

The result in the *Hoffman Radio* case should be judged according to its peculiar circumstances. In any event, contingent compensation arrangements with key and executive employees and certainly stockholder-employees should be covered by formal contracts executed well in advance of the services to be rendered and written in language keeping in mind the principles of the regulations. [*Hoffman Radio Corporation,* 177 F.2d 264 (9th Cir. 1949).]

FRINGE ALLOWANCES

Are fringe allowances, other than those referred to in deferred compensation plans, subject to the reasonableness test? Regulations covering certain employee benefits say nothing about reasonableness. Amounts paid for dismissal wages, unemployment benefits, guaranteed annual wages, vacations, or under a sickness, accident, hospitalization, medical expense, recreational, welfare, or similar benefit plan, are deductible as ordinary and necessary business expenses. [Regs. 1.162-10(a).]

In *Lincoln Electric Co.,* a deferred-compensation case, the Court held that the payment of premiums on an employee's retirement annuity policy, and certain other expenditures for contributions to a trust for the benefit of some of its employees, were noncompensatory in nature and hence not subject to the specific test of reasonableness. However, the Court stated that the element of reasonableness is inherent in the phrase "ordinary and necessary." Further:

"Clearly, it was not the intention of Congress to automatically allow as deductions operating expenses incurred or paid by the taxpayer in an unlimited amount." [*Lincoln Electric Co.,* 176 F. 2d 815 (6th Cir. 1949).]

The Revenue Service has ruled that premiums paid by an employer on an individual income replacement policy for an employee are deductible if, when added to all compensation paid the employee, the result is reasonable. [Rev. Rul. 58-90.]

Although certain salaries were found to be unreasonable, premiums paid on accident and health policies on the same employees were found to be reasonable and deductible. In another case, premiums paid on small policies of insurance on officers in a company-wide group insurance plan were allowed. In the latter case, there was no finding as to the unreasonable or reasonable nature of the premiums. [*Ernest, Holdeman & Collet, Inc.*, TCM 1960-10, aff'd (7th Cir. 1961); *Huckins Tool & Die, Inc.*, TCM 1959-190, aff'd (7th Cir. 1961).]

In theory, fringe allowances are probably subject to the reasonableness test and are to be included with total compensation. As a practical matter, if the amounts are relatively small, the test of reasonableness might not be applied.

The reasonableness test as applied to contributions to qualified pension and profit-sharing plans is clearly prescribed in the regulations. A contribution which is in the nature of additional compensation for services performed in prior years is deductible, if reasonable, even if the total of such contributions and other compensation for the current year is in excess of reasonable compensation for services performed in the current year. The total of all compensation and contributions paid to or for such employee in prior years must stand the test of being a reasonable allowance for all services, past and present, rendered by the employee by the end of the current year. [Regs. 1.404(a)-1(b).]

Credits for past services with a former employer can be given under a present employer's pension plan to an employee under certain conditions. In this respect, it is considered a unit of measurement as to the reasonableness of current compensation for services to the present employer. [Rev. Rul. 62-139.]

Although the law and regulations require the disallowance of an excessive amount of the total nondeferred and deferred compensation, they are silent as to the manner in which the disallowed amount should be allocated between the deferred and nondeferred portions. As between current compensation and contributions to a qualified pension or profit-sharing plan the Revenue Service requires an adjustment or a reallocation of the portion of the contribution determined to be unreasonable to the other participants in the plan to prevent discrimination. The position taken in the ruling is quite arbitrary and without foundation. An adjustment could easily have been devised without having an effect on the nondeferred portion of the compensation paid. [Rev. Rul. 67-341.]

NONQUALIFIED DEFERRED-COMPENSATION PLANS

The reasonableness of payments under a nonqualified deferred-compensation plan is to be tested against total compensation for all past years as well as for the current year, and is to be judged in relation to total services over the same period of time. Payments to a nonqualified deferred-compensation plan are deductible by the employer only when paid. A showing of reasonableness is necessary at the time of the deduction with reference to services rendered either at the date the plan was adopted, or during the term of the plan or at the date of payment, depending on the plan adopted and its terms.

AGGREGATE COMPENSATION

The reasonableness of aggregate compensation paid to all employees as a group or to a number of executives as a group cannot be used to justify an unreasonably high salary paid to one employee or one executive in the group. [*L. Schepp Company*, 25 B.T.A. 419 (1932), *acq.*]

In *Miller Manufacturing Company, Inc.*, 149 F. 2d 421 (4th Cir. 1945), the Fourth Circuit sustained a disallowance of compensation on grounds of unreasonableness, pointing out that aggregate compensation is not a proper test. The company failed to shoulder the burden of proof to support individual salaries as reasonable. The presumption of correctness of the Commissioner's findings had not been overcome.

In a case, previously referred to above, involving 1,900 employees, aggregate compensation paid as to all employees, considered with a number of individual tests, was held to be reasonable. [*R. J. Reynolds Tobacco Co.*, 260 F.2d 9 (4th Cir. 1958).]

TREATMENT ACCORDED EXCESSIVE COMPENSATION

The income tax liability of a recipient in respect of an amount ostensibly paid to him as compensation, but not allowed to be deducted as such by the employer, will depend upon the circumstances of each case. Excessive payments by corporations bearing a close relationship to stockholdings may be found to be a distribution of earnings or profits. The excessive payments will be treated as a dividend.

If the excessive payments are in substance payments for property, they should be treated by the payor as capital expenditures and by the recipient as part of the purchase price. Any amount paid in the form of compensation, but not in fact the purchase price of services, is not deductible. [Regs. 1.162-7 and 1.162-8.]

The Court of Claims in *Sterno Sales Corp.* stated that: "Thus, disallowed payments consist of two general types — true compensation which is barred because excessive, and payments which are not compensation but something else." Compensation which is barred because excessive might not lose its character as compensation and thus remain taxable to the executive. As a practical matter, he may find it very difficult to argue that the payments are anything other than compensation.

Payments which are described as compensation but are something else will be characterized as determined by all the facts of each particular case. If they are determined to be dividends, they will be taxable as such. On the other hand, if they conceivably can be said to be payments for property, they will be treated as payment of the purchase price.

The Court in *Sterno Sales Corp.* further stated:

"Compensation remains compensation even if it is held unreasonable in amount and, accordingly, not deductible as a business expense. The payment does not change in character solely because it is characterized as excessive or undue.

"The nondeductibility of the expense of the payor, because it is unreasonable in amount, does not transform the payment in the hands of the payee."

The case serves as a warning that a taxpayer must normally accept the tax consequences of the way in which he deliberately chooses to cast his transactions, although the Revenue Service may not be bound by his choice. [*Sterno Sales Corp.*, 345 F. 2d 552 (Ct. Cl. 1965).]

The portion of compensation paid which is determined to be

unreasonable cannot be taken as a business deduction in another form. [*Roehl Construction Co., Inc.*, 17 T.C. 1037 (1951).]

EVIDENCE OF REASONABLE COMPENSATION

Advance planning and a clear record are prerequisites to supporting reasonable compensation. Although corporate minutes may be essentially self-serving declarations, they are a place to describe facts and show as many of the favorable factors as is possible, as to why the compensation of an executive is as high as it is, or why it was necessary to give an increase.

In appropriate situations, a Subchapter S election can be made so as to eliminate any question of unreasonable compensation for shareholder-employees. However, care must be exercised in such cases to avoid an assertion that compensation levels are being used to shift income among the stockholders of the Subchapter S corporation.

One of the ways to defend against the threat of unreasonable compensation is to provide for a repayment of the portion denied as a deduction to the employer. The repayment is not taxable to the employer since it was not allowed a deduction and therefore resulted in no tax benefit from the original payment. It returns to the employer the cash in the year of repayment in the amount of the lost deduction.

As to the executive, the repayment has no effect on his receipt of the unreasonable compensation in the year in which he actually received it. However, if repayment is made under a legal obligation existing at the time the original compensation was received, a deduction is possible for the amount of repayment for the year in which it is made.

Agreements to repay made after the time the original compensation is received are considered purely voluntary acts, and therefore, do not support a deduction. An agreement to repay should be specific at the time the executive receives the compensation, requiring that he repay any part determined excessive and subsequently disallowed to the corporation. Such agreements, however, do have an obvious drawback in that they call attention to the matter. Since the repayment to be deductible must be made in accordance with a legal obligation which exists before the original compensation is received, the agreement to repay should be clearly spelled out in corporate minutes or other written instruments at the time the payments are made. [*Vincent E. Oswald*, 49 T.C. No. 68 (1968); *Ernest H. Berger*, 37 T.C. 1026 (1962).]

If the deductible repayment is $3,000 or less, the executive's tax in the year of repayment is reduced to the extent of the deduction allowed under Section 1341. However, if the repayment is in excess of $3,000, the law permits the executive to recover the tax he incurred when he reported the compensation in the earlier year, if that amount is greater than the decrease in tax for the year of repayment resulting from the deduction of the amount repaid.

CONTROLLED ENTITIES

It is usually immaterial whether an executive employed by several related corporations is paid directly by several payrolls, or has his compensation paid by one corporation which is allocated by intercompany charges among several corporations. However, the application of Section 482 in which the Commissioner is given the power to allocate income and deductions among the members of a group of controlled entities, as that phrase is used in the regulations, can create some odd results.

There are two problems in this connection. On one hand, total compensation paid to an executive must stand the test of reasonableness for total services rendered. On the other hand, an allocation among several controlled entities must result in what would have been done in what is otherwise an arm's length situation. The question of reasonableness is to be resolved by the application of Section 162(a)(1) while the fairness of allocation is to be tested under Section 482.

In many cases, the question of reasonableness is not raised and only the fairness of the allocation between the related parties is considered. [*Glenmore Distilleries Co., Inc.*, 47 B.T.A. 213 (1942), acq.] In other cases, the fairness of an allocation is determined on the grounds of whether services rendered to the controlled entity were commensurate with the compensation allocated.

In one case, the employees of a Philippine subsidiary rendered no services to the United States parent which had paid 50% of their salaries. The 50% paid by the parent corporation was disallowed as a deduction. However, although the president of the Philippine subsidiary performed no services for the subsidiary, the deduction of the parent's payment of his full salary was allowed to the parent because it was shown that his services were in substance performed for the parent in the capacity of supervising the parent's significant investment in the subsidiary. [*Columbian Rope Company,* 42 T.C. 800 (1964), *acq.*]

Where the reasonableness and fairness of allocation are questions to be raised in a particular controlled situation, the Commissioner should not be permitted to have the option to use either Section 162(a)(1) or Section 482. Both sections should be applied together, rather than independently, since otherwise odd situations can occur. Assume, for example, that X is an employee of parent corporation P at $30,000 per year. He is also an employee of subsidiary corporation S at $20,000 per year. Assume also that $50,000 is reasonable compensation for X from both corporations.

P and S file separate returns. Both corporations are profitable and pay income taxes at the time the Commissioner proceeds against P, claiming that the compensation paid X was unreasonable in the amount of $10,000. Since Section 482 has been interpreted as not giving the taxpayer a right to use it or to force the Government to use it, if the Commissioner does not reallocate in this instance, P might lose a $10,000 deduction — and if so, it might be lost to everyone. [Regs. 1.482-1(b)(3).]

Under the regulations of Section 482, correlative adjustments are required when Section 482 is used. [Regs. 1.482-1(d)(2).] If the deduction is denied one taxpayer because another is entitled to it, there is to be an allocation to the other taxpayer who is then allowed the deduction.

In the above example, there is no correlative deduction allowed to S, since the disallowance by the Commissioner is based on grounds of reasonableness rather than the fairness of an allocation. However, if the $10,000 when added to the $20,000 paid by S is reasonable, a valid basis for a deduction exists, since payment by the parent is either an advance or a contribution of capital to the subsidiary and is a constructive payment by the subsidiary allowing the subsidiary a deduction.

EFFECTS OF COMPROMISE

A disallowance of unreasonable compensation in one year can have an effect on deductions in future years. Assume that a corporate employer recognizes and admits that there are certain weaknesses in his case and concludes that he should arrive at a settlement with the revenue agent. He realizes that any disallowance will also act as a stimulus to the next revenue agent who examines future years.

In such a case, negotiating a settlement with the revenue agent should be done on a decreasing scale. Thus, if there are several years involved, the maximum agreed-to disallowance should be proportionately greater in earlier years and lower in later years. In fact, in the last year, if appropriate, no adjustment should be made. Of course, the results depend on individual circumstances and the factual situation presented.

Federal Estate Tax

EXCLUSION UNDER SECTION 2039(c)

BENEFITS RECEIVABLE. The value of an annuity or other payment receivable by any beneficiary (other than an executor) under certain qualified plans and under certain annuity contracts, to the extent the annuity or other payment is attributable to employer contributions, is excludable from the decedent's gross estate for Federal estate tax purposes. The exclusion applies to amounts receivable by any beneficiary (other than an executor) from qualified pension, stock bonus, or profit-sharing plans which at the time of the decedent's separation from employment, whether by death or otherwise, or at the time of the termination of the plan, if earlier, met the requirements of Section 401(a). [Regs. 20.2039-2(b).]

The exclusion also applies to the value of a retirement annuity contract purchased by an employer under a qualified plan which met the requirements of Section 403(a) at the time of the decedent's separation from employment, by death or otherwise, or at the time of the termination of the plan, if earlier. Similarly, in the case of a decedent dying after December 31, 1957, the exclusion applies to the value of a retirement annuity contract purchased for an employee by a religious or educational organization or by an organization which normally received a substantial part of its support from the United States or any state or political subdivision thereof and is exempt from tax under Section 501(a). These organizations are identified in Section 503(b)(1), (2), and (3).

For benefits other than from exempt religious, educational or government-supported organizations, the exclusion applies to estates of all persons dying after December 31, 1953.

Example 1: Under a qualified pension plan, an employer makes contributions to a trust which is to provide the employee and his wife upon his retirement at age 60 with an annuity for their joint lives. The employee dies at age 61 after the trustee began making payments of his annuity. Since the wife's annuity is receivable under a qualified pension plan, no part of the value of the annuity is includable in the decedent's gross estate since the employer was the sole contributor. [Regs. 20.2039-2(b), Example (1).]

Example 2: If an employee dies before reaching retirement age and his wife receives payment of amounts credited to the employee's account in a qualified profit-sharing plan, no part of such payment is includable in the decedent's gross estate if the employer was the sole contributor under the plan. [Regs. 20.2039-2(b), Example (2).]

The exclusion applies if the amount is paid from a qualified plan even if the payment constitutes the proceeds of life insurance. [Rev. Rul. 67-371.]

Example 3: Under the terms of a qualified pension plan, the employer made contributions to a trust which were used by the trustee to purchase a contract from an insurance company for the benefit of an employee. The contract was to provide the employee, upon his retirement at age 65, with an annuity of $100 per month for life, and was to provide his designated beneficiary, upon the employee's death after retirement, with a similar annuity for life. The contract further provided that if the employee should die before reaching the retirement age, a payment equal to the greater of (a) $10,000 or (b) the reserve value of the policy would be paid to his designated beneficiary in lieu of the annuity described above. Assume that the employee died before reaching the retirement age and that at such time the plan met the requirements of Section 401(a). Since the designated beneficiary's payment was receivable under a qualified pension plan, no part of such payment is includable in the decedent's gross estate by reason of the provisions of Section 2039(c). It should be noted that for purposes of the exclusion under Section 2039(c), it is immaterial whether or not such payment constitutes the proceeds of life insurance under the principles set forth in paragraph (d) of Regulations 20.2039-1. [Regs. 20.2039-2(b), Example (3).]

Example 4: Upon retirement, an employee elects under a qualified profit-sharing plan to have the amount credited to his account left with the trustee under an interest arrangement. Under the plan, the employee retains the right to have the principal paid to himself in a lump sum up to the time of his death. At the time of his death the employee had not exercised this right. The amount payable to his beneficiary at his death is includable in his gross estate since the employee is considered to have constructively received the amount credited to his account upon his retirement. The exclusion under Section 2039(c) is not applicable. [Regs. 20.2039-2(b), Example (4).]

The above rules apply to qualified plans under which the employee makes no contributions. However, if a qualified plan is contributory (i.e., if the employee makes contributions as well as the employer) to the extent that the value of the benefits payable to a beneficiary is attributable to employee contributions, the portion of the benefit so attributable to employee contributions is includable in the gross estate of the employee.

Example: An employeee retires and, after receiving a pension for ten years, dies. His widow receives an annuity for her life in a lesser amount, which is worth $8,000 at her husband's death. During the period of his employment, the employee contributed $5,000 and the company $15,000. The value of the widow's annuity is includable in the employee's gross estate in the amount of $2,000 ($5,000 divided by $20,000 is 25%; 25% of $8,000 is $2,000). [Regs. 20.2039-2(c).]

In an annual-election-type qualified profit-sharing and savings plan where the employee may elect all or one-half of his share of the company's annual contribution to be transferred to a trust fund and credited to his account, or, upon his failure to so elect, receive a distribution equivalent to such share to be paid directly to the employee, a contribution to the trust fund is considered to be a payment made by the employer and not by the employee for the purpose of the exclusion provided under Section 2039(c). [Rev. Rul. 68-89.] There is also no constructive receipt for income tax purposes. [Rev. Rul. 63-180.]

EXCLUSION ALLOCATION. In certain cases, employer contributions to a qualified plan on the employee's account cannot be readily ascertained. The regulations provide the following example to determine the amount excludable from the employee's gross estate.

Example: Under a qualified pension plan, the employer and the employee contributed to a trust which was to provide the employee, upon his retirement at age 60, with an annuity for life, and which was to provide his wife, upon the employee's death after retirement, with a similar annuity for life. At the time of the employee's retirement, the pension trust formed part of a plan meeting the requirements of Section 401(a). Assume the following: (*a*) that the employer's contributions to the fund were not credited to the accounts of individual employees; (*b*) that the value of the employee's annuity and his wife's annuity, computed as of the time of the decedent's retirement, was $40,000; (*c*) that the employee contributed $10,000 to the plan; and (*d*) that the value at the decedent's death of the wife's annuity was $16,000. On the basis of these facts, the total contributions to the fund on the employee's account are presumed to be $40,000 and the employer's contribution to the plan on the employee's account is presumed to be $30,000 ($40,000 less $10,000). Since the wife's annuity was receivable under a qualified pension plan, that part of the value of such annuity which is attributable to the employer's contributions ($30,000 is 75% of $40,000; 75% of $16,000 is $12,000) is excludable from the decedent's gross estate by reason of the provisions of Section 2039(c). Compare this result with the results reached in the examples set forth in subsection (b) of this section in which all contributions to the plans were made by the employer. [Regs. 20.2039-2(c)(2).]

Note that the above example is more favorable to the employee than when the employer's contributions can be ascertained, in that in the example all accretions are treated as being contributed by the employer. Such treatment is consistent with similar treatment under Regulations 1.101-2(b), dealing with the $5,000 exclusion from income of certain payments made because of death. The first $5,000 paid from a qualified plan on account of the death of the employee, to the extent it is attributable to employer contributions, is excludable from gross income. However, if the employee had a vested (nonforfeitable) right to receive such payment while living, the exclusion only applies if all amounts standing to the credit of the employee are paid in a lump sum. [Reg. 1.101-2(b).]

The value of a survivor annuity is to be computed in accordance with the rules set forth in Regulations 20.2031-7 to determine the amount excludable from the gross estate under a contributory plan. Table I, which sets forth the present value of an annuity based on the continuation of one life, is to be used for this purpose. Table I assumes a 3½% interest factor.

In some cases an insurance company makes the benefit payments under a group annuity contract directly to the beneficiaries of a qualified pension trust. To the extent that the benefits payable are attributable to employer contributions, they are exempt from Federal estate tax. [Rev. Rul. 59-401.]

The Revenue Service generally will not issue advance rulings or determination letters on a matter involving the prospective application of Federal estate tax to the property or the estate of a living person. [Rev. Proc. 64-31.]

ESTATE AS BENEFICIARY. Designation of an employee's estate as the beneficiary of benefits payable at his death from a qualified pension or profit-sharing plan is to be avoided. The law grants no exclusion from the employee's gross estate for the value of such benefits which are so payable. [Sec. 2039(c).]

ESTATE TAX DISADVANTAGE OF CAPITAL GAIN DISTRIBUTION AT RETIREMENT. The income tax attraction of capital gains on lump-sum distributions from qualified pension and profit-sharing plans is an inducement to many employees, especially executives in high income tax brackets, to request such distribution. In the interest of estate tax economy, however, the employee should realize that the amount he receives in a lump sum, to the extent that it is retained by him at his subsequent death, is subject to estate tax, and will not qualify for the exclusioin under a qualified plan.

If such an employee has an option to receive his retirement benefit over a period such as life and ten or twenty years certain, a balance payable at his death will be entitled to the estate tax exclusion. In addition, the amount payable at death in a lump sum will be entitled to capital gains treatment. [Section 402(a)(2).]

The exclusion is not available to a lump-sum distribution from a qualified plan before an employee dies — e.g., on his retirement. Since the benefits from the plan have been paid and reduced to possession of the employee, it is treated in the same way as any other property he owns and has full control of before his death.

If a retired employee draws down minimal installments

after retirement with the expectation that, in so doing the bulk of his account will go to his beneficiary, this may be evidence of an intent that the plan is being used to avoid estate tax. Section 401(a) is not intended as an escape hatch for estate tax purposes. It is intended to give employees certain favorable tax treatments. In such a case a plan is not being used for the primary benefit of the employee; and thus, the exemption from income tax may be in jeopardy. [Speech by Isadore Goodman dated October 7, 1966, Questions and Answers, Q. 3; *Prentice-Hall Pension and Profit-Sharing Service*, ¶ 19,036.11.]

If a qualified profit-sharing plan allows an employee to withdraw a portion of his account at a certain time and he dies before having exercised that right, the amount he could have withdrawn is subject to estate tax. Also, the mere fact that the employee could not have withdrawn the portion available in his account until the trustee computed the value of his share made no difference in estate tax consequences. [Rev. Rul. 67-37.]

If the pre-retirement withdrawals are voluntary and subject to, say, a cash penalty of 6%, the amounts not withdrawn before retirement will not be subject to estate tax. This assumes that the employer made all the contributions and that the benefits are paid by reason of death.

A wife's interest in a qualified profit-sharing account of an employee living in a community-property state is included in her gross estate if she dies before he does. The Revenue Service reasons that the employee's wife is not an employee participating in the profit-sharing plan. Since her community-property interest is a receivable by her executor, it becomes a part of her probate estate and thus subject to estate tax. [Rev. Rul. 67-278.]

NONQUALIFIED PENSION BENEFITS. An employee decedent was entitled to payments under a nonqualified annuity plan. The payments to his beneficiary arising because of survivorship were includable in the employee decedent's estate. [*James Gray, Exr. v. U. S.*, 278 F. Supp. 281, (D.C. N. J., 1967).]

Where the employee's rights are nonforfeitable except for his own actions — e.g., working for a competitor — the value of a retirement contract under a nonqualified plan providing for payments to specific beneficiaries was includable in an employee's gross estate under Section 2039(a). [*Estate of Edward H. Wadewitz*, 39 T.C. 925 (1963), aff'd (7th Cir. 1964).] The value of certain death benefits to a widow of a deceased employee, were not included in the employee's gross estate, where the employer awarded the amounts voluntarily. The employee had no property right to the benefits. [*Estate of William E. Barr*, 40 T.C. 227 (1963), *acq.*]

Death benefits payable under a nonqualified, noncontributory plan to a survivor in 120 equal monthly installments in accordance with the decedent's revocable direction are includable in his gross estate at their commuted value. The Tax Court rejected the Revenue Service's proposal that the entire amount of such payments should be included because of the employee decedent's control of the method of payment at the date of his death. [*Estate of Henry C. Beal*, 47 T.C. 269 (1966), *acq.*]

SELF-EMPLOYED PERSONS. The Federal estate tax exclusion does not apply to annuities and other payments made under qualifying trusts and plans attributable to contributions on behalf of the self-employed while he was a self-employed employee within the meaning of Section 401(c)(1). Contributions for that period are attributed to the employee, and such attribution bars the exclusion. [Section 2039(c).]

SERVICEMEN. Under the Retired Serviceman's Family Protection Plan, the gross estates of servicemen dying after December 31, 1965 do not include the value of annuities for a surviving spouse or certain child beneficiaries except to the extent of amounts deposited by a retired member in accordance with Section 1438 Title 10 of the U.S. Code. [Section 2039(c).]

MARITAL DEDUCTION UNDER SECTION 2056

In a great number of instances, the employee's principal beneficiary will be his widow. Since large payments from profit-sharing trusts are no longer considered unusual, Federal estate tax might be paid unnecessarily if the employee fails to consider an important estate-splitting principle known as the "marital deduction." For Federal estate tax purposes, a deduction is allowed under specified conditions for interests in property that pass from the decedent to his widow. The amount allowed as a deduction cannot exceed one-half of the adjusted gross estate — in general, the gross estate less debts and expenses. The value of a pension benefit payable to a widow and includable in the gross estate of the deceased employee (as, for example, the portion of the payment from a qualified plan which is attributable to the employee's contribution) may qualify for the marital deduction if it meets the conditions specified. [Sec. 2056.]

In general, the conditions of the terminable–interest rule will determine qualification for the marital deduction. The terminable-interest rule provides that an interest in property passing to a surviving spouse will not qualify for the marital deduction if it is a life estate only or other terminable interest and the property interest has passed or passes to someone (other than the spouse or spouse's estate) who has not paid adequate consideration in money or money's worth for it and such other person may possess or enjoy the property after the spouse's interest ends.

If the spouse is given a general power of appointment over any proceeds exercisable by her alone to revoke contingent beneficiaries and name her estate instead, or if she can withdraw the principal sum for her own use, the value of the interest subject to such a power may qualify for the marital deduction, if certain other conditions are met. See Section 2056 generally for exceptions and limitations.

If, at the decedent's death, any portion of his contributions is payable to anyone other than the decedent's spouse or, in the event of her death or remarriage, her estate, the value of a survivor's annuity will not qualify for the Federal estate tax marital deduction.

In Revenue Ruling 64-310 the decedent had retired from Federal employment and at the time of his death the total amount of annuity received was less than his contributions to the retirement fund. He had elected to receive a reduced annuity in order that his widow receive a survivor's annuity until her death or remarriage. The ruling held that —

- If the decedent designated his wife or her estate as the beneficiary of any unrecovered contributions, the marital deduction would be allowed.
- If any part of the contributions, plus interest, would pass to anyone else, the marital deduction would be disallowed.
- If the contributions, plus interest, had been recovered by the date of death, the value of the survivor's annuity would be allowable as a marital deduction.

Federal Gift Tax

EXEMPTION UNDER SECTION 2517

MECHANICS. The exemption from Federal gift tax for employee annuities or other payments under qualified pension, stock bonus, or profit-sharing plans parallels the Federal estate tax exclusion. In general, Section 2517 exempts from Federal gift tax the value of the right of a beneficiary to receive an annuity or other payment when an employee irrevocably designates a beneficiary under a qualified noncontributory plan at the employee's death. However, if the plan is contributory—i.e., if both the employee and the employer make contributions—the employee may be subject to gift tax on that part of the value of the beneficiary's interest which is attributable to employee contributions. [Section 2517(b).]

In general, an employee makes a gift of an annuity if he has an unqualified right to an annuity but takes a lesser amount with the provision that upon his death a survivor annuity or other payment will be paid to his designated beneficiary. He has made a gift at the time he gives up his power to deprive the beneficiary of the survivor annuity or other payment, but such gift may or may not be excluded from gift taxation depending upon whether the plan is (1) a qualified plan and (2) contributory.

The employee makes such a gift in any of several ways:

1. By irrevocably electing to take a reduced annuity and designating the individual who is to receive the survivor annuity or other payment. In this case, the gift is made at the time election and designation are irrevocably made.
2. By permitting a prior revocable election of a reduced annuity and designation of beneficiary to become irrevocable through failure to revoke during the period in which revocation could be made. In this case, the gift is made at the time the prior election and designation become irrevocable.
3. By permitting an option to expire under which the employee could, by exercising the option, have defeated the beneficiary's interest in the survivor annuity or other payment, and thereby regain for himself the right to a full annuity. In this case, the gift is made at the time the employee permits the option to expire.

FUTURE INTEREST. The value of the gift is the value, on the date of the gift, of the survivor annuity or other payment, computed in accordance with the principles set forth in Section 25.2512-5, Table I. Such a gift is a gift of a future interest and hence does not qualify for the $3,000 annual gift tax exclusion. [Regs. 25.2517-1(a)(1).]

EXEMPT GIFTS. The transfers described above are exempt from gift tax to the extent of employer contributions if the value of an annuity or other payment, upon death of an employee, will become payable to the employee's beneficiary under:

1. An employee's trust forming part of a pension, stock bonus, or profit-sharing plan which at the time of such exercise or nonexercise, or at the time of termination of the plan, if earlier, was qualified.

2. A retirement annuity contract purchased by an employer under a plan which, at the time of such exercise or non-exercise, or at the time of termination of the plan, if earlier, was a qualified plan.
3. A retirement annuity contract purchased for an employee by an employer which is an exempt religious or educational organization or an exempt organization which normally receives a substantial part of its support from the United States or any state or political division thereof. These organizations are described in Section 503(b)(1), (2), and (3).

As to 1 and 2 above, the exemption applies if the gift would otherwise be considered as having been made on or after January 1, 1955. As to the retirement annuity contract in 3, the exemption applies if the gift would otherwise be considered as having been made on or after January 1, 1958. [Regs. 25.2517-1(a) and (b).]

PORTION TAXABLE. If the employee contributes to the qualified plan, the irrevocable designation of a beneficiary subjects the value of the annuity or other payment to the beneficiary to gift tax on the portion attributable to employee contributions. The regulations show the following example of the computation of the amount excludable:

Example: Under a qualified pension plan, contributions were made by employer and employee to a trust which was to provide the employee, upon his retirement at age 60, with an annuity for life, and which contained a provision for designating, either before or after retirement, a surviving beneficiary upon the employee's death. Assume that the employee made an irrevocable election on January 20, 1955, whereby he would receive a lesser annuity and that after his death annuity payments would be continued to his wife. At the time of making the election, the pension trust formed part of a plan meeting the requirements of Section 401(a); contributions to the plan on the employee's account amounted to $20,000, of which $15,000 was contributed by the employer and $5,000 was contributed by the employee; and the value of the survivor annuity was $8,000. Since the wife's annuity was receivable under a qualified pension plan, that part of the value of such annuity which is attributable to the employer's contribution ($15,000 divided by $20,000 equal 75%; 75% of $8,000 is $6,000) is excludable from gifts by reason of the provisions of Section 2517(b). [Regs. 25.2517-1(c)(1).]

In some cases, the amount of employer contributions is not ascertainable. In such situations the value of the annuities or other payments payable to the employee and his beneficiary is considered to be the total contribution to the plan on the employee's account by both employer and employee. By subtracting from such value the amount of the employee's contribution to the plan, the amount of the employer's contribution on the employee's account is obtained. For example, if the employee contributed $10,000 and made an election at retirement, when the value of his annuity and his wife's totaled $40,000 (of which his wife's annuity alone was worth $16,000), the amount excludable is computed as follows: Total contributions are presumed to be $40,000. The employer contribution is presumed to be $30,000 ($40,000 minus $10,000). The amount excludable is $12,000 ($30,000 divided by $40,000 equals 75%; 75% of $16,000 is $12,000). [Regs. 25.2517-1(c)(2).]

CHANGING BENEFICIARIES. Generally, an employee covered by a qualified pension, profit-sharing, or stock bonus plan is given the right to designate and change beneficiaries up to the time of retirement. Since such designations and options are revocable, there is no gift until the time they become irrevocable.

SELF-EMPLOYED PERSONS. The Federal gift tax exemption does not apply to annuities and other payments made under qualifying trusts and plans attributable to contributions on behalf of the self-employed while he was a self-employed employee within the meaning of Section 401(c)(1). Contributions for that period are attributed to the employee, and such attribution bars the exclusion. [Section 2517(c).]

SERVICEMEN. Under the Retired Serviceman's Family Protection Plan (Title 10 U.S. Code, Chapter 73), the exercise or nonexercise of an election to provide an annuity for a survivor in lieu of a single pension is not a taxable transfer for gift tax purposes in calendar years after 1965. [Section 2517(a) & (b).]

MARITAL DEDUCTION UNDER SECTION 2523

Married persons making gifts to a spouse after April 2, 1948 may under certain conditions exclude one-half of the value of the gift in determining gift tax, if any. However, since the designation of a spouse as a beneficiary under a qualified plan generally relates to a life interest only, a marital deduction may not be available. The $30,000 lifetime exemption may be used if it has not previously been used.

In general, the same conditions necessary to qualify a terminable interest for the estate tax marital deduction must be satisfied. The donee spouse must have a right to income for life with a general power of appointment over any principal. See Section 2523 generally for exceptions and limitations. See also page 329.

Current and Future Trends

REFORM

The private retirement plan system in the United States is truly a financial giant. In recent years, private pension plans have grown dramatically. Some 26 million persons are now covered by such plans in contrast to 9.8 million in 1950. The forecast is for even more growth and further improvement. But it is also true that the private retirement system is under criticism, and there is a clamor for more legislative controls.

Reform activity in Washington at the Executive, Administrative, and Congressional levels is reaching new peaks. Numerous bills affecting retirement plans have been introduced in Congress, public hearings have been held, and private industry and others are apprehensive that, in an effort to attain national social goals, correct alleged deficiencies, and protect beneficiaries, legislators may impose regulations that could stifle private retirement plans.

PRESIDENTIAL COMMITTEE REPORT

In March 1962, Congress passed and President Kennedy signed the Welfare and Pension Plans Disclosure Act Amendments of 1962. The amendments were intended "to provide the enforcement teeth which are lacking in the existing law, as well as to make certain other necessary improvements" in the original Act of 1959. At the same time President Kennedy appointed seven Cabinet-level members to a committee known as the President's Committee on Corporate Pension Funds and Other Retirement and Welfare Programs. The Committee's assignment was:

"... to review legislation and administrative practice... [and] the implications of the growing retirement and welfare funds for the financial structure of the economy, as well as a review of the role and character of the private pension and other retirement systems in the economic security system of the nation, and consideration of how they may contribute more effectively to efficient manpower utilization and mobility."

In January 1965 the findings of the President's Committee were published in a report entitled, *Public Policy and Private Pension Programs: A Report to the President on Private Employee Retirement Plans.* The report emphasized the greater importance of the social security program although giving a vote of confidence to the manner in which private retirement plans had been established and administered. The report concludes with reference to the social security public retirement program:

"The public program will continue to be the nation's basic instrument for assuring reasonably adequate retirement income to workers, their widows and dependents.

"Private pension plans should continue as a major element in the nation's total retirement security program. Their strength rests on the supplementation they can provide to the basic public system.

"The basic justification for the indirect public subsidy involved in favor of tax treatment lies in the social purposes served by private pension plans. In view of these social purposes, public policy should continue to provide appropriate incentives to private plan growth and by improving the basic soundness and equitable character of such plans, set a firmer foundation for their future development. Because protection will always be far from complete, private pension plans cannot be a substitute for public programs, but public policy can encourage developments which will provide supplementary retirement benefits to a growing proportion of the nation's workers and will provide greater assurance that the promised benefits will be paid.

The report contained repeated references to preferential tax treatment and, in effect, a tax subsidy granted by the Federal Government justifying Federal control of private plans for social purposes. It contained numerous recommendations, some diverse and unrelated, many of them extremely controversial. The recommendations included: compulsory vesting, minimum funding, portability and reinsurance of benefits, protection of participants' rights, inspection of funds, a 10% restriction on investments in securities of the employer, integration restrictions limited to no more than 50% of social security benefits, fixed-formula contributions to profit-sharing plans, and a reduction or elimination of certain allegedly unjustifiable tax benefits applicable to amounts distributed.

INTER-AGENCY STAFF COMMITTEE

With the appointment of the Inter-agency Staff Committee on Private Pensions, proposals for comprehensive retirement plan legislation appear likely to increase. The committee consists of representatives from Commerce, Justice, Labor, Treasury, Bureau of the Budget, HEW, Council of Economic Advisors, Federal Reserve System, and the SEC. Meetings have been held by this committee with representatives of interested parties in the business community on the subjects of vesting, fiduciary responsibilities, broadening of participation, funding, and reinsurance.

SENATE ACTION

Introduced in the Senate by Senator Yarborough (D–Texas) is the Welfare and Pension Plan Protection Act of 1967, S.1024. The bill proposes to amend the Welfare and Pension Plans Disclosure Act by changing it from a disclosure law to a protection law. It proposes to give the Secretary of Labor power to regulate pension and welfare plans by increasing his investigatory and enforcement powers. Included are provisions for Federal standards imposing the "prudent man" rule for fiduciary responsibility on trustees, a requirement for annual independent audits of funds, and a limit of 10% on investments in the stock and securities of the employer company.

At the same time, the Inter-agency Committee on Private

Pensions conducted studies on problems connected with minimum vesting and funding recommendations with a view to specific proposals for legislation. In May of 1968, Senate Bill S.3421 — a Labor Department Bill with proposals on vesting, funding, and reinsurance — was introduced by Senator Yarborough. In introducing the bill, Senator Yarborough made the following remarks:

"First, the legislation I am introducing today will impose minimum standards for all pension plans in order to provide vested retirement benefits to all participants who have worked for the same employer for ten or more years after reaching the age of 25.

"Employees may now work a lifetime for the same employer and yet be entitled to nothing on leaving, even though a sound pension plan exists. More than 12 million employees are now covered by pension plans under which benefits do not vest after ten years' service. Some 3 million of these persons will — in the absence of this bill — never receive any benefits from these plans. It is not just or equitable that a man, when he changes jobs, should lose rights acquired over so long a period even though the necessity of private circumstances may compel him to seek employment elsewhere.

"Secondly, some 500 pension plans covering more than 25,000 workers terminate each year with all the losses that this entails. The bill will require minimum standards of funding to assure that sufficient assets are accumulated to carry out promises to employees and their dependents. Too often, the protection offered by private pension plans is illusory, and a worker, at the age of 60, suddenly discovers that he will not get the promised monthly income so important to his future plans.

"Thirdly, to assure that such promises are kept, the bill provides insurance against losses to pension funds caused by involuntary termination of a plan before it is fully funded, as in cases of bankruptcy or plant closure.

"The bill will avoid a severe immediate impact upon current pension plans by permitting various arrangements by which such plans can make careful transitions in order to permit easy adjustments. In addition, the Secretary of Labor is authorized to approve alternative methods of meeting standards in special cases.

"Finally, the bill provides for continuing studies of all aspects of pension plans, including the possibility of portability of pension credits."

Out of the plethora of legislative activity and the studies recently and now still taking place, it is prudent for the employer who is contemplating adopting or amending present plans to be aware of the changes that are being proposed, some of which ultimately seem destined for adoption. He should be cognizant of these current and future trends which are bound to vitally affect his relationships with his employees, the Government, and his business.

INDEXES

Subject Index

H.R. 10, *116, 125*
Hypothecation of stock, *187, 199*

Inactive self-employed, *116*
Incidental benefits, *18*
Individual annuity plan, *237*
Information requirements, *37, 45, 92, 155, 190, 203, 246*
Insurance company reserves, *72*
Integration with social security, *34, 119, 257-263*
Investments, *13, 38, 111, 122, 229, 239-255, 303*

Joint ventures, *32, 80, 254, 291, 303*

Keogh plans, *115, 125*
Koppers-type stock bonus **plan, 300**

Leases, personal property, *220, 224, 229, 232, 244, 249, 303*
Leases, real property, *220, 227, 244, 248, 251*
Liability, accrual of under profit-sharing plan, *21, 90*
Life insurance, *3, 19, 21, 39, 44, 56, 58, 59, 61, 64*
Limitations:
  Deductions, test of reasonableness of, *81, 94, 96*
  Method binding with return, *79*
  Multiple or overlapping plans or trusts, *80*
  Pension plan contribution deductions, *7, 74-80, 278*
  Profit-sharing plan contribution deductions, *7, 80, 278*
  Self-employed contribution deductions, *119, 120, 125*
  Stock bonus contribution deductions, *7, 80, 278*
Liquidations (*see* Business combinations)
Loans to employee, *26*
Loans to employer, *205, 211-214, 247*
Local law, *166, 241, 245, 303*
Lump-sum distribution, *48, 49, 50, 51, 52, 55, 65, 66, 144, 149, 269, 295, 327*

Management decisions, *8*
Marital deduction, estate tax, *329*

Marital deduction, gift tax, *334*
Medical benefits for retired employees, *37*
Medical expense plans, *3, 18, 21, 60*
Mergers (*see* Business combinations)
Method of payment of contribution under qualified plan, *91*
Methods of computing deduction for contributions under qualified plans (*see* Limitations)
Money purchase plans, *17, 27*
Multi-employee trust, *19*
Multiple plans of affiliated corporations, *82*

Nonqualified pension benefits, estate tax, *328*
Nonqualified plans, *285*
Nonqualified plans, contributions under, *94*
Nonqualified stock bonus plan, *298*
Nonqualified stock options, *158, 191*
Nonstatutory stock options, *158, 191*
Normal cost, definition of, *76*
Normal cost, unpaid, *76*

Officers' compensation plans, *285*
Offset plan, integration of, *260*
Overfunding, *17, 26, 27*
Owner-employee, definition of, *117*

Partners and partnerships, *115, 119, 120, 125, 222, 303*
Past service cost, definition of, *76*
Pay plans for executives, *285*
Pension plan, comparison of with profit-sharing plan, *5*
Pension plan, definition of, *17*
Pension plan costs, *17*
Percentage requirements, *28*
Permanency of plan, *24, 100*
Personal property leases, *220, 224, 229, 232, 244, 249, 303*
Phantom stock plan, *300*
Pooled investment funds, *235*
Presidential Committee Report, *337*
Professional man, tax planning for, *125*
Profit-sharing plan, comparison of with pension plan, *5*
Profit-sharing plan, definition of, *20*
Prohibited transactions, *123, 203, 205, 241, 242, 247*

Property used for payment, *91*

Qualified plans, comparison of, *5*
Qualified plans, requirements of, *16,
99, 108, 135, 141, 149*
Qualified stock options, *157, 159, 165*

Real property leases, *220, 227, 244,
248, 251*
Reasonableness test for compensation,
40, 81, 94, 96, 212, 305-321
Reform activity, *337*
Reorganizations (*see* Business com-
binations)
Restricted stock options, *157, 177*
Restricted stock plans, *198, 302*
Retired employees, *95*
Retirement bonds, *99, 105*
Retirement income, levels of, *5*
Retirement plans for self-employed
individuals, *115, 125*
Retirement programs, *4*
Retroactive amendments, *36*
Revaluation of investments, *26*
Revocable trusts, *287*
Royalties, *220, 249, 250, 290*

Salaried employees' coverage, *30, 34*
Savings and loan associations, *122,
209*
Savings plans, *107*
Securities and Exchange Commission,
113, 153
Securities laws, Federal, *113, 156*
Security, adequate, definition of,
211, 247
Self-employed retirement plans, *37,
66, 97, 99-100, 105, 115, 125, 215,
237, 327, 334*
Separation from service, *47, 51, 65,
113, 144, 149, 269, 295*
Sick-pay exclusion, *60*
Social security, *34, 141, 143, 145,
148, 201, 257-263, 295*
Sole proprietor, *115*
Split funding, *237*
Step-up plan, integration of, *260*
Stock bonus plan, definition of, *23*
Stock bonus plan, nonqualified, *298*
Stock options, *151*
Stock purchase plans, *173*
"Stockless" stock bonus plan, *300*

Supplementary compensation, exempt
organizations and, *71*
Suspension of contributions, *19, 25*

Tax planning for the professional man,
125
Taxation of employee annuities, *63*
Tax-exempt trusts, *41*
Tax-exempt trusts, employees', *203-
232*
Ten-year rule, *50*
Terminal funding, *234*
Terminations, *19, 24, 48, 62*
Three-year rule, *67*
Thrift plans, *107*
Time of payment of contribution un-
der qualified plan, *89*
Time of taxation, *66*
Total distribution, definition of, *50*
Trust investments (*see* Investments)
Trustee responsibilities, *9, 203, 240,
339*
Trusts for employees, foreign-situs
(*see* Foreign-situs trust)
Trusts for employees, revocable, *287*

Unfunded plans, *233*
Union-negotiated plans, *18, 24, 31,
96*
Unqualified plans, *285*
Unqualified stock bonus plan, *298*
Unqualified stock options, *158, 191*
Unrealized appreciation, *26, 45, 53,
54, 113*
Unrelated business income, *204, 217-
225, 242, 243*

Valuation, *13, 17, 26, 27, 154, 178,
185, 192, 212, 268*
Vesting (*see also* Forfeitable vs. nonforfeitable), *6, 24, 25, 36, 118,
339*
Voluntary contributions, *7, 19, 35,
110, 120, 131, 132*

Wage and Hour laws, *82*
Welfare and Pension Plans Disclosure
Act, *94*
Western Hemisphere trade corpora-
tion, *135*
Withdrawal from plan, *19, 22, 110,
132*
Withholding, *45, 200*

Index of Rulings

MIMEOGRAPHS (MIM.)

MISCELLANEOUS

REVENUE PROCEDURES (REV. PROC.)

REVENUE RULINGS (REV. RUL.)

Index of Cases

Glenshaw Glass Co., 13 T.C. 296 (1949), *acq.*, *310*
Glinske, Edward Joseph, 17 T.C. 562 (1951), *48, 271*
Gray, James, Exr., v. U.S., 278 F. Supp. 281 (D.C. N.J., 1967), *328*
Greenwald, Harold D., 44 T.C. 137, 366 F.2d 538 (2nd Cir. 1966), *33*
Harold's Club, 340 F.2d 861 (9th Cir. 1965), *307*
Hicks v. U.S., 314 F.2d 180 (4th Cir. 1963), *22, 45, 47, 67, 108*
Hoffman Radio Corporation, 177 F.2d 264 (9th Cir. 1949), *313, 314*
Huckins Tool & Die, Inc., TCM 1959-190, aff'd (7th Cir. 1961), *315*
Jewell Ridge Coal Sales Co., Inc., TCM 1957-30, *309*
Johnson, U.S. v., 331 F.2d 943 (5th Cir. 1964), *270, 274, 275*
Kane Chevrolet Co., 32 T.C. 596 (1959), *25*
Kuchman, Harold H., 18 T.C. 154 (1952), *acq.*, *196*
Lehman, Robert, 17 T.C. 652 (1951), *nonacq.*, *196*
Lincoln Electric Co., 176 F.2d 815 (6th Cir. 1949), *315*
Lincoln Electric Co. Employees' Profit-Sharing Trust, 190 F.2d 326 (6th Cir. 1951), *20*
LoBue, Com. v., 351 U.S. 243 (1956), *192, 196*
Lucas v. Ox Fibre Brush Co., 281 U.S. 115 (1930), *311*
Martin, Lester B., 26 T.C. 100 (1956), *271*
Mayson Manufacturing Company, 178 F.2d 115 (6th Cir. 1949), *307*
McGowan v. U.S., 277 F.2d 613 (7th Cir. 1960), *272*
Miller Manufacturing Company, Inc., 149 F.2d 421 (4th Cir. 1945), *316*
Miller, Mary, 22 T.C. 293 (1955), aff'd (6th Cir. 1955), *271*
Mississippi River Fuel Corp. v. U.S., 314 F.2d 953 (Ct. Cl. 1963), *95, 287*
Oates, Com. v., 207 F.2d 711 (7th Cir. 1953), *296, 297*
Olmsted Incorporated Life Agency, 35 T.C. 429 (1960), *nonacq.*, aff'd (8th Cir. 1962), *296*
Oswald, Vincent E., 49 T.C. No. 68 (1968), *319*
Peebles, U.S. v., 331 F.2d 955 (5th Cir. 1964), *271*
Pepsi-Cola Niagara Bottling Corp., 48 T.C. 75 (1967), rev'd (2nd Cir. 1968), *32*
Rank v. U.S., 345 F.2d 337 (5th Cir. 1965), *161*
Ray Cleaners, Inc., TCM 1968-6, *32*
Reynolds, R. J., Tobacco Co., 260 F.2d 9 (4th Cir. 1958), *307, 316*
Rieben, Edward I., Estate of, 32 T.C. 1205 (1959), *271*
Robinson, Ray S., 44 T.C. 20 (1965), *291*
Roehl Construction Co., Inc., 17 T.C. 1037 (1951), *318*
Roth Office Equipment Co. v. Gallagher, 172 F.2d 452 (6th Cir. 1949), *311*
Russell Manufacturing Co. v. U.S., 175 F. Supp. 159 (Ct. Cl. 1959), *95, 287*
Russell Manufacturing Co., U.S. v., (D.C. Conn., 1964), aff'd (2nd Cir. 1965), *287*
Rust-Oleum Corp. v. Sauber, (D.C. Ill. 1958), *310*
Saalfield Publishing Co., 11 T.C. 756 (1948), *78*
Safety Engineering & Supply Co., Inc. v. U.S., 374 F.2d 885 (5th Cir. 1967), *312*
Schepp, L., Company, 25 B.T.A. 419 (1932), *acq.*, *316*
Schlegel, Jack E., 46 T.C. 706 (1966), *271, 274, 275*
Sheridan, Bank of, (D.C. Mont., 1963), *287*
Sherwood Swan & Co., Ltd., 42 T.C. 299 (1964), *nonacq.* aff'd (9th Cir. 1965), *32*
Sproull v. Com., 194 F.2d 541 (6th Cir. 1952), *289, 297, 298*
Steele Wholesale Builders Supply Co. v. U.S., 226 F. Supp. 82 (D.C. Tex., 1963), *92*

Index of Regulations

PROPOSED REGULATIONS (PROP. REGS.)